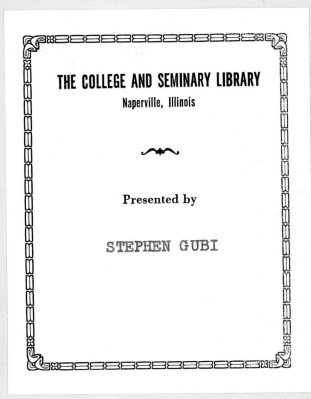

NEW FAITH FOR OLD

OTHER BOOKS BY SHAILER MATHEWS

HISTORICAL

Select Mediaeval Documents
The French Revolution, 1789-1815
New Testament Times in Palestine
The Spiritual Interpretation of History
The Validity of American Ideals
The Making of Tomorrow
The Messianic Hope in the New Testament

SOCIAL ASPECTS OF CHRISTIANITY

Jesus on Social Institutions
The Social Gospel
The Individual and the Social Gospel
The Church and the Changing Order
Christianity and Social Process
Creative Christianity
Patriotism and Religion

RELIGIOUS BELIEF

The Growth of the Idea of God
The Atonement and the Social Process
Immortality and the Cosmic Process
The Gospel and the Modern Man
The Faith of Modernism
Contributions of Science to Religion
   With Thirteen Scientists
A Dictionary of Religion and Ethics
   With G. B. Smith
A Constructive Life of Christ
   With E. D. Burton
The Student's Gospels
   With E. J. Goodspeed

NEW FAITH FOR OLD

An Autobiography

By
SHAILER MATHEWS

NEW YORK
THE MACMILLAN COMPANY
1936

PREFACE

I NEVER expected to write an autobiography. The life of a theological professor does not abound in adventure, nor is it conducive to that rhetorical exhibitionism so popular in recent years. As a matter of fact this book started in response to a suggestion that someone ought to describe the changes which have come over Protestant religious life during the last half century. It is surprising that so little has been written about them, so I set off on a historical exploration only to find that I was dealing with events with which I had been more or less closely associated. In mentioning this to one of my friends for whose opinion I have high respect, I was surprised to be urged to make the book not only one of historical reminiscence and criticism but something autobiographical. Such a proceeding seemed to me to be highly immodest and to treat one's own life altogether too seriously. But I must confess it was not unattractive. As the future grows shorter the past grows more vivid. And since one always tries to rationalize his decisions, I recalled how in my various attempts at writing history I had found that autobiographies, even of unimportant persons, enabled one to get at the human side of social change. And that, I honestly think, is how I came to write this personal account. I have tried to be as objective as possible and I have not lost sight of my original purpose to trace the development of those religious changes which have resulted from new elements in our social life. It might perhaps have been better to treat matters more impersonally, but after all these changes were not impersonal, but the outcome of discussion, committees and, in many cases, controversy. As the past has been revived in my memory it has become all the clearer that

v

a religion is not to be identified with the intellectual process by which it has been justified. To be understood as a phase of individual and social behavior it must be shared. It must affect action in every phase of life. The aim of such action is personal values rather than information. It becomes intelligent as it recognizes new conditions and answers new questions. All those who have lived in two eras and have seen how one has passed into the other will, I am sure, agree with me that there has been progress which is more than change. And not the least of these changes are those which have resulted from efforts to make the ideals of Jesus influential in all aspects of social process.

SHAILER MATHEWS.

CONTENTS

NEW FAITH FOR OLD

CHAPTER I

MID-VICTORIAN EVANGELICALISM

THE WORLD in which we of the older generation were young seems today incredibly simple. There were no telephones, automobiles, radios, electric lights, or very much plumbing. Even a city like Portland, Maine, where I was born, had no water supply or sewerage system. Most of the streets were still paved with cobblestones and the introduction of wooden blocks was revolutionary. Street cars were "horse cars" and the nearest approach that we had to airplanes was the satirical poem by J. T. Trowbridge, "Darius Green and His Flying Machine." There were no baseball leagues and football had hardly acquired any character beyond a miscellaneous kicking of an inflated round rubber ball. Boys played baseball, "New York Scrub," and various other simpler games. Golf and tennis were yet to be played. There were few gymnasiums, fewer athletic parks, and no stadiums. There were athletic groups like the Portland Turnverein, but their membership was limited. Streets of a city were lighted with gas, country roads with an occasional kerosene lamp. Indeed, kerosene was only beginning to be used and farmers' wives still made tallow candles by dipping strings in melted tallow or by filling iron moulds. There were few mowing machines. Men cut grass with scythes. Immigration in Maine was almost entirely limited to the Irish and the French Canadians.

The Yankee stock had not been depleted by the migration to the Middle West. In fact, the territory between the Mississippi and the Rockies was still so uninhabited as to offer careers for Indian fighters and furnish the buffalo robes which every owner of a wagon or a sleigh used. Factories were built where there was water power. An ocean-going steamer was so much of a rarity that pictures of the Great Eastern in the harbor of Portland were published, although that all but legendary side-wheel steamer never entered the port. Shipyards of Maine were still active and most commerce was carried in sailing ships.

Recreation and play were simple, all but unaided by mechanical means beyond a hand cart or a horse and wagon. In the country and along the coast there were, of course, boats and streams and ponds in which to fish and forests and marshes in which to hunt, but the contrast between such a simple life and our modern world strikes those who are old enough to remember it when they visit some little country town. Motor boats line the side of ponds—lakes they are called now—where once rafts, canoes and flat-bottomed square-ended boats were the implements of adventure.

I

In the seventies simple things could be enjoyed. The city boy nowadays has small need of sitting on the wharves watching the schooners come and go. The smell of fish and salt, the swash of the tug's wake on the piles, are quite outside his sphere of interests. His father has his cottage with wide verandas, where he may spend his days in neither country nor city, with neither work nor play. He does not need to learn the meaning of the clouds or the wind—unless he has a motor boat which may serve himself and his young women friends as a means of obtaining the coat of tan prescribed by fashion. The boy like the man has been swept into the current of machine-made conventionality.

He misses more than he knows. It is bad enough for the city boy to grow up ignorant of the daily toil of the farm and never share in the joy of harvest. But the son of well-to-do city people is doubly unfortunate in that he has so much done for him. Let a boy wander into the outskirts of life like that which still lingers along the water fronts of our seaboard cities, and he has not only come close to elemental humanity, but he has tasted, be it never so diffidently, the world of romance.

At least this is as it appears to one who remembers the days when Custom House Wharf was a world of mystery and delight. Is there a man of us old Portlanders who does not remember the awakening of life that came just about marble-time, when the ice drifted away from the muddy ends of the docks, and the fishing-boats once more began to drive up the bay to the wharves on the islands? That was before the day of the packing monopolies and the huge pickling works. Up and down Casco Bay were the little wharves, left high and dry when the tide went out, where some fishing smack unloaded and its haul was spread out to the ministration of sun and air and salt. How new the world seemed to us as we swung our feet over the sunny side of the wharf and listened to the longshoremen speculate upon the luck of some fisherman swinging around Bug Light on the breakwater, or tell of the fortunes of some man from the Foreside. Even to watch the tiny steamer known along the coast as the "Ferry," push its occasional way across to the Cape—now reached by a noble viaduct —was to discern the advance of summer, for it no longer wore its winter coat of boards about its deck. And when the "Express" and the "Forest City"—peace to their ashes!—took up again their regular trips to Peaks and Cushings, we knew that summer indeed had come.

Do boys still sit on Custom House Wharf and smell its unforgettable odors, and try to convince themselves that their mothers would not be quite implacable if one were to yield to the temptation of a rowboat at fifteen cents an hour?

It is hard for any one who today for the first time sees the serried ranks of cottages along the Maine coast to realize that there was a time when they were a novelty. In those bucolic days Little Diamond was Little Hog Island, and on the bar that joined it to Great Hog you could dig the best of clams for clambakes. Over against you was Trefethren's Landing— or was it Evergreen?—and off to the southeast was that *terra incognita,* Long Island. I forget now what mystery hung over that island. Was it a tradition of wild calla lilies and twin-flowers, or was it a hotel with red plush furnishings that disappeared in an opportune fire? Farther down were the Chebeague Islands—Little catering to Sunday-school picnics, and Great with actual roads and schoolhouses.

In spring there was always safe recourse to Cape Elizabeth. There were the little coves among the cliffs where you could count on starting up a sandpeep on which to train your new, and generally inoffensive, gun. There, too, were the shelving rocks where you could just steady yourself as you fished for rock cod and cunners. There were the Portland Light and the earthworks that shared with Forts Scammel and Preble and Gorges the task of guarding the entrance to the harbor. In those days we never thought that House Island would become a quarantine station, and that a foreign war would give such importance to the earthworks on the Head. And then there were the woods on the Middle Road where you were sure to find the earliest flowers for the botany class, and which incidentally furnished a most satisfactory supply of spruce gum, a luxury which, in those days before gum-chewing had been commercialized, could be justified on hygienic grounds.

Yet best of all were the islands. You could even row down to them if your cousin came from the country, and so added caution as well as fortune sufficient for the exploit. And once there you were outside even the very imperfectly conventionalized world in which you lived. The sea stretched out to the sky, the firs sung in the wind, the long breakers—every seventh one a monster—struggled to seize you. There were fish to catch, potatoes to roast, driftwood and seaweed for the clambake. And the city was far away!

In the winter there were snowball fights that sometimes acquired almost the importance of military operations with snow forts and icy snow balls. The picture in Thomas Bailey Aldrich's incomparable, *Story of a Bad Boy,* is a historical photograph of a world in which I passed my boyhood.

A boy's life, even if denied dancing and social excitement, had plenty of fun. I was never very musical, but I experimented in playing the piano, the clarinet and the viola. I never became proficient with either instrument but for a while I was a member of an amateur orchestra. For one winter I did the best I could to play the viola in a string quartette. And after a rather long and sometimes strenuous apprenticeship as organ-blower for our local musical genius, Hermann Kotzschmar, I sang in a church chorus.

My summers were spent on an old farm cut by my great-grandfather from the forest of Maine, on which my father had been born. It was in the little town of Monson a few miles south of Moosehead Lake. It backed up against the vast forest which covers the northern half of Maine and gave a boy not only the opportunity to learn how to drive oxen, harness horses and carry on "haying," but also the chance to fish in trout streams and ponds and to learn something of life in the woods. The "Old Farm" is now mine, a motor truck replaces oxen, and although life in the big farmhouse is far from that I knew as a boy, my children and grandchildren share my love for the beauty of the location and the sense of family born of more than a century's ownership. My grandchildren are the sixth generation of my name which has lived on the place. No family lives north of us short of Canada, and despite all our modern conveniences bears and deer debouch from the forest upon the orchard. One year twelve bears were killed on my land. This year there were eleven.

Holidays and celebrations like a boy's recreations continued the spirit of the practices of earlier New England. Christmas—without mistletoe—was observed but not as a religious festival. That would have been too great a concession by New England Puritanism to Episcopalianism. This was even truer in the case of Holy Week and Easter. I cannot recall that there was any celebration of either. The holidays sprang from colonial and revolutionary days. The observance of Fast Day in the spring had dwindled until it had become a day in which few if any persons went to church and fewer still fasted, but for boys the day meant that they should ride horseback *fast*. On Washington's birthday boys had their bonfires for which fuel had been collected for weeks. The Fourth of July began with a procession of "antiques and horribles"—a burlesque of the Ancient and Honorable Artillery of Boston—and in most of the small towns notables marched to groves or public halls and listened to the reading of the Declaration of Independence and patriotic addresses. Memorial or Decoration Day was observed in the spirit of its founding. It had not yet become a holiday to be exploited by commercialized sport. Thanksgiving was the great day of New England, although it was not nationally observed. As an offset to the current criticism of Puritanism it is worth recalling that the social order which dared, at least conventionally, to practice self-control gave to the United States its single feast day. It is not difficult to imagine what would have been the reaction of New England to a proposal to establish Labor Day or Columbus Day.

II

This simple life of my boyhood days was a phase of a social order that had not yet felt the results of that capitalism already developing because of the increase of population and exploitation of the Central West. It is now hard to realize that the steel industry was only beginning to develop and that most factories produced textiles. New England was still basically agricultural; grist mills, saw mills, and small woolen mills were to be found in many of the small towns. Except in wheat there was little competition with the agriculture of the West and the South sent its cotton to the North to be made into cloth.

Commercial methods did not differ radically from those of the first half of the nineteenth century. The distribution of goods varied little from that which had come over from the earlier days of New England. My father was in the wholesale trade, and by virtue of the fact that for a number of years I kept books for his business, I came to know something of the depression of 1878, unwise bankruptcy legislation, the place of the middle man in trade and the limitations of banking and credit institutions. Competition was still regarded as the life of trade and the interference of the government with the economic life was avoided although there was a growing conviction that infant industries should be protected by a high tariff. Corporations were beginning their rapid growth, but trusts were as yet unknown. Larger business houses were individual with an occasional branch but their development was due to superior wealth and ability of their owners. Commercial Street in Portland was lined with wholesale dealers in foodstuffs, but I doubt if any one of them did a business of half a million a year. It was a good era for the middle class!

With this limited development of the inherited economic life in Maine the older generation in the period immediately following the Civil War was apparently satisfied. So far as I can recall, there was no serious economic readjustment or even criticism. Labor, it is true, had begun to organize in the Knights of Labor. From our present point of view, the twenty-three principles which this, at first, secret organization set forth, do not seem particularly radical, for many of them have been embodied in legislation. In the late seventies, however, and early eighties they were too radical for the New England mind. For some unaccountable reason, I made "Mechanical Industry" the subject of my high school graduation address in 1880. I don't know what wisdom I there expressed but thanks to the severe discipline in committing the declamation to memory, I recall that the opening sentence was "In these days of strikes and riots our minds naturally turn to that branch of industry in which they occur." The declamation could not have had any particular value for I knew nothing about economics or social process but it showed that my generation early began to give attention to matters in which it later was to be deeply concerned.

But new movements within the economic order did not seriously affect Maine. Neither in journalism nor in education was there any serious inquiry into economic affairs. The prevailing political interests were the struggle between the Democrats and Republicans and the reconstruction of the Southern States. The Greenback party was in process of growth but it was not until 1880 that it became a serious contender with the other political parties. In New England its influence outside certain labor groups was small, although it gained some significance as a protest party.

The commercial group in which I grew up was essentially conservative. Responsible leaders had preserved the point of view and methods of the first half of the nineteenth century. The exploitation of the natural resources of the country made possible by the application on a gigantic scale of principles which had been unquestioned in the older economic order, raised no moral questions. Economic theory was largely dominated by John Stuart Mill but economic practice was rationalized by appeal to national pride and pre-industrial practices. In the Grange which spread rapidly among the farmers of New England was the only organized attempt to limit the "rugged individualism" of the middle man by co-operative buying. In such conditions it was natural that moral vision should be obscured. The years following the Civil War were marked by as low political morality as America has ever known. The loss of ideals which usually mark post-war periods was intensified by political rancour and graft. The rapid expansion of the West through building of transcontinental railroads made American politics a field of corruption. The consequent scandal served, however, to evoke a new moral interest in government and gradually the laws were shaped to control the action of rapidly growing corporations. But the danger of ill-distributed wealth began to be seen and such movements as the Knights of Labor and the Grange sounded a note of social readjustment. Their proposals, however, were so far out of keeping with current economic interests as to seem opposed to sound economic conditions. The era of reform in politics which followed the uncovering of the evils of the carpet-baggers in the South, graft in great cities and the Federal government did not concern itself with more than the punishment of the grafters. One recognizes the justice of Professor Muzzey's characterization of the period as one of "national dead-center." It was, however, by the generation that was too young to have political power that the moral issues involved were later to be faced.

III

It was natural for this indifferently social individualism to express itself in Protestantism. The morality of the late seventies and early eighties was probably no higher than that of today, but it was more conventional. At any rate I have no ambition to join those who make autobiography a form of literary exhibitionism. Church services had to face no rivals in Sunday amusements. The Christian was supposed to avoid dancing, card-playing, and theatres. He might, indeed, play dominoes or authors but he was not supposed to know that they were denatured forms of forbidden games. When *Pinafore* came to Portland, only the fact that the company played in the City Hall rather than Fanny Ward's Theatre justified attendance on the part of the church members.

As far as the relation of the sexes was concerned there was

no frankness of discussion. Those of us who were brought up by intelligent parents were probably more innocent than children of intelligent parents today, since sex was taboo in conventional religious circles. Even divorces were hardly to be mentioned. The Christian was to keep himself unspotted from the world, even to the extent of avoiding smoking. The use of liquor and beer was something which in a prohibition state was to be limited to members of the commercial aristocracy or the drunken wretches which one so frequently saw in the poorer sections of the city.

Until my generation did undertake leadership in religious life, the attitude of churches was one of aloofness from other forces in society. They were indifferent to them because religion in the evangelical churches was something outside of group morality. Church-going was perhaps more general than at present but the message of the pulpit was essentially for the individual. Respectable people went to church in the morning; their children went to Sunday School in the afternoon. The more active church members met on Tuesday night in prayer meetings which were popularly regarded as the thermometer of church life. On Friday night there was a young people's meeting led by some person who at least had once been young. Hell and the devil were very real. A person could be saved from them only by acceptance of the atonement worked through the death of Jesus Christ. Salvation and morality were not to be confounded. A saved person was supposed to be moral to the extent of keeping the ten commandments and avoiding worldly practices but morality in the unsaved was dangerous. It served to deceive its possessor and to make him indifferent to the need of faith in the atoning Christ. The religious life was conventionally pietistic. The head of the Christian family was supposed to hold family prayers and to say grace at the table at meals. God was a very distinct personality and prayer was a recognized means of inducing Him to aid the Christian in all the affairs of life.

The observance of Sunday as the Sabbath while strict was tempered by certain concessions. We children could play with our blocks on Sunday but were supposed to build meeting houses rather than railroad stations. My grandfather, Dr. Wm. H. Shailer, was a minister of the old school, genial but conscientious. With him Sunday was still the Puritan Sabbath. During its hours no cooking was to be done except boiling water for his tea. The family always had cold corned beef which had been cooked on Saturday, which was uniformly treated in New England as a "baking day." How strict was his Sabbatarianism may be observed from a curious regulation of the house. The piano had a melodeon attachment which, by turning a switch, could be played with the piano keys. On Sunday only the melodeon part of the instrument could be played.

I doubt if my own experience was different from that of those men and women with whom later I was to be associated in various religious undertakings. Loyalty to the religious institution became ingrained in us. Even trivial matters had their significance in maintaining this loyalty. I suppose the adolescent in those days as in these had his characteristic problems and moments of rebellion from conformity to practices and religious services in which he saw little meaning, but I cannot help feeling that the insistence upon attendance at church services served to fix in my unconscious life a conviction as to the importance of the church. My running errands for the Burmah Missionary Society when its members held a "levee" for the benefit of missionary funds, brought action to the support of this attitude. I can still hear the jingle of the box of three tined steel forks which I dragged in a hand cart from Aunt Hattie Radford's to the church.

But quite as important for the development of the consolidation of my religious life, such as it was, must have been our family life. My parents were both sincerely religious in the then current sense of the term. I do not recall that they ever raised philosophical or theological questions although I remember my father was rather terrified lest his conviction that God was swayed by love rather than by justice was heretical.

But life in our New England home was not sombre. While my father was never rich and sometimes found his business in serious distress, we were never poor. The discipline of the family was steady but not severe. When the street lights were lit we children came into the house. This was a rule which my mother administered inexorably. In the light of today's psychology I can see how influential was the absence of controversy within the family and the treatment of religion as a matter of course. In the case of my younger brothers and sister there was a lessening of the restrictions upon our social life, but this was not marked until after I had left home for college. As the grandson of the minister and the son of a deacon I had to be an example of virtue. It was a heavy handicap for a boy! But thanks to the mingling of discipline with a sane liberty in sports and other interests of a healthy boy, religion became a normal item in my life. As a member of a Christian family I accepted it as a matter of course and joined the church when I was a lad of fourteen.

It was while I was a boy in high school that the wave of evangelism inaugurated by Dwight L. Moody swept across New England. These evangelists were not as commercial as some of their successors but their theology was that of orthodoxy; in many cases committed to premillennarianism. George C. Needham conducted in 1877 a series of largely attended revival meetings in the city of Portland and one phase of the revival was the meetings for boys. A number of boys of high school age, among them myself, became members of the church. Churches unfortunately had little experience in dealing with youth beyond the conventional young people's meetings and so far as I know only a few of these boys continued in church life. Yet from a sense of need of the young was to come the Young People's Society of Christian Endeavor, organized by the Pastor of Williston Congregational Church of Portland, Francis E. Clark, in 1881. This in turn was followed by a number of denominational young people's organizations like the Epworth League and the Baptist Young People's Union of America. These movements, however, did not reach maturity until the late eighties and early nineties when the younger generation was able to give expression to religious interest which was less concerned with theology than with practice.

It would be a mistake to think of nineteenth century evangelicalism as exclusively theological. Its orthodoxy was unquestionable but it was also devoted to the culture of the inner life. Despite its revolt from the liturgical forms of worship it made the public service of the church a very formal succession of hymns, bible reading, prayer and sermon, but it also laid great emphasis upon the prayer meetings and experience meetings in which there was no set order of service, and those present were free to participate in prayer or religious exhortation. The prayer meeting undoubtedly ministered to the religious life of the church but it also developed formulas of its own. Persons would confess to being sinners but would have been insulted if they had been asked to specify their sins. The hymns of the time emphasized the religious mode. P. P. Bliss and Ira D. Sankey were the leaders in organizing a new type of music known as gospel hymns. For a long time these were not used in regular church services but in revival meetings and prayer meetings. In them one finds the heart of evangelicalism. Men were not only to accept but to experience their Saviour. Fellowship with him became for the Protestant what the sacrament was for the Catholic. Prayer had no liturgy. It was to be the free expression of religious faith in the divine presence and aid.

Without any full consciousness of this fact, the evangelical movement was thus centered upon religious experience that was personal and recognizable. Conviction of sin was universally felt to be a prerequisite for the consciousness of salvation. It was long before any serious attempt was made to study religion scientifically. The final appeal for meeting doubt and philosophical uncertainties was the appeal to the feelings. On its more liberal side this evangelical movement found in Tennyson's *"In Memoriam,"* a treasure house of aspiration and faith. The later developments of religious education and the psychology of religion came naturally from this emphasis upon religious experience when once the evangelical movement came in contact with scientific method.

CHAPTER II

THE BEGINNING OF A YOUTH MOVEMENT

THE ATTITUDE of unsophisticated superiority which marked the New England life in general was to be found in education. My generation was perhaps the last to be unaware that there are problems in education. What our forefathers had done we were to do. The discipline in the grade schools was severe, whispering was punished and children were taught to sit upright with folded arms. High school training was modeled after that of the English public schools. If a boy expected to go to college—the higher education of women was just beginning to attract attention—he was expected to study Geometry, Latin, Greek, Ancient History, elementary Chemistry and Botany, and possibly English Literature. The teaching of the ancient languages consisted largely in memorizing grammatical rules and construing word by word whatever was being translated. We were supposed to know something about facts of Greek and Roman history, but we got little insight into classical life and thought. Evidently the ancients were well acquainted with Goodwin's Greek Grammar and Hadley's Latin Grammar. Occasionally the personality of a high school teacher broke across the routine of recitations and stimulated something more than a desire to repeat what had been committed to memory. One of our teachers developed interest in Virgil by setting up competition as to who could translate the greatest number of lines in four minutes. I owe an interest in plants to the enthusiasm of my teacher in Botany. About all that I can remember about my chemistry class was the attractiveness of the teacher, the smell of chlorine gas, and the oracular statement that we do not pant because we are warm, but we are warm

15

because we pant. I do not know just what this important truth had to do with chemistry but I am sure it came from the text book.

I

A college education in the last decades of the nineteenth century was not radically different from that given the parental generation. Much that was then taught in college would be excluded from thoroughly modern high schools as too elementary, but it formed the substance of what was known as the higher education. Instruction was almost entirely by text book which we were supposed to commit to memory. Among these text books were Huxley's *Physiology,* and Whately's *Rhetoric.* The aim of recitation was to repeat as near verbatim as was humanly possible so many paragraphs of each book. Such methods of study were not conducive to independent thinking to say the least, although it might acquaint a class with dignified and clear literary style. The methods of high school were continued into the college and there was little or no effort to arouse independent thought unless it was in debates and orations. Running over the various programs for public exercises during my four years in Colby College, I can find no indication of interest in the transition through which the social order was passing. It may be that Maine was too much on the periphery of American life to have its colleges affected by the new problems which had developed since the Civil War, but it is more probable that all colleges looked with suspicion on any questioning of the *status quo.* Graduate study in the sense of research was practically unknown in the American universities. Johns Hopkins had just been founded and the educational system of the past held the present in *mortmain.*

In one particular, however, a college education was breaking loose from the past. Political economy and history were increasingly gaining recognition. Political economy was largely an adaptation of John Stuart Mill and found itself in sharp opposition to the practical economics which was developing the idea of protective tariff in the interest of the rapidly developing industry. Historical study was beginning to feel the effects of the German university training which many of the younger teachers of history had. At Colby we had the stimulating personality of Albion W. Small who later became head of the department of Sociology in the University of Chicago. In the early years of his teaching in both the economic and historical fields he laid little or no emphasis upon the acquisition of method and demanded memoriter recitation. But some of us owe a great deal to him personally. He brought to the college an interest in modernity that the elderly members of the faculty ignored. Yet, even he, who in after years was to be protagonist for intelligent study of social trends, could criticize an extension of social concepts into economic thought.

Colby had pioneered in co-education. The number of women in any class was small. They had little or no influence on the student life beyond an occasional courtship.

What was true of educational methods might well be expected true of the religious life of undergraduates. A student body of America in the eighties was largely limited to those who planned to enter one of the professions or school teaching. The proportion of men in my class studying for the ministry was large, judged by modern statistics, but the motives which led men toward theological education were not altogether religious. Outside of law and medical schools the theological seminary furnished about the only type of graduate study available. An examination of the catalogs of university appointments in the last decade of the nineteenth century will show that many members of faculties had attended theological seminaries. Such had been the case of Professor Small. Such as it turned out was to be true of myself. The ministry had not yet been subjected to the inundation of untrained men and theological controversies were of the general sort from which denominations emerged. In most colleges the religious life was that of conventional evangelicalism. Students were compelled to attend chapel and were supposed to go to church. The Boardman Missionary Society, named after a missionary who had been a student at Colby, held weekly prayer meetings and there were class meetings attended by the more religiously active minority of the student body. But there was no serious interest in theological thought. The nearest approach to it was hostility to evolution. I remember going to our professor of Biology, himself a very stimulating personality although without any apparent interest in research, and asking him for a book which showed that evolution was untrue.

"Why do you want to know it is untrue?" he asked.

"Because," I replied, with the assurance of complete ignorance, "it is contrary to Christianity."

"If science shows," said the professor, "a fact which is contrary to Christianity, Christianity must be changed."

Such a reply shocked me but stirred me to undirected reading in the field of evolution. I have an impression that I am the only living person who read through Lionel Beale's *Protoplasm*. For weeks I deluged my friends and my fraternity with discussions of evolution until they gave me to understand that I was becoming a nuisance. For the first time I began to think critically. It was very poor thinking but it at least amounted to the organization of a tolerant attitude toward that which was not in current evangelicalism. Such an experience was typical of many college students of the time. They came under the influence of Darwin, Tyndall, Huxley and Spencer. They were forced to make some sort of decision as to their religious life. In some cases as in that of my exceedingly able and lovable friend, later dean of the Divinity School of Harvard, W. W. Fenn, this decision led to an abandonment of evangelical affiliations. In the case of others who like myself remained within the evangelical group, it led to an attitude of mind which was sensitive to theological adjustment. Scientific method, however, was so limited to the fields which were neither religious nor social, that its bearing upon religious thought was small. Most youths of the eighties were unaware of the new trends in philosophy and theology.

I never committed myself to the ministry, but my sympathies and acquaintances were chiefly among those who were planning to go to theological seminaries. Periodically this group felt the pressure of what seemed to them to be the duty of active religious work. Like our evangelical forebears we would hold occasional meetings in schoolhouses in the country. Our chief interest was to convince those who attended these meetings that they were sinners and needed to be converted. About that we had no doubt. The people themselves, however, seemed to be less convinced and I recall that when we were to hold a second meeting in a schoolhouse where we had endeavored to convince our hearers of the dangers which lay in their future, we found it empty. As we approached we saw the young man who had made a fire in the stove, escape through a window.

There was, of course, danger that our consciousness of moral superiority and religious mission might have made us prigs. I do not think that this was the case although we had little to do with the students who in our small college were regarded as "fast." I dare say their habits were not as strict as ours but most of them in later years became highly respected school teachers, lawyers and doctors. In fact, my long acquaintance with student life has made me rather skeptical as to the hopelessness of young men who in college are supposed to be dissolute. When responsibility comes, they are likely to lead respectable and useful lives.

I was by no means at the head of my class in scholarship but I did succeed in getting a senior prize for a highly metaphysical and, I fear, rather unintelligible disquisition on "Progress." Coming interests evidently cast the shadow of their vocabulary! The last year of my college life I paid my incidental expenses by running the college book store. I organized voluntary athletic classes in our sadly inadequate gymnasium, and brought a teacher from Portland who taught us some gymnastic accomplishments. During winter vacations I practiced gymnastic exercises in the Portland Turnverein. I never learned to turn a back-somersault or satisfy my ambition to do the giant swing, but I did progress far enough to win a second prize in the mile walk and on the horizontal bar. I played second base one year on the baseball team and in my senior year caught. In those days we had no mattress-like protection from foul tips, and while the pitcher was supposed to deliver the ball below the shoulder he was only forty-five feet away from the catcher. After graduation I had several invitations to join local professional teams. A few years ago a reporter from one of the Chicago papers called on me to tell me that while his paper had some biographical material concerning me they would like to bring it up to date. I suggested that such a prospective obituary made hardly a cheerful interview, but told him to ask his questions. Among them he wanted to know what in my life I was most proud of. I replied that after graduating from Colby I played one professional game on the Portland team against Providence, that year the champion of the National League. My answer was not scientifically accurate but it illustrates how one takes pleasure in the exceptional. Was not Raphael proud of his sonnets?

II

The student body in the colleges of the last decades of the nineteenth century as a rule had at least some nominal connection with a Protestant church. There were few Jews. Habits of religious thought and practices were carried over from the churches. It was natural, therefore, that a religious movement among college students should embody conventional ideals and purposes. Social problems did not bulk in the undergraduate mind. Moral questions were those of the individual. There were, it is true, a

few voices which were heard pleading for the application of
Christianity to social affairs, but they met with as little response
in colleges as in the churches.

It was characteristic of the period that the first expression of
new interests in the younger generation should have been in the
field of religion. During the years following the Civil War wage-
earners, baseball players, farmers and manufacturers began to
organize agencies for joint action in the protection and increase
of their rights. It was not strange that at the same time college
fraternities should assume new significance, or that the religious
life of the colleges should also respond to this social trend. By
the eighties most colleges had religious organizations which had
become more or less acquainted with each other. This tendency
was stimulated by the organization of Young Men's Christian
Associations both in cities and in colleges. In colleges these societies were interested in and sought to develop the Christian life of
their members by holding meetings, generally prayer meetings.
In 1876 Luther D. Wishard had conceived the idea of an intercollegiate movement which would gather the various societies
into one body. In 1880 under his leadership the various religious
societies and associations in colleges were brought together into
an intercollegiate body. In Colby we transformed the Boardman
Missionary Society into a Young Men's Christian Association.
On the campus of many colleges buildings were erected and secretaries employed. At the start an Association was devoted to
conventional religion, but in a short time it took on increasingly
the nature of a club. Its house still was the center of religious
life of the students on campus but was largely used for social,
athletic and other student activities. The elaborate "Unions" had
not supplemented the "Y." The conception of religion was enlarged and devotional and evangelistic interests were brought into
rivalry with others which were destined to grow increasingly
important. The Associations set up elaborate bible study pro-

grams with enormous registered attendance. In fact, in the course of a few years there developed intercollegiate competition among these bible study classes and the statistics of enrollments were so much greater than the actual attendance as to put an end to the competition.

Such developments as these were not foreseen in the early days of the intercollegiate movement. It was the day of evangelists. The spirit of the Association was largely shaped by Dwight L. Moody. His Northfield Conference to which a large number of colleges sent delegates was centered around the development of a Christian attitude toward life and had a profound influence on Associations in the colleges. In the later eighties there developed among college students an interest in foreign missions. The Student Volunteer Movement, one of the most remarkable student movements in history, was organized in 1888. John R. Mott then became a leader. It was a youth movement still under the influence of the older generation. To it religious expansion meant evangelism. Sociology was all but unknown and the social implications of religion if not ignored, were not emphasized. This movement, however, contained a promise of new religious development. Though their initial outlook on life was highly individualistic, these new organizations were to travel a road which their founders did not foresee, and to become agents in the transformation of evangelicalism itself. Changes in personnel of a religious movement always result in redefinition of inherited beliefs and practices.

It was probably fortunate that this movement among the students of the latter part of the nineteenth century should have had the guidance of broad-minded men of the older generation and that its early leadership should have been more concerned with consolidating religious attitudes and habits rather than with social reform. The social sciences were not yet sufficiently developed to discover the full meaning of the great changes which new economic forces were making. With other leadership young men and women might have been less interested in the development of character and more in economic problems which neither they nor their elders had yet fully grasped. Evangelical religion gained a sense of its social responsibilities and assumed new character, as my generation of college students gained influence in the religious thought and organization at the turn of the century.

CHAPTER III

UNCRITICAL PIETISM

I GRADUATED from Colby in 1884 and entered Newton Theological Institution. I did so rather as a matter of course and without any particular sense of vocation to the ministry. On my mother's side there was a long line of ministers and I went to the seminary in much the same way that I had gone to college. The evangelical heritage was still untroubled. I had no questions to be answered and no serious doubts to be settled. Professor Albion W. Small was one of my heroes and I remember that one of my classmates had suggested that I should, like him, plan to enter a teacher's life. But there was nothing very definite in my mind. The next thing to do was to go to the seminary. My father enabled me to purchase a book store in the seminary and for three years I was able to support myself without any further call upon the family exchequer. The first two years of my course I did not preach but taught a Sunday-school class in Ruggles Street Baptist Church for which I was paid $1.50 a Sunday and given a forty-cent allowance for travel and accommodations and board from Saturday to Monday. I also taught a term in a night school in Newton, my one experience in public school teaching. During the holiday seasons I was clerk in the large book store of the American Baptist Publication Society. I infer that I made a fairly good clerk for I was offered a permanent position at a salary which seemed to me to be larger than I could ever hope to receive as a minister or teacher.

I

The early years in Newton were an Indian summer of college life. Without any particular sense of mission I did my class work,

24

played tennis, learned to ride a high-wheeled bicycle, made social calls and on Sundays listened to Phillips Brooks preach. Those of us who can remember the Phillips Brooks of those years before he became a Bishop will remember his inspiration. His sweep of imagination and freedom from slavery to orthodox formula carried one into a new religious atmosphere. The old inhibitions of conventional Christian life lost something of their control, and the genuinely religious outlook upon life which he gave made life rather than formula important. Those of us who heard him every Sunday were preserved from that professional conformity which a Baptist Seminary in those days made almost inevitable. Less desirable was his influence as a preacher. More or less consciously we copied him. In my own case this amounted to over-rapid speech and the habit, fortunately short-lived, of stuttering in public address. It was easier to reproduce his weakness than his genius!

Theological seminaries in the nineteenth century had been founded to prepare men for denominational ministries. Their curriculum was based upon a conception of the church and the ministry which was unaffected by new currents in scientific thought. Their object was in effect to produce private chaplains co-operatively sustained. There was little incentive to independent religious thought. An infallible and authoritative Bible was the source of the truth they were to preach and from its pages were to be drawn the arguments for rejecting what denominational opponents preached. In controversies which arose over various interpretations of an infallible revelation the Protestant denominations could not appeal to the church as the source of divine authority. By their origin and history they could rely only upon the Bible as the sole rule of faith and practice. A theological seminary was therefore chiefly concerned in training prospective ministers in that particular interpretation of biblical teaching which was held by the denomination it represented. The student body was almost never interdenominational. Congregationalists went to Congregational, Baptists to Baptist, and Presbyterians to Presbyterian seminaries. In the nature of the case our theological education was indifferent to changes in scholarly method or in giving new content to doctrine. The Bible was to be studied in its original languages. Theology was to be committed to memory, the history of the church was to be sketched, homiletic and pastoral methods were to be inculcated. There was very little stimulus to research beyond the exegetical study of the Bible. The minister was supposed to be able to read Hebrew and Greek with sufficient ability to appreciate scholarly commentaries. Indeed, an extraordinary interest in the study of Hebrew had been aroused by William Rainey Harper who was just beginning his work as professor in Yale. The faculty of Newton Theological Institution had two professors in the Old Testament department, one in the New Testament, Theology, Homiletics, Church History and Public Speaking, respectively. One of these instructors, Ernest DeWitt Burton, was to achieve international reputation as a New Testament scholar. At that time he was beginning his career, and his chief interests lay in furthering the method of biblical study which he had inherited from his own teacher, Wm. Adam Stevens of Rochester Theological Seminary. It consisted in word studies, that is to say, an extension of lexicography to biblical exegesis. A striking illustration in the results of this method somewhat modified by historical considerations is to be seen in Burton's great *Commentary on Galatians* published many years later, as well as in various word studies which represent enormous labor in discovering the use of New Testament words in all types of Greek literature. Professor Charles R. Brown was a young man who had something of Harper's contagious devotion to Hebrew. College training did not prepare students for meticulous accuracy in grammar which was demanded by these two teachers, but some of us caught Brown's enthusiasm and I read the Bible through in its original languages.

Associated as I have been during most of my life with theological education, I look back over those years in Newton with the feeling that despite the dominance of educational methods which I have opposed, their influence upon persons of my temperament was helpful. The study of Hebrew induced accuracy in detail, and the teaching of theology taught caution as well as open-mindedness. Orthodoxy, of course, was regnant, but it was not tinged with intolerance. The influence of Dr. S. S. Curry, who became a national figure in the substitution of "expression" for "elocution," evoked an open-minded attitude. He was not only a fine teacher of public speaking but, what was more important in my case, he was alive to literary and philosophical questions. If he did not make us great preachers, he did extend the horizons for those of us who like myself, were unaccountably developing an attitude of dissent.

A movement within biblical study had appeared which was to have unexpected results. That was Biblical Theology. This was really an introduction of historical relativity into theological thought. While it did not deny the authority of the scriptures it undertook to present the religious thought of the different biblical writers from the historical rather than the dogmatic point of view. There was much more implicit in its method than in its findings. Its recognition of the development in biblical thought tended to undermine the basis of evangelical orthodoxy. But this was not perceived by the American biblical students and for a number of years Biblical Theology was treated as a field coordinate with that of Old Testament and New Testament interpretation. It was the first stage in that understanding of the scriptures which a whole-hearted application of historical methods was to accomplish.

II

In my student days at Newton, theological differences and discussions were largely within the field of denominational theology. The philosophy of the time was dominated by idealism and its use by theologians was largely apologetic. Joseph Cook, that cross-section of errant omniscience, had introduced Lotze to Boston audiences and had even made certain concessions to the evolutionary thought, but so far as my recollection goes, the real center of anything like progressive religious thought was in Andover Seminary. There the focus of attention was eschatological. The arguments of Universalists were met by insisting that while there was no second probation after death, there was a continued probation. This in turn had a bearing on the doctrinal treatment of the Bible. In 1885 the professors of Andover Seminary published essays that had previously appeared in the *Andover Review* in a volume entitled *Progressive Orthodoxy*. In it were clearly expressed views which later became widespread. The influence of historical method is to be seen in its discussion of the scriptures. The apostles were the bearers of a revelation made immediate to each of them by the spirit of God, but in the exposition of this revelation they were affected by the conditions under which they wrote. The apostolic teaching was therefore not fixed or absolute but subject to development. Such a view was naturally regarded by evangelical leaders as dangerous and from it arose a controversy which became historic. I doubt if it greatly affected the theological thought of the seminaries or the churches. The "Andover controversy" popularly centered around missions and the basic doctrine of origin of sin and consequent doom of the heathen. At Newton we heard little about it except that such views "cut the nerve of missions." Evangelicalism was too thoroughly presumed to be self-conscious or introspective. The discussion as to the composition of the Pentateuch between William Rainey Harper and William H. Green of Princeton Seminary was too technical for us students, although Dr. Green gave lectures on the subject at Newton. Professor Brown was suspected, with justice, of being sympathetic with the critical position, and Dr. O. S. Stearns, senior member of the Old Testament Department, gave us a series of lectures on the higher criticism which made none of us higher critics although he himself intimated that he thought "there might be something in it." Our outlook was that of orthodox evangelicalism. Social problems, group morality or economic life did not concern us. The business of the ministry was to save souls and produce lives that would not yield to the temptations of the world. The nearest approach to any presentations of the wider significance of religion was given in a series of lectures by David J. Hill then President of Bucknell University. I do not recall that they had any influence on our point of view. The training which we received and which was characteristic of practically all seminaries developed conformity rather than enquiry. Such an attitude was inevitable so long as the scientific method was not stressed in college training. Occasionally students would raise questions in the theology classroom but they were answered from a point of view of an authoritative scripture. Such a method made me theologically restless and I was told by one of my classmates that unless I became a missionary I should become an atheist. Paradoxically this champion of orthodoxy now regards me as a conservative!

Theological students are as human as others but they have their peculiar temptations. Perhaps the most subtle of these is that toward professionalism. Their education not only tends to set bounds to their interests but the position which a young minister holds in the church is singularly subject to both contempt and adulation. Unlike the priest the minister is not believed to have a supernatural influence, and his calling is sacred only in the sense that he is the representative of others' religion. Politeness gives the minister a shadowy priestly status, but his position is determined largely by his personal popularity and service. On Sunday he stands apart from his congregation, on week days he is in demand for funerals and weddings, but his actual status is conditioned largely by the estimate his people place upon his life as a minister. Theological training has largely centered around the two foci, ministerial efficiency and personal piety. In my student days there was no formal training in the latter field. Chapel sessions made no particular appeal to the student body, but class prayer meetings were held by a few members of my own class. The institutional life was not conducive to religious warmth. Those students who possessed genuine spiritual experience turned toward the type of religious life which looked to God for specific guidance in life's affairs. An effort of a student from the theological seminary of Boston University to convert some of us to his doctrine of perfection, however, was wrecked when he told us he thought he was as good as Jesus. Undoubtedly the interest in foreign missions served to deepen religious feelings. The evangelization of the world was a real cause. It appealed to the imagination as well as the conscience of those of us who came under its influence. To go as a missionary in those days meant more of a sacrifice than today. Motives to which appeal was made were religious rather than social or philanthropic, and the state of the non-Christian world was interpreted from an uncompromising evangelical point of view. So many pagan souls died every second, and all were bound to perdition. They needed to hear of an atoning son of God, and it was our duty to carry them the needed message.

The inner conflict involved in deciding upon a life work had a religious meaning. Prayer and the devotional reading of the Bible were sources of peace. We never heard of the psychology of religion and did not become scientifically interested in our own experiences, but there was developing a conviction of divine fellowship and guidance that was genuine. Our God was not under investigation. He cared for us and could be trusted to direct our lives. However one may psychologically account for such implicit faith, and however far I may have moved from its naïveté, it developed a mind-set which made religion something more than a philosophy and has helped me to sympathize with the mystic and the Fundamentalist even while recognizing the limitations of their views.

With its avoidance of worldly pleasures pietism was about the only form of religious experience. I was too much of a Down East Puritan not to distrust excessive emotion and I was not temperamentally a mystic, but providence was no mere rhetorical word. One could expect divine guidance if only one had faith. To search the scriptures was a necessary part of piety.

This habit had sometimes unfortunate results for the scriptural material is not altogether suited for all occasions. The first time I preached in a city church my stage fright was increased by my forgetting the order of petitions as I led the congregation in the Lord's Prayer. For the scripture lesson I had chosen to read the beautiful prayer of Habakkuk. But when I tried to find it Habakkuk was no longer in the canon. In my desperation I turned the leaves of the Bible back and forth as long as I dared and then read the first paragraph my eye fell upon. It happened to be one of Ezekiel's explicit and startling comparisons of the nation of Israel to a prostitute.

Which reminds me of an even more untoward incident which happened in the family of one of my friends. The father was a successful merchant but not much concerned with personal religion. A friend of his, a devotee to the discovery of daily messages from God's word, was much concerned. When my friend's father was confined to his bed by some illness this earnest soul called upon him.

"Charles," he said, "I felt that I ought to come and speak to you about your soul's salvation. Let us open the Bible and get a message from God."

"Very well, I have no objections."

The visitor saw on the bedside table a book bound in limp black leather. Taking it up he said, "Now I will open this and the first verse that I touch with my finger will be the message." So he opened the book and, of course without looking, put his finger down to find a text. It was the description of the Moulin Rouge. The book was a leather-covered guide book to Paris.

But irreverent tales of this sort played no part in such religious life as some of us undertook to lead in the seminary. While I was just enough sophisticated to distrust anything like divination, the Bible had its daily message. I fancy that my experience in this regard was that of most of the young men who shared the new religious enthusiasm due to the appeals of foreign missions and Young Men's Christian Associations and the evangelistic fervor which Moody and his fellow-workers aroused. Pietism with its reading of the Bible and devotional books, its periods of prayer, its avoidance of "worldliness" and above all its conviction that life has a meaning because God makes its plan, may easily become formal and censorious. But it may also give a direction and coloring to religious life which even the scientific study of religion and absorption in practical affairs cannot efface. It would be safe to say that men of my generation who have become religious leaders owe much to these experiences of late adolescence. One may have come to distrust the theological formulas with which such religious habits were rationalized but the experience of these years was too real and too intimate to be discarded.

One new element did enter into my theological thinking. The discussions which arose in a class in theology were within the circle of evangelicalism. Orthodoxy lost something of its sharpness of outline, but any changes were conditioned upon the teaching of the Bible which, however romanticized, was none the less authoritative. For some reason it occurred to me that even the tempered theory of inspiration which we were being taught needed still further modification in the way of recognizing the effect of historical situations upon the thought of the biblical writers. I dare say that this suspicion, for it was hardly more than that, arose from the reading of two books which dealt with the relation of other religions to Christianity. The one was by Trench, *Unconscious Prophesies of Heathenism,* and the other by Kenningale Cooke entitled *The Fathers of Jesus.* The first was thoroughly apologetic and recognized the worth of various pre-

Christian religions in that they foretold the coming of the Christ. The other had been purchased by our professor of history with the belief that it was a history of the Jesuits, but it really was a pioneer in the religious-historical method. I can still recall how it left me bewildered. If the teaching of Jesus was to be derived from that of the rabbis and the oriental religions, what divine authority would he have? That was rather too searching a question to be settled except by recourse to piety. But whether Paul's conception of the work of Christ was not an expression of his rabbinical training was quite another matter. Historical study might help to some conclusion. My interest in the matter became a nuisance in the classroom and President Hovey asked me to write a paper on the subject. So far as I can recall this was the first piece of independent research I had ever made. I do not suppose that I produced a remarkable paper but I made my first approach to a field and a method of study to which I was to give years of effort.

III

It would be a mistake to think that students in colleges and seminaries from 1880 to 1890 were altogether indifferent to world affairs. It was natural, however, that since the new movements among them were directed and stimulated by religious leadership that when the new expansion of interest developed it should have taken the form of a crusade to evangelize the world in their own generation. Whether this same interest could have been directed toward social reconstruction is uncertain for religion for the youth of those days was the only organized movement. In fact, the Northfield Conference and the intercollegiate Y.M.C.A. furnished the initiative for this wider movement. R. P. Wilder, Princeton 1886, John R. Mott, Cornell 1888, C. K. Ober, an associate of Wishard's, and John N. Foreman, a classmate of Wilder's, visited many colleges and seminaries. The missionary interests which had been aroused at Mount Herman spread like wildfire among the colleges. In a single year, 1886 to 1887, more than 2,000 students volunteered for missionary work. This interest swept into the seminaries. The Interseminary Missionary Alliance had been formed in 1881, but in 1898 when at the recommendation of a committee of which Professor J. Ross Stevenson, then at McCormick Seminary, and I were members, it was dissolved, delegates reorganized a theological section in the intercollegiate Y.M.C.A. with Robert P. Wilder as secretary. In the theological seminaries this interest in foreign missions was furthered by persistent endeavor. Men who had never given the foreign missionary work a thought were swept along by the new enthusiasm of its leaders. In 1887 the theological seminaries in the vicinity of Boston held a largely attended convention in Newton Center, and as chairman of a committee I drew up an appeal to the churches to furnish means for sending out new missionaries.

Our enthusiasm was born of an expanding evangelicalism. We heard little about social service except education and nothing of those other forms of mission work which have developed more recently. We were out to evangelize the world in our generation. For years the Student Volunteer Movement did much to break the indifference of students to world affairs.

As I look back upon it I can see this new interest on the part of students for the ministry was the beginning of a wider conception of Christianity and its relations to the world. Expressed as it was in the patterns of evangelicalism, it none the less aroused interest in a world very much larger than New England or even the United States. Many of the leaders of religious expansion in the twentieth century were the outcome of this world-wide movement among students of the last two decades of the nineteenth century. Some of them, it is true, never realized that evangelization was only one aspect of the interpenetration of Western and Eastern cultures, but the psychology of a generation stirred to religious enthusiasm by the call to transform a world was changed. Within it there was no surreptitious imperialism. The church of Christ with its message of salvation and its ideals of individual conduct was to spread throughout the world. What would have been the result if industrialism, militarism and science had been the only forms of the interpenetration of the East by the West is not difficult to imagine. But thousands of young men and women supported by the Protestant churches of America and Europe interpreted the ideals of the West to peoples who otherwise would have known only exploitation.

The religious life was thus being socialized without our being really conscious of the fact. If one can judge from the religious literature of the time, and the appeals of the leaders of the new youth movement, no one had any intimation of the possibilities of this aspect of Christianity. Our interests were primarily with the heathen as subjects of divine justice and love. It was not sociology but religion that was at work in American churches. The new interest was destined to be directed by intellectual and social forces but it was also to furnish ideals and motives for social change.

IV

Between the middle and the senior years of the seminary I had my only experience in the pastorate. For three months I had charge of a church of twenty-two members on the eastern frontier of Maine. The community was made up largely of families whose men worked in saw mills. Church membership was all but unanimously feminine, and young men were almost never present.

As a minister I was the confidant of those who wanted advice. I buried the dead, visited the sick, helped adjust domestic difficulties, kept peace between deacons and made innumerable pastoral calls. I lectured on Luther and Savonarola and organized Sunday-school concerts. It was all very strange and the summer would have seemed interminable if I had not made the acquaintance of some young people in the neighboring city of Calais. Despite all my determination to be a good pastor I must confess that I welcomed tennis and a camping party on Grand Lake.

I undertook to put into operation what was then known as muscular Christianity. I coached the baseball nine and taught some of them how to pitch a curved ball. It was a very different world from that to which I was accustomed but at least I learned that the religious man can be normally interested in human affairs.

I learned another lesson. As I was preaching one Sunday I noticed that a young woman was smiling at me. A theological student cannot preach the gospel under such influence, and I directed my attention to the other side of the church where members of the baseball nine were endeavoring to keep awake. When I reached my boarding house my hostess asked me if I noticed the girl as she sat grinning at me. When I said I had she wanted to know whether it made me nervous.

"No," I replied, "I looked the other way."

"Well," she said, "there was a minister preaching here once and the girl grinned at him, so he stopped in the middle of the sermon and said that the sister should show less levity in the house of God. After the service the mother of the girl came up and demanded of the minister what he meant by abusing her daughter in public. 'I did not know she was your daughter,' said the minister, 'but she was grinning at me and it made me nervous.' 'Well,' she replied, 'she is my daughter and if she grinned at you that is all right. That is the way she worships.'"

I suppose hundreds of times I have found that extraordinary definition of worship occurring to me as a solace for some unintelligent act of good people. That was the way they worshiped.

There was individuality in the men and women who lived on the border of the United States and Canada. Some of them would have made fine characters for books. Indeed, I actually did write the opening chapter of a story and sent it off to a friend for criticism. It never was returned and my literary ambitions subsided.

I recall meeting one original character who lived on the most rocky farm I have ever seen. In fact it illustrated the saying that Satan while carrying a load of rocks had stubbed his toe and spilled the rocks. None the less the owner was proud of his farm and he boasted that his potatoes were the best raised on the river. As I was looking over the stony field he suddenly said, "Elder, did you ever see a mushtang?" As I hesitated to speak he said, "It's a sort of horse that has mushtaches. That's why they call it a mushtang." As I must have still showed my surprise he went on to say he had one down in the barn if I would like to see it. So I went down to the barn and there sure enough was a mustang. The old gentleman suspected I was looking for the mustaches which obviously were not there. "Well," he said, "that critter is a mushtang and in the spring he has mushtaches just like a man, but when I turn him out into the field the darn rocks wear the mushtaches off."

My little parish was exceedingly kind to me, although I suspect I must have been the subject of general discussion. My boyish liking for cocoanut-frosted cake evidently was published, for when the Sunday school went on a picnic to Grand Lake the luncheon was served on a little steamer which had been moored to the shore. When the luncheon boxes were opened every woman had brought a cocoanut-covered cake for the minister. It was quite impossible to refuse their hospitality or to eat all the cake. I did not know how to refuse the offerings but after tasting the cake and praising the culinary achievements of its donor I surreptitiously dropped it overboard. After this had gone on for some little while I happened to look out over the lake and to my horror found the steamer all but surrounded with cocoanut-frosted cake!

This summer experience convinced me that my interests did not lie in the pastorate. Although I preached occasionally during my last year at Newton I decided that I would neither be ordained nor go as a missionary but would become a teacher.

I do not know just what led to this decision. Long ago I destroyed a journal which I kept during these months of new experiences. My last year in the theological seminary was to demand decisions as to what in those days seemed to be providential guidance. A few months ago when I was in Madras I was reminded that during the last months of my theological course I made a solemn promise to myself and, as I believed, to my God that I would go to Madras as a missionary if a decision as to a position at Colby was not reached within two weeks. Probably it was fortunate for the work in Madras that the decision was reached and that I became Assistant Professor of Rhetoric and Instructor of Elocution in my *alma mater*.

CHAPTER IV

THE DISCIPLINE OF COLLEGE TEACHING

THE FACULTY of Colby University, as it was then called, numbered eight, most of them elderly men. There had been very little change in the courses of study and the institution did not differ radically from what it had been when I graduated three years before. Shortly after my appointment Dr. W. S. Bailey joined the faculty as Professor of Geology. He and I kept house together for a year or more and I owe much to his influence. A doctor from Johns Hopkins University he brought to Colby a conception of independent research and scientific method such as the institution had never known.

I

I was barely twenty-four, impatient and, I fear, opinionated but with an enthusiasm for teaching I have never lost. A teacher's life can easily become a deadly routine. To be creative it needs to be supplemented by interests outside its own field. Fortunately I was given opportunity to experiment in new courses as I saw fit. My appointment in Colby was not conditioned by any specialization in the field to which I was called. Professor Small had for several years taken charge of what was then known as elocution but had tired of its drudgery and so arranged matters that I should take over the work he was abandoning, and in addition take classes in rhetoric. The combination of rhetoric and public speaking was sound and not unusual in those days. When I began my teaching I immediately substituted modern text books for Whateley's *Principles of Rhetoric,* and introduced theme writing. I worked faithfully over the themes and public speaking. I had

39

taken summer work with Professor Curry, but I had no gifts as a public reader, and my classes in public speaking, I fear, were taken as an unavoidable evil. Once when I was a few minutes late in meeting a class its members did not take advantage of the traditional right to "cut" if a professor did not appear when the college bell stopped ringing. I felt much flattered. One of the students afterwards told me, however, that if it had been anything else but a class in elocution they would not have waited.

I suspect that my experience with Professor Curry made my criticism sometimes intemperate. My brother, Edward B. Mathews, now chairman of the Department of Geology in Johns Hopkins, has never quite forgiven me for the brusque way in which I dealt with his attempt to declaim the poem "Lives there a man with soul so dead . . ." "There never did," I interrupted and told him to take his seat.

The teaching of elocution carried with it the duty to coach students for declamation in various public exhibitions. For hours I dealt with these young fellows endeavoring to put into application the admirable principles which I had learned from Professor Curry. I certainly did not turn men into orators and about the only compliment I ever had was from Arthur J. Roberts who afterwards became President of the college. He said, "I remember your instruction in training me for the Freshman reading. You told me that there was no absolute necessity of a hiatus between my vest and my pants."

Routine work in English composition did not exhaust my energies. I tried to organize a group of the more mature students for the study of Browning. I also ventured on an elective course in the history of English idiom. In preparing for it I was led into a study of Early English as well as modern literature. I doubt if the course was valuable to anyone but myself, but I have been surprised that more competent persons have not undertaken to make a study of the subject. It still seems to me an attractive field midway between philology and literature. I must have made some sort of success in my teaching of English for I was asked by David Starr Jordan to consider a position in that department in Indiana University. After a good deal of effort, I persuaded the faculty to let me give a course in elementary Hebrew for the benefit of those who planned to go to theological seminaries. The first article that I ever had published, "The Rhetorical Value of the Study of Hebrew," appeared in the *Old and New Testament Student,* edited by William Rainey Harper and George S. Goodspeed, both of whom were then at Yale. My interest in Hebrew ended with my declining to teach it in Newton Theological Institution. People were rapidly becoming more interesting to me than detached scholarship.

II

Although the discipline was good for me I doubt if I could have carried on in my two tasks much longer. Unexpectedly I was directed into what was to have permanent and growing appeal.

In 1888 Dr. Albion W. Small, who was professor of History and Political Economy, was made President of Colby. He caused me to be transferred from the department of rhetoric to that which he was leaving. He chose only to give courses in sociology. It shows how novel social studies were outside of Johns Hopkins, where our new President had just been made Doctor of Philosophy, that it was the first time I had heard the word. I asked him what sociology might be. He undertook to tell me, and in so doing entered upon the major task of his brilliant career—determining the meaning of sociology.

A few years later with John Dewey I was present as an extra-departmental examiner at a doctor's examination in Dr. Small's department at Chicago. The candidate showed monumental ignorance and the examiners' hearts were softened. After a long and sympathetic silence as a last resort, Professor Dewey in his gentle voice asked the candidate to tell us what sociology is. He immediately straightened up and in loud tones said, "I have a definition of sociology but do not care to give it for fear Dr. Small would use it."

One of my many obligations to Dr. Small was that he made it possible for me to have a year's study in Germany. In 1890 I was married to Mary Philbrick Elden, and with her went to Berlin where we set up housekeeping. I entered the University of Berlin for the purpose of studying history and political economy. So far removed was I from the field of theology that I never heard even so distinguished a man as Harnack lecture. The detachment was fortunate. My introduction to critical historical study was not complicated by apologetic interest. One could learn objective historical research without concern as to its results.

The Germany I saw was the Germany of the young Emperor. Only a short time previous Bismarck had been retired. Moltke was still living, and the grandiose policies which were to play such a role in later history were in the making. German scholarship was unquestioned and academic freedom of the instructors was assured. There was a growing dislike of the Jews, but they were members of the faculties. Socialism was developing but it had not acquired the political position which it was later to attain. Von Treitschke was still the prophet of Prussianized imperialism, and Wagner the prophet of scientific economics. I discovered what thoroughness of research meant when in a seminar under Sehring I wrote a paper on *Homestead Exemption Laws of the United States,* and found that his treatise on the subject was more exhaustive than any American literature available in the libraries of Berlin. The courses with Delbrück, Scheffer-Boichorst and Jastrow were guides to the study of sources, the development of a critical historical sense and the impartial accumulation of data. An attempt to study the campaigns of Frederick the Second in a seminar under Jastrow was soon abandoned as I found myself quite lacking in a knowledge of military affairs which the German students possessed.

In later years I recommended students who were going abroad to attend German universities to gain mastery of the language but not to expect that they could gain more effective methods of study than those available in America. In Europe and the Near East, however, it is possible to study geography and monumental remains until the past ceases to be literary and archaeological and becomes instinct with human values. A realization that history is human conduct comes from historical sites and well-organized museums. True, no one can be a genuine historian without severe discipline in the critical study of historical sources, but history itself is not a collection of notes united by a card catalogue. It is the behavior of real people which, often in unexpected ways, survives in or affects the social behavior of the present. To realize this fact is the first step in any reconstruction of today's thought and life. The neglect of this preliminary discipline in historical method accounts for the failure to appreciate social process which marks so much of the theology of today.

In a German university a student of history had all but no contact with students of theology. The university was an institution of research, not for professional training. Students who were planning to win a Doctorate in theology naturally found themselves drawn toward technical questions, particularly of literary criticism. The Ritchlian school was freeing theological thought from metaphysics but its influence was academic. Most of the American theological students were planning to become teachers, and inevitably carried into American theological education this attitude of the German university. Different results might have followed had they attended the German institutions devoted to the practical aspects of the ministry. As it was the technical interests of German scholarship reappeared in American religious life. A rift between scientific theology and the rank and file of church members was a natural consequence. American theological education has for a generation suffered from the unwillingness of theological faculties to recognize that the ministry deals with contemporary people and institutions. I have always been thankful that my apprenticeship in historical method was not in the theological field.

The sudden transition from Maine to Germany was calculated to change inherited attitudes. It would be hard to find a sharper contrast than that between *mores* of a small New England town and those of the great city of Berlin. An evangelical church member in Maine was not supposed to use any form of liquor (Maine was the home of prohibition), smoke, play cards, go to the theatre, work or play on Sunday. Religion was largely a matter of inhibition. In Berlin one found the precise opposite. The meetings of the Historical Club were held in a beer hall. Duels were fought by the members of the corps. Stores were open in the afternoon of Sunday and its hours were given to recreation rather than to church-going. Social practices, which in New England would have been regarded as possible only for the unregenerate, were in Germany regarded as matters of course. American students easily took over and brought back to America new conceptions of personal liberty. My generation of the emancipated did not break with conventions to which they returned, but it was natural that its successor when once it became articulate should look upon vestigial late-Victorian attitudes as hypocrisy. In any social process the third generation is apt to be rebellious. The apprehension with which American religious circles of the mid-Victorian period looked upon German thought is understandable. It was not merely that the universities were free to examine the major premises upon which evangelicalism rested, there was for American students also the disintegrating influence of living in two moral climates. After one had breathed the atmosphere of life in a German university the inhibitions of New England evangelicalism might be observed because of social pressure but their moral infallibility was lost.

III

The three years which followed the year of study in Germany were devoted primarily to the development of my courses in history and political economy. In the latter field I came under the influence of the social conception of economic problems emphasized by Professor Richard T. Ely, and the generation of economists which he taught at Johns Hopkins University. The influence of Mill which had been all but standardized by President Walker, grew rapidly weaker. Economics grew increasingly quantitative and historical. German and Austrian economists, as well as British, furnished technical methods for the revamped science, but the social implications of economics were increasingly realized. As one looks back on those early days of the revolution in economic thought it is hard to realize that Marx was treated in almost an antiquarian spirit and that championing municipal and state ownership of public utilities and the national control of corporations was regarded as radical. In my own teaching, radicalism was certainly not in evidence. I was feeling my way. I printed a little syllabus for my classes, but it must have been an immature attempt to restate Marshall and Roscher and the Austrian theories of value. I doubt whether my classes learned as much as I. About the only clear recollection I have of their reaction is a proposal of a young woman that the dangers of Malthusianism should be met by segregating men and women. But a detached study of theoretical economics certainly tends to realistic rather than impressionistic reforms. Too many religious champions of social reconstruction base their programs upon sympathies and current enthusiasm for untried major premises rather than on historical and economic study. Like my young woman student they forget that all reforms would be easy if it were not for folks.

As the youngest member on the faculty I was impatient of the conservatism of the older members and I became aggressive.

Indeed, about the only regret which my colleagues expressed to me when I left Colby was made by Professor Julian D. Taylor. "I shall miss my constant fight with you in the faculty meetings," he said. The opportunity offered by the institution for other than classroom work was not great, although I did gain permission and funds for rebuilding the gymnasium and installing in it shower baths. I was called upon to do detailed work in the preparation of schedules of class hours, but there was little inspiration in college routine. I fear that I should have degenerated into a mere task master if it had not been for the ideal of independent research which Professor Bailey illustrated in his daily work on the United States Geological Survey. I undertook to assist in the preparation of a concordance for Chaucer, and was assigned his *Boethius*. I worked on it faithfully for some time but soon discovered that I was inept for the making of concordances. Concordance makers are born and not made.

Somewhat later we organized a sort of bureau at the college to meet the possible demands for extension lectures. I wrote a series of articles on "Money" for the *Lewiston Weekly Journal* for which I was paid nothing except the sense of initiating a new phase of popular education. In three centers I gave a series of lectures on the French Revolution. Maine, however, was not keen for university extension and so far as I know there were only one or two other courses of lectures given. There was, however, satisfaction in feeling that one was sharing in a widespread movement and a few years later those lectures were developed into a book.

During my year's study in Germany I became interested in the struggle between Church and Empire, especially from the days of the Carolingians to the Hohenstaufen. This period is valuable for teachers of history, for it shows the elements of social struggle and development so dramatically as to make it interesting for the undergraduate. There was, however, no book of sources available for the study of such a period and during my stay in

Berlin I made such a collection. In 1892 I published *Select Mediaeval Documents,* a collection of material derived pretty largely from works at my disposal in the room of the historical seminar in Berlin. The book was a pioneer in its field and although it passed into a second edition it was superseded by more elaborate collections of materials in an English translation. But the selection of illustrative material from a mass of published documents was a good discipline in developing a sense of significant steps in a social process.

During these years at Colby I got first lessons in the organization of a Cause in an attempt to raise the salary for a professor of the English Bible. I think the plan was originated by President Small but the work of putting it into effect was passed on to me. It consisted in getting contributions of ten cents from every member of every Baptist Sunday school in the state of Maine. As there were no funds for secretarial assistance the amount of work was considerable, but it was a good introduction to the technique of raising money.

So far as professional religious work was concerned I supposed that the matter was closed. I did occasionally preach and used to conduct a fairly large voluntary Bible class at the college Sunday mornings. But there was no incentive to participate or even to become intimately acquainted with religious movements.

Nor was I specially interested in theological thought. Even Mrs. Humphrey Ward's *Robert Elsmere,* which created such a stir in church circles, gave rise to no serious doubts. The bearing of the historical method upon Christianity was still overlooked. But it had some effect upon my thought of the atonement and it was characteristic of the evangelical attitude which I still possessed, that I should be concerned. At the suggestion of our common friend Henry Kingman, I went to Portsmouth, N. H. to see if Rush Rhees, later President of the University of Rochester, who was then pastor of the Baptist Church in that city, might help resolve what I considered doubts. His thought was much more mature than mine and he assured me that I was not losing my Christian faith by thinking that Paul's teaching was colored by his Jewish inheritance! The matter was settled in a buggy ride through the rain and thereafter we talked about a great many matters that were not connected with theology.

Thanks to the writings of Washington Gladden, Josiah Strong and Richard T. Ely my interest was aroused in the social bearing of Christianity. *The Outlines of Economics* by Professor Ely which I used as a text book in the place of Walker's *Principles of Political Economy* served to systematize a growing interest in the subject. But in a small town it was impracticable to attempt to organize any social body and I doubt whether it ever occurred to me to undertake it. What little share I had in politics consisted in serving as delegate to a Republican state convention where I saw a political machine in actual operation. I supposed that my connection with religious affairs had ended except as a member of a church.

IV

This interlude of seven years between my graduation from the theological seminary and the beginning of work in Chicago was significant in many ways but in none more than accustoming me to deal with historical problems on their merits rather than in the interest of some theological position. Historical minded-ness will never be developed by those who undertake to manip-ulate history in the interests of theological conclusions. Our libraries contain many volumes which have an encyclopedic mass-ing of facts but are often mere special pleading. Historical method and historical mindedness can be gained only in a devo-tion to history itself. It is, of course, much easier to select data that prove some thesis than to let historical facts interpret them-selves as observable points in a social process. Scientific attitude can be gained only by scientific study. President Mason of the University of Chicago used to insist that ministers' training should include a year's training in some chemical or physical laboratory where men actually performed experiments rather than generalized about "science." The proposal doubtless has its value, but the real field for such experimentation is that of the social sciences such as history, economics and sociology. Such discipline is indispensable for those who deal with religion. Otherwise they are likely to be swayed by that to which they respond emotionally as truth. It is certainly significant that so much of our new appreciation of religion is due to the work of men who acquired their techniques in non-religious fields. I did not realize when I was getting up my extension lectures on the French Revolution that in the attempt to approach the problems of the Revolution from the point of view of social forces there was being shaped a method for the approach to Christianity as a religion.

When in 1892 President Small left Colby to become the head of the department of Sociology in the new University of Chicago, he planned to have me enter his department as soon as it was practicable. In consequence I set about, under his direction an independent study of the literature of sociology beginning with Spencer. Such studies and my attempts to introduce genuine historical study in undergraduate classes served to give me a mind-set which saw history as a social process with elements of the past continuing in the present.

Fortunately the classes with which I had to deal contained men of exceptional ability. Not a few of them later reached distinction in academic and legal circles. I have to confess, however, that they did not become historians. The example of Professor Bailey turned several of them toward the field of geology. Perhaps my excess of zeal helped in the decision. At any rate George Otis Smith, who subsequently became Director of the United States Geological Survey, says that I made him a geologist by abusing him in my courses in the French Revolution.

The years have brought notable changes to the college and the institution as I knew it has became thoroughly modern. All in all it was an exceedingly comfortable life at Colby in those days. Our income was sufficient to enable us to satisfy a reasonable desire for travel and some luxuries. Yet the security and quiet of a small college in a small town gradually became burdensome. There is no incentive to ambition in such surroundings. Before I was thirty I realized that I could do my classroom work without any necessity of severe study. Opportunities to participate in the major movements in thought and social reform were lacking. I was isolated in a world in which I had been born.

Yet, I remember joining a group which included E. Benjamin Andrews, at that time President of Brown University, Frances Bellamy, Philip S. Moxom, Charles Rufus Brown, and Norman Fox. It was my first experience in uninhibited dissent. Nothing, however, came of our meetings, although there was a half-hearted attempt at publication of a progressive journal. Rebellion expended itself in criticism of denominational policies. There was no connection with the Brotherhood of the Kingdom which had been established in 1892.

Just at this time Professor Ernest D. Burton proposed that I should come to Chicago as Associate Professor of New Testament History. My first reaction was one of hesitation. Although I had taught two winters as his substitute in Newton Theological Institution I knew I was not adapted to conventional New Testament instructing. In fact, I had declined a call to a professorship in New Testament in Newton. I had never worked in the field proposed and knew nothing about it. In that I had plenty of company for the historical method had not yet been applied in any serious way to the study of the New Testament. I doubt if Dr. Burton himself foresaw the revolutionary effect of such a method. Then, too, remembering my experience I had no desire to join a theological school. More than that, a visit which my wife and I made to the Columbian Exposition had left an unfavorable impression of Chicago. But Professor Burton overcame our hesitation. I caught his enthusiasm for a university in the making. My inherited interest in religion took form in an ambition to have a part in extending its frontiers. A new age was in the making and religion was needed in social change. I had at least some mastery of historical method which could be applied to the New Testament field. The appeal of an adventure, an opportunity to share in the life of a university, the possibility of escape from limitations of which I was growing daily more conscious pointed to only one decision. In the summer of 1894 I took up my work in the University of Chicago.

CHAPTER V

ACADEMIC FREEDOM IN RELIGION

FOR ONE accustomed to the ways of college professors in a small New England town the atmosphere of the new university was exhilarating. The fact that no titles were used by members of the faculty except in the case of physicians, emphasized human rather than professional relationship. At the time when I joined its faculty the institution was a novelty in Chicago life. To many persons a professor was some one who had unaccountably overlooked opportunities to make money. I remember once asking the partner of the leading bond house of Chicago as to how a young man I had recommended to him was getting on. "That young man," he said, "will never make a business man. He ought to be a professor." But it was not long before it was evident that the faculty of the University was anything but indifferent to the municipal affairs. President Harper served on the Board of Education. Charles E. Merriam, after serving as alderman, barely missed being elected mayor. Professor J. Lawrence Laughlin had a part in the building up the Federal Reserve System, Professor Charles R. Henderson was a leader in charities and correction. Other faculty members were on commissions and many public enterprises.

I

The University of Chicago at the time of my arrival on its campus was sprawled over an all but unredeemed prairie. No one looking at the majestic buildings which today face the Midway can realize the institutional crudity I found. The buildings which had been erected had many of them unfinished brick ends, the athletic field was a section of open prairie and the gymnasium was in a one-story temporary building which housed also the university press and library. But the air was charged with enthusiasm and hope. On the faculty there were men who had already won distinction, and whose co-operation inevitably set the highest standard of research and scholarship. They were indeed Olympians. But I look back also upon a group of young men, some of them barely thirty, whose career has been noteworthy. Some of them are still with us; others have passed into that empyrean atmosphere in which dwell the presidents of Foundations and universities; others are dead; still others are partaking of a meteorological last sacrament in the climate of California. To them was given the opportunity of contributing their own growth and spirit to the collective growth and spirit of the University. To them as they matured every addition to knowledge was a frontier to be extended. Their sense of mission, one might almost say in ecclesiastical terms, of vocation, gave to the University of Chicago a quality which older institutions often lack. A sense of an uncompleted task faced us in the prophetic brick walls of buildings waiting for additions and in the crudities of our surroundings.

In 1894 the educational world of America was only beginning to break from the conventional ideals of the American college. Graduate study outside the professional schools was just beginning to be made possible in Johns Hopkins and Harvard. Many of the older men of the faculty were products of theological seminaries, although they were ready to forget the pit from which they had been dug! The University of Chicago represented principles and practices which were, in the very nature of the case, experiments. To read the first bulletins of Dr. Harper is to find one's self in the midst of educational projects and novelties which make the reorganized University of today appear almost conservative. There was little in the accepted educational organization of the day that was not scrapped or modified. The University was to be kept open the year round. Semesters and terms were to be replaced by quarters. The summer was to be devoted to University activities on the same level as the rest of the year. Instead of an educational *table d'hôte* of one-hour and two-hour courses, the student was to take two courses, a major two hours a day, and a minor one hour, during six weeks. Instead of diffusion, there was to be concentration in study, with the minds of the students centered rather than distracted by a variety of interests.

Intercollegiate athletics had been treated by most educators either as a sort of prophylactic against student disorder or as a means of keeping students together while the faculty sprayed them with education. The University of Chicago made physical culture a phase of university life, and, to the amazement of the educational mind, made Alonzo A. Stagg the Director of Physical Culture a member of the faculty, and put the control of athletics in the hands of professors instead of students and alumni.

The University was not to be a college, but was to include a college. At once the problem of curriculum and organization took new form. The junior college came into existence on our campus and, so far as I know, the institution first of all dared to break across the established educational respectabilities of college "years" and miscellaneous electives by sharply distinguishing between the types of study of the junior college and the senior college. The institution has dared to risk making educational mistakes in the interests of educational progress. Freedom for institutional introspection, criticism, and reorganization has made the University of Chicago a laboratory where educational experiments have been made.

Criticism of the University's daring to break with convention and to experiment in self-organization has ranged from bitter attack to alleged humor. One of the leading journals of the East, with that fine detachment from the American spirit that characterizes the outposts of European culture on the Atlantic

Coast, prophesied that soon the output of doctors of philosophy in the University of Chicago would rival the output of pigs in the stock yards. The most familiar form of humor, however, was to refer to our institution as a continuation of the Midway shows, or "Harper's Three-Ring Circus."

But neither satire nor opposition stopped our attempts to give order and outlook to educational reconstruction. A reformer whom nobody criticizes is no reformer. It is better to be damned than ignored.

II

If a university is to conduct research, academic freedom is indispensable. As far back as 1899 the Congregation of the University adopted the following resolution:

Resolved, 1. That the principle of complete freedom of speech of all subjects has from the beginning been regarded as fundamental in the University of Chicago, as has been shown both by the attitude of the President and the Board of Trustees and by the actual practice of the President and the professors.
2. That this principle can neither now nor at any future time be called in question.
3. That it is desirable to have it clearly understood that the University, as such, does not appear as a disputant on either side upon any public question; and that the utterances which any professor may make in public are to be regarded as representing his opinions only.

It is to the lasting credit of the Board of Trustees and the Founder that they have never sought to prevent free expression of views held by members of the faculties. President Harper in a Convocation address stated this fact distinctly:

In the University of Chicago neither the Trustee, nor the President, nor anyone in official position has at any time called an instructor to account for any public utterances which he may have made. Still further, in no single case has a donor to the University called the attention of the Trustees to the teaching of any officer of the University as being distasteful or objectionable . . . Neither an individual, nor the state, nor the church has the right to interfere with the search for truth, or its promulgation when found.

This position was that of President Harper's successors in office, notably of President Robert M. Hutchins. Those who were given this freedom did not turn it into license. The University has suffered from only a few men with rhetorical halitosis born of ill-digested omniscience. It is true that some of our number have resorted to epigrams that found journalistic publicity, and an epigram is often a half-truth so expressed as to irritate people who believe the other half-truth. But freedom evoked a sense of responsibility.

Unless one dares face unexpected and, it may be, undesired results of research in any field, such research is impossible. For those who in all fields of thought are scientifically minded, there is the abiding conviction that good method in the hands of honest people will correct false conclusions; develop intellectual independence; evoke a cautious, tentative presentation of conclusions; and arouse the conviction that youth is not merely the inheritor of the achievements of its elders, but fellow-seeker for reality.

III

It was into this atmosphere that the Baptist Seminary, in which President Harper had taught, entered as the Divinity School of the University.

Its relationship to the University was more than formal. It brought the Divinity School faculty into the atmosphere of research. It was inevitable that they should be increasingly sensitive to the problems which arose from the social, economic and scientific approach to life. I suspect that a great many of our colleagues on other faculties thought that we were perpetuating traditional attitudes and beliefs, but as the struggle over academic freedom in the field of religion grew more intense, this feeling of suspicion was appreciably diminished. Especially was this the case as the older members of the faculty who came over from the Morgan Park Seminary retired or died, and the faculty was developed by the addition of those who were frankly committed to research in the field of religion.

When the University was founded, the Baptist Union Seminary in Morgan Park, Illinois, was made the Divinity School of the University as one of the conditions under which Dr. Harper assumed the presidency. This was done through a contract which left the trustees of the seminary responsible for the conduct of the Divinity School. As a matter of fact, however, the Baptist Union has never had sufficient funds to carry on the school and its budget has been met from the general funds of the University and such specific gifts as were made for its support. The situation was liable to serious complications but, thanks to the fact that the most influential trustees of the Baptist Theological Union were members of the Board of Trustees of the University, no serious issue ever arose between the two Boards. Large gifts to the University for the benefit of the Divinity School served to make the administration of the school a phase of the total university life. By vote of the Baptist Theological Union trustees its faculty possessed the same academic freedom as that enjoyed by members of the other university faculties.

There has never been any requirement that the faculty of the Divinity School should belong to any single denomination, and although at the start its members were all Baptists, at the present it is genuinely inter-denominational.

All theological professors are exposed to the danger of being drawn away to the technical interests of their own fields and of becoming detached from anything except formal ecclesiastical relations. This and the fact that most theological seminaries are under denominational control may explain why it is that theological professors, insofar as they attempt independent studies, tend to center upon technical problems or those associated with their own denominational organization. We were, of course, not free from this attitude of detachment but from the start I felt that the training of men for religious professions necessitated participation in the activities into which they were to enter. A theological professor in the best sense of the word ought to be a man of the world. However respectful he should be of the prejudices of those with whom he is associated in organized religious life, he must be first of all a man interested in human affairs. Professional piety and the censorship of others' morals are non-conductors between one's self and the actual world.

The prevailing theological interest at the time of its organization is to be seen in the size of the various departments in the Divinity School. There were as many in the field of the biblical and Semitic studies as in all the other departments combined. Biblical study was the representative of the new scientific interest in religion. The Divinity School coming into the atmosphere of academic scientific freedom naturally found itself confronted with the question as to its own attitude toward similar freedom in the field of religion. We suffered from no such segregation as sometimes marked the relations of theological seminaries with universities. The members of the faculty of the Divinity School were members of the various university boards and the school was integrated into the general university life. In my last year I was a member of practically every university board. Professor Burton, head of the New Testament Department, became President of the University. Furthermore, members of our faculty shared in the general social life of the University. When the Quadrangle Club was formed I was for a number of years its treasurer and in 1903 was its president.

It was inevitable that we should share in the enthusiasm for scientific research which has always marked the University of Chicago. But scientific research is tentative, and theology has always been the organization of an authoritative group belief. The two attitudes seemed incompatible with each other. The

Divinity School must either remain as it had been, an adjunct of the Baptist denomination or exercise the freedom of research in its own field. This was to raise the question of academic freedom where both custom and tradition were bound to be shocked. It was hard for the laity as well as the clergy to realize that the University as an institution did not have opinions and could not be quoted as taking attitudes on religious matters. Freedom of research, too, involved the possibility of different views being held by members of the same department, and academic courtesy as the only limitation set upon the expression of one's own findings, and the criticism of those of others, even though they were colleagues.

In the case of a divinity school academic freedom is not quite so simple as in the case of chemistry or any of the natural sciences. For religion is not merely philosophy, and a divinity school is in a real sense of the word a professional school training leaders of groups whose efficiency has always depended upon theological coherence. The Divinity School as an integral part of the University, had to decide whether it should become a detached school of religion or a leader in a religious movement. As a matter of fact it chose to do both. On one side it endeavored to train men for the leadership of organized religion, and on the other it undertook to introduce them to the methods of the scientific study of religion. It would have been much simpler to have chosen one or the other of these alternatives. There have been times during the forty years of my association with the school in which the temptation to do so has been great. But President Harper bequeathed to us a policy of maintaining a relationship with organized church life which at the start was naturally closest with the Baptist denomination. However, the Baptist denomination as such had no control over the school, and the relationship of the various members of the faculty to organized religious life was largely one of their own choosing. They were all members of evangelical church bodies and carried into the atmosphere of academic freedom a sense of corporate relations which were based upon a sound sociological understanding of religion itself.

The struggle between academic freedom and ecclesiastical authority occurred under favorable conditions. On the one side was the University granting the Divinity School as full a measure of freedom as was shared by any department of the University, and on the other were the members of the faculty who undertook to administer such freedom in such a way as would further the interests of the Christian movement. That they should increasingly come to question theological formulas was to be expected. But their great problem was the extension of a religious movement along the new frontiers which they saw rapidly expanding in the various fields of investigation in which their colleagues on the University faculties were engaged.

IV

It was natural that the first contact of the scientific spirit with the evangelical church life should have been in the biblical field. The conflict between scientists and theologians had served to concentrate attention upon the first chapter of Genesis. In so doing it had raised the question of scriptural infallibility. Historical criticism found its way into American Christianity as men educated in Germany applied their new skills to biblical instruction. It became the *bête noire* of orthodoxy. Yet it did not at first affect the general theological position of the critics. The controversy and trials which arose within the Presbyterian churches were explicitly within the confines of confessional theology. Their storm centers were Charles A. Briggs of Union Theological Seminary and Henry P. Smith of Lane Theological Seminary. The former was tried for heresy and acquitted by the presbytery of New York in 1892, but was suspended by the General Assembly the following year. Two years later he joined the Protestant Episcopal Church. His theology was conservative and he defended the articles of creedal dogma. Professor Smith was forced to leave Lane Theological Seminary, not so much for his theological heresy as for his critical views.

It may be difficult for the younger ministers of today to realize that the initiation of popular interest in biblical study came through enthusiasm for the study of Hebrew. In large measure this was due to the influence of William Rainey Harper. While a young professor in the Baptist Theological Seminary at Morgan Park, Illinois, he gave correspondence lessons in Hebrew which were taken by a rapidly increasing number of clergymen. When he became professor at Yale his ability as teacher and his application of the historical method to the study of the Bible attracted widespread attention. He founded the American Institute for Sacred Literature, which carried on instruction by correspondence. He himself at one time held three professorships in Yale University. Those of us who were young men in the last two decades of the nineteenth century will recall the zeal with which men turned to the study of Hebrew. The interest was not merely literary or historical. It was really born of the evangelical belief in the Bible itself as the word of God. By the study of the Hebrew one could come closer to inspired teaching. The stories of those who studied Hebrew because they believed they would use it in Heaven were doubtless exaggerated, but they expressed a current belief in its worth as the language of inspiration. At one time there were hundreds of men as well as many women studying the language by correspondence and in summer schools. By the end of the century this linguistic enthusiasm had cooled but the new interest in the Bible continued. Appreciation of its literary value was fostered by lectures and books and correspondence lessons. Courses in the literary study of the Bible appeared in many colleges and universities. It became popular to distinguish sharply between the theological and literary use of the Bible.

With few exceptions, theological seminaries regarded critical methods as dangerous and as having a direct bearing upon the acceptance of the Bible as the volume of revealed truth. There was, for instance, the question as to the authorship of the Old Testament books. This would have been of hardly more than academic interest if it had not been urged that it affected the orthodox belief in the deity of Jesus Christ. His reference to Moses, David and Jonah was not literally correct if the conclusions of the critics were accepted. It became increasingly impossible to avoid theological alignment in critical and noncritical groups.

The issue was more than doctrinal. It was personal as those of us who were free from denominational control can testify. The recasting of religious faith differs with different people. Most generally the beginning is one of bewilderment born of the surprise which follows the examination of beliefs which rest upon presuppositions which had never been questioned. Suddenly they seem to be, as it were, hanging in mid-air. It is probably true that all persons have a limit beyond which they do not care to have investigation go. In the case of a natural scientist it would probably be confidence in method. In the case of a Catholic it would be the church as a preserver and enricher of the revelation given in the Bible. In the case of those of evangelical background it was the Bible itself. Whenever a presupposition is subjected to examination the effect is the same. What happens next is largely a matter of temperament or of circumstance. Some people are born dissenters and doubts make them rebels. Other persons are naturally conservative and hesitate to break with existing relations. Criticism of presuppositions leads to a change in perspective of value that is unconscious. Early loyalties and associations are maintained and realization of the change of attitude comes unexpectedly. I was once conducting a class in the teaching of Paul, which I had worked out in some detail, and had found that Paul agreed with my views rather satisfactorily. (It was a procedure in which I was not without companions!) A student asked me a question. When I had answered it my lecture notes were of no value, and I abandoned them then and there. For the first time I saw meaning in data which I had either overlooked or romanticized. I had the same experience in a course on the life of Jesus. I was giving what I believed was a historical view of Jesus when suddenly I thought, "How does it happen that the person you are describing ever had the significance which he has had?" I never again used those lectures. The external history of New Testament times became an approach to the psychology of Jesus and the early Messianists.

In moments of solitude also one sees kaleidoscopic recombinations of questions and answers, doubts and faith, of which one had not been aware. Sometimes this unexpected discovery of how far one has progressed into new religious convictions is painful. Dr. Harper once told me that when first he realized that his critical conclusions involved a denial of the Davidic authorship of one of the psalms quoted by Jesus, he paced his study for hours struggling with the question as to whether he should follow his findings. I well remember how questions I had pushed into the closets of my mind assailed me as for days I rode alone along the side of Mt. Hermon. It was hard for any of us to accept conclusions which a respect for intellectual integrity demanded. It would have been easy to take the position of a theological professor who said in his classes that his mind showed him that there were two Isaiahs but that his heart told him there was one, and that in religion he followed the dictates of his heart. Later he outgrew this obscurant position but it expressed a conflict which could not be avoided. Others than he romanticized orthodoxy and attempted by more or less casuistical devices to conserve the value of the Bible as the word of God. Indeed, there sprang up a short-lived discussion as to whether the Bible contained the word of God or was the word of God. It would be unjust to say that these adjusters of orthodoxy were insincere. Their conservatism was due to a lack of method and loyalty to church affiliations. In the case of scholars who were outside the evangelical churches the need of conserving accepted religious beliefs was unnecessary. But such men were few in America. Biblical scholars were not only members of evangelical churches but they were professors in evangelical seminaries. They could not act as if they were not.

It was natural that there should be bitter opposition to the critical study of the Bible. The term "higher," itself was an irritant. We were charged with feeling an arrogant superiority to other Christians. Theological discussion is always intense because the disputants believe that they are the representatives of the higher powers. Evangelical orthodoxy rests so largely upon a theory of biblical inspiration that the critical approach to the scriptures seemed tantamount to an attack upon God himself.

It is not difficult to appreciate the somewhat illogical position in which we were placed who were loyal to the religious bodies to which we belonged. We did not realize how criticism would disintegrate the evangelical position itself. The religious press, with almost no exception, was denominationally controlled and pressed home the charge that in the critical findings as to the authorship of the biblical writings we were really attacking the deity of Christ. The argument was simplicity itself. Jesus had referred to the fact that Jonah had been three days in the belly of the great fish. If this were not a historic fact then Jesus was either mistaken or untruthful. In either case he could not be the Saviour who was the incarnate Son of God. And this in turn resolved itself in the discussion as to whether a whale could really swallow a man, and if so, whether it would be possible for a man to live when once swallowed. As evidence of the truth of the Bible we were told of men who had had this experience and lived. One champion of orthodoxy, realizing that the biblical account speaks of a great fish and not of a whale, declared that his God was capable of making a fish large enough to hold an apartment building. One of the Chicago daily papers published a cartoon illustrating this belief. All this seemed to me to be less a matter of theology than of ichthyology, but the issue certainly could not be avoided. Our critical position relative to the Mosaic authorship of the Pentateuch, the integrity of the book of Isaiah, the historicity of Jonah, and the Davidian authorship of the Psalms had theological consequences of real magnitude. It was, I suppose, inevitable that we did not at first realize this fact and undertook to meet the difficulty by giving new content to the evangelical vocabulary and by activity in church life. In so doing, we exposed ourselves to charges of dishonesty and hypocrisy from those who held similar critical views but were not attempting to conserve evangelical values. I do not think that the charge was justified, but neither do I believe that those who made it were intentionally offensive. The fact is that all three parties, the orthodox, the detached radical and the evangelical critic were sincere. The real issue appeared in the later struggle between Fundamentalists and Modernists for the leadership of the evangelical denominations.

V

During the twenty years or more during which this controversy was incubating, the Divinity School of the University of Chicago was educating itself in the matter of academic freedom. In the earlier days the faculty contained men who differed frankly as to the worth of the higher criticism. The unwillingness on the part of biblical scholars to assume radically negative positions could not satisfy those who held to Gladstone's "impregnable rock of holy scripture." It was, indeed, a new policy for a divinity school to permit theological differences among its members. I remember a conversation I

had with the president of one of the leading theological seminaries of America on this subject. His faculty included leaders
in the critical school, and had been involved in heresy trials. To
illustrate the freedom of his faculty he told the following
anecdote.

"I was recently on a railroad train and fell into conversation with a professor in a certain Theological Seminary. We
naturally discussed conditions in our respective schools. I remarked that we were seeking after truth and endeavoring to
train men to preach the truth. My companion said: 'Such investigation does not trouble us. We are not seeking truth. We
are teaching our men to teach the Westminster Confession.' "

The story was good-natured and was intended to show the
freedom of the speaker's own institution. I asked him, however, what would happen if in the search for truth a member
of his faculty should decide that he ought to become a Unitarian. The reply was, "We should ask him to resign!"

There was plenty of pressure brought upon President Harper
to take a similar position. Some of the religious newspapers of
the country were unqualified in their demand that certain
members of our faculty, including the President himself, should
be disciplined, if not dropped. It was President Harper's policy
never to get into controversy, and attacks made upon him personally he let go unanswered. But he took the bold step of
asking the Baptist Conventions of the Central States to appoint
members of a committee to come and investigate the teaching
of the Divinity School and to decide as to what the proper
policies should be. This committee had a number of meetings
and had various members of the faculty, including the President, state their general position relative to the Bible. The body
of course had no authority, but gave an opportunity for President Harper to offer an alternative as to whether in their opinion it would be better that the Divinity School should have
academic freedom or to cancel the contract existing between the

Baptist Theological Union which historically had oversight of the Divinity School, letting the Union take its funds and organize an independent school in some sort of affiliation with the University, thus giving the University an opportunity to develop its own independent Divinity School. As a matter of fact, at his request, I had drawn up plans to meet this contingency. But the decision of the committee was practically unanimous. It wished to maintain the existing relations with the consequent academic freedom on the part of the members of the Divinity faculty. From that time the interest of the Committee of One Hundred, as it was called, gradually waned, and one of the first acts of my administration as Dean of the school was to let it disappear.

A generation earlier, undoubtedly, the result would have been the dismissal of a number of us from the faculty. As it was, a definite step was taken in the process of adjusting evangelical Christianity to new conditions. If biblical studies were to be controlled by theological considerations, scientific study of the Bible in any real sense was impossible. If, however, such studies were to be strictly free and genuinely scientific, the practical question arose as to what bearing their results should have upon the religious life, organized as it was in denominational groups loyal to an authoritative Bible. Such a question was more than academic or even scientific. It involved the psychology of groups and an evaluation of the importance of the past as it exists in the present. Quite as truly was it a question as to whether the organized religious life of the country should oppose or utilize the rapidly developing scientific spirit.

VI

In the earlier days President Harper had been the center of attack and the issue centered about the Bible. But it could not well remain so limited. Professor George B. Foster unintentionally became the center of the inevitable theological contro-

versy. He was asked to give an address at a convention in Iowa.
Before going he told me that he planned to state his position,
telling his audience that what he was about to say was the very
worst that could be said as to the position of the Divinity
School. Knowing as I did the religious temper of Iowa I urged
him to do nothing of the sort but give an excellent sermon of
his on "Patience." But he insisted that his plan was desirable
and that the result of his speech would be that every one would
see how unwarranted was the hostility toward our faculty. It
turned out as I feared. So far from quieting criticism it furnished new fuel to the critics. Professor Foster was a wonderful spirit but lacked persuasiveness. In fact, his presentation
of his position was apt to be irritating even to those who agreed
with him. When asked to repeat his Iowa address at a Ministers' Meeting in Chicago he aroused a veritable storm of criticism. Pressure was brought to bear upon President Harper for
his dismissal from the faculty. The hostility to Professor Foster
was deepened after the publication of his volume *The Finality
of the Christian Religion* in 1906, an important contribution
to the development of religious thought. I remember his saying to me that it represented the maximum of Christianity that
could be retained by the modern mind. The volume however
greatly disturbed some of the Baptist ministers of Chicago and
it was proposed to expel Professor Foster from the Baptist
Ministers' Meeting. The result was a series of heated discussions which finally resulted in his being dropped from the Ministers' Meeting, although a few years later the constitution of
the body was so changed as to prevent the repetition of any
such heresy trial. The opposition to Professor Foster's view
was led by persons who were not particularly well-grounded in
theological thought but correctly saw that his position was anything but orthodox. One of the charges made against him was
that he said that any one who believed in miracles was a knave.
The author of the charge, when challenged to bring forth the

evidence of such a statement found a sentence in which Professor Foster had said that those who believed in miracles were *naïve!*

President Harper would not consent to dismiss Professor Foster but as there was a vacancy in the department of Systematic Theology he determined to appoint a man who would represent a different type of theology. He finally came to the conclusion that I should be transferred from the department of New Testament to that of theology. I agreed to accept the transfer under certain conditions. When those conditions were known Professor Foster immediately wrote me a courteous letter in which he said he planned to ask to be transferred from the department of Systematic Theology to that of Comparative Religion. This was accomplished and he became thus a member of the faculty of Arts and Literature. His students, however, were almost exclusively from the Divinity School.

Professor Foster was one of the noblest and bravest souls I ever knew. He faced misfortunes with courage which was sublime. I met him just after one of his children had been drowned. He was suffering deeply and cried out, "There must be a God somewhere in the universe." He passed later through successive philosophical stages which led him away from the evangelical theology of his earlier days but he always had a profound faith in God. One evening as we walked home together after a lecture he had given on pragmatism, I remember his calling out in his penetrating voice, "Mathews, we need a God, a real God, a God to whom we can pray for rain."

Professor Foster was a good representative of the movement in thought which was increasingly removed from the perception that Christianity is a religious movement rather than merely a system of truths. The importance of non-church-going religious philosophers is great but their influence is indirect if not negligible so far as operative Christianity is concerned. They find themselves increasingly out of sympathy with Christian groups and tend to dissociate themselves from organized religious work. The choice between such an attitude and that of a continued participation in organized church life sooner or later has to be made. Academic freedom in teaching religion involves something more than a mere presentation of beliefs. There remains also a question as to whether one will approach religious problems from the point of view of the religious community or from that of a detached search for truth. Clearly enough there is involved here the still more profound choice between religion as a form of social behaviour rationalized and directed by intelligence, and religion as a philosophy in which the historical and social elements of an organized movement are to be ignored. If the former conception be chosen, attention will be centered upon the reorganization of religious institutions, the adjustment of religious education to intellectual and social conditions and the extension of the values preserved in the Christian movement to the morality of groups.

In other words freedom in teaching presented the choice between an introvert or extrovert religion, between philosophical techniques and participation in the actual recasting of the Christian movement.

It may be that I am making the antithesis too distinct, but one has only to look at the religious history of the last thirty or forty years to see the different attitudes of men who hold approximately the same religious convictions. If one is to withdraw from the strain and problems of human life it is comparatively easy to discuss any question involved in religious belief and treat Christianity as if it were independent of human action. But if Christianity is a religion it cannot be treated as if it were a group of absolute truths. However important may be a philosophy of religion, the religious life which furnishes material for the philosophy is more fundamental.

I do not think that the distinction between these two conceptions of religion was very much in my mind at the turn of the century, but I increasingly felt that my approach to religious reconstruction should be from the point of view of an existing religious group rather than from that of abstract philosophical thought. The Christianity with which I was concerned was not so much an essence of truth as the organized Christian movement which carried forward permanent values in its beliefs. It was only gradually that the current of my thinking led to decreased emphasis upon evangelical formulas.

CHAPTER VI

DEMOCRATIZING RELIGIOUS SCHOLARSHIP

THE DEMOCRATIZING of an idea must have instruments and technique. One has to choose between participation with going social movements and a detached criticism of such movements. In religion as in politics radicals have their place as irritants, but religious progress is possible only when religious groups are affected. To accomplish this end is an educational task. However much its leaders may criticize existing situations and beliefs the influence of the Christian religion rises and falls with the development of the mind-set of a group. In the early days in Chicago we felt ourselves to be something more than observers or critics of conventional church life. We had a Cause, the extension of correct, and as we believed, inspiring views of the Bible. We could not be cloistered scholars; we were to serve a religious movement.

I

We had at our disposal two agencies for educational propaganda, *The Biblical World* and The American Institute of Sacred Literature. Both owed their origin to President Harper who until his death directly or indirectly edited the *Biblical World*. The members of the biblical departments were contributing editors of this journal, but the detailed work of the office was carried on by George S. Goodspeed, then by Clyde W. Votaw, then by Professor Burton, and in 1912 by myself. The character of the journal varied somewhat under its different managing editors. In its earliest days it showed the effect of the Parliament of Religions and Professor Goodspeed's interest in the field of comparative religion. In its later days it reflected my own

72

interest in group ethics and the relation of theology to historical process. It never was self-supporting and needed subsidy from the University. After the War rising costs made too heavy a demand on the general funds of the University and the *American Journal of Theology,* which had an even smaller circulation and the *Biblical World* were replaced by the *Journal of Religion.* It was our hope that the new journal should represent the growing interest in the psychology and history of religion, and only incidentally deal with biblical and theological subjects. To a considerable extent this has been true but our difficulty has been to find writers who are interested in the field of religion as distinct from the field of theology. If anything was needed to make us feel that we were moving into an unexplored field of investigation it was the lack of interest by professors in theological seminaries in the scientific study of religion.

As the need of sociological technique for an understanding of religion grew more evident, we undertook to develop co-operative work on the part of some of the hundreds of missionaries who studied with us during their furloughs in America. Our plan included selecting those who were particularly interested in the study of the religions with which they came in contact in Asia and giving them some acquaintance with the methods which were being used in the research carried on by various members of the departments of sociology and anthropology. Furthermore, I had ambitious plans for the development of a museum for the study of the history of religions and I felt that the missionaries might be of particular value in finding material. I drew up elaborate plans for such a museum which, unlike the Musée Guimet of Paris, should actually show the genetic relations of different religions and also make it possible to make comparative study of cults. I also felt that it might be possible to carry on explorations in the Greek or Roman burial grounds, and I made tentative approaches to the Italian Government looking toward our being permitted to do in Italy what the Oriental Institute of the University was doing in the Near East. We were able to make small beginnings in carrying out these plans. A few of the missionaries who sympathized with our methods became really expert in the collection of significant religious implements. Unfortunately the depression as well as lack of interest prevented the administration of the University from permitting me to raise funds for the undertaking and the plans are now in some secure pigeonhole. In the meantime the *Journal* continues and is making a real contribution to the study of religion on the part of those intelligent enough to understand its articles. With the disappearance of the *Biblical World* American Christianity was left without any magazine distinctly standing for the popularizing of historical and literary methods in biblical study. I have not heard any loud lamentations over this fact, doubtless for the reason the development of Religious Education has been away from biblical study. Uncritical and unhistorical biblical study has been left in possession of the journalistic field.

The American Institute of Sacred Literature was one of President Harper's contributions to the religious life of the country. In its earlier years it was not a part of the University, although Miss Georgia L. Chamberlin, for forty-four years its secretary, had her office in a University building. It became an important agent of that optimism, in which we all shared, that it was possible to give new vitality to the church by proper methods of Bible study. In its earlier years it was nominally administered by the Council of Seventy which included many biblical teachers in theological seminaries. But they did not do much more than meet annually and after discussion approve plans which were really being formulated at the University of Chicago. During the lifetime of H. Clay Trumbull it furnished lessons for the *Sunday School Times*. In those that I prepared my first paragraph was frankly called the criticism of material. As may well be imagined such lessons were not very radical and for two reasons: we ourselves were not radical, but emphasized the positive rather than the negative results of our criticism; and we were concerned not so much with the discovery of truth as in persuading those who used our material to share our enthusiasm for making biblical characters and times vivid. We also hoped that they would find in their study the moral and religious principles which would be applicable to our own day. It may be added that after the death of H. Clay Trumbull the *Sunday School Times* had no further use for our lessons, however gratuitously they might be contributed!

Before his death, President Harper arranged for the American Institute of Sacred Literature to be taken over by the University. It was under the general direction of a committee of the Divinity faculty of which Professor Burton was chairman. With his election to the presidency of the University I was appointed to the position. Each year we published the *Institute* containing a series of studies. Sometimes we had as many as ten thousand people studying the material contained in the little monthly. It soon became apparent that helpful as might be a scientifically directed study of the Bible, there was need of a much wider education than our classes could give. So in 1917 the Institute began the publication of tracts under such serious titles as "Why I Believe," "Science and Religion," and "Biblical." We have circulated several hundred thousand of these pamphlets and believe that they have been helpful in developing a new religious spirit. Their circulation has not been limited to America, but has extended through Young Men's Christian Associations and missionaries to Asia. In many colleges they have been used by student groups discussing religion. Where legislation relative to teaching evolution in tax-supported schools threatened intellectual liberty, they have been used by thousands.

II

While it is true that interest in religion as a more or less organized philosophy is shown by those who do not share in religious activity, millions are being reached through churches. Sympathetic appreciation of their attitudes is demanded if one would help them adjust moral conduct to the world in which they live. It was largely an ambition to remake religious opinion among church members that led me to assume in 1912 the position of Director of Religious Work in Chautauqua Institution. I had lectured in Chautauqua in 1896 when President Harper was in charge of the Summer Schools. Apparently my social application of the gospel displeased some of the conservative ministers who were present, but the opportunity to get in touch with the type of people who compose the churches and women's clubs, I saw was really great. Chautauqua Institution is attended by many thousands of people each year and has been a great influence in the development of intellectual life of America. In it religion is given distinct recognition but the Institution itself is not religious. Its interest is quite as great in music, education, recreation and current affairs. Many outstanding figures in these various fields have had a share in developing its influence. The majority of those attending it are undoubtedly conservative economically and theologically, but there is also a considerable number of persons distinctly progressive.

With the invaluable co-operation of Miss Georgia L. Chamberlin, the Secretary of the American Institute of Sacred Literature, the Department set up classes, invited chaplains, maintained a Sunday School, arranged public lectures, all intended to help organized Christianity inspire new conditions with intelligent religious faith. For twenty-one years we carried on the religious work, getting in contact with a wide range of persons through whom we were able to reach innumerable churches throughout the country. I became a member of the Board of Trustees and for years was chairman of the Executive Committee. The effect of the depression, however, was so serious that it was necessary for the Institution in 1933 to go into the hands of a receiver for the benefit of the bondholders. In this crisis a committee was organized to raise funds to meet the obligations of the institution, the members of which were to speak euphemistically, theologically conservative. My active participation in the work of the Institution then ended. I did not wish to become a center of controversy.

This experience confirmed my belief that silence as to the infallibility of the scriptures as a basis of Christian faith is as certain to weaken its significance as is theological polemic. Once the Bible is felt to be only one of many religious literatures it is liable to have no authority for modern life. Such an attitude may easily drift over into religious indifferences. It is not strange that those who did not approve of the critical method should look upon its representatives as attacking the basis of Christian belief. Yet nothing could have been farther from our purpose. What we were trying to do was to show how by the aid of scholarship, the Bible could be used for stimulating and directing the moral life of our own today. But it soon appeared that something more was needed. Historical and critical study of the Bible needed to be supplemented by an understanding of the Christian religion itself. That was the next step to be taken if, on the one hand, the study of the Bible was not to become merely technical, quite detached from the development of individual and group morals, and on the other hand, those who held to the Bible as an infallible revelation of God's will were not to become consolidated in belligerent reaction. In reality both results followed. Biblical study grew technical, and reaction became Fundamentalism. But at the same time theology grew ethical and churches, under the inspiration of new ideals, grew socially minded.

The creation of a public mind is a phase of education. Education has to begin where people are not where they ought to be. If this be recognized, conflict between the progressive and the reactionary elements in religious thought may not be avoided but it will at least be postponed long enough to make some type of co-operation between the two elements possible. Whether or not one calls it compromise, co-operation between liberals and conservatives will always be in the direction of the liberals. Progress may be slow but to one who takes a long view of social process it is certain.

Those who take a realistic view of progress through co-operation rather than through conflict must be educators rather than agitators. And education demands patience.

Our early efforts at popularizing the historical study of the Bible and the social teaching of Jesus were supplemented by the more or less scientific study of the Bible and religion in colleges and universities. As a rule state universities cannot move into the theological field, although a department of philosophy apparently has full liberty to make *ex parte* attacks upon religion. But considerable biblical teaching is permitted under the guise of the study of Hebrew and comparative religion. It was believed that sectarianism could not control these two fields. Despite the fact that college students in large numbers had some instruction in Sunday Schools, their notion of the Bible was exceedingly vague. Professor H. Morse Stevens told me that once in one of his courses in ancient history he referred to roads which were said to have been built by Solomon. After the class was dismissed a young woman came to him and said, "Do you mean to tell me that Solomon was a real person? I thought he was just somebody in the Bible."

Another way in which the Bible had been introduced into college curricula was as literary study. The influence of Professor R. G. Moulton here was great. He was one of the most remarkable lecturers of his day, and his work both on the platform and in his *Modern Readers' Bible* and other volumes had a wide influence among those who were unwilling to abandon the study of the Bible and yet could not make it a basis of any theology. But the separation of the literary from the historical religious character of the Bible always seemed unsatisfactory. That it has literary value is, of course, true. But to use a literature that is primarily religious as if it were merely literary is to overlook its character.

For instructors to say that they are not interested in the contents of the Bible but only in its literary quality discounts religion itself. It is like making Plato's *Republic* illustrative material for a Greek grammar. In the study of biblical literature one is brought face to face with the religious movement from which it sprang and by which it has been used. To neglect this relationship is as misleading as to treat the Constitution of the United States of America as if it had literary but no historical significance.

III

Early in 1895 President Harper told me that he had arranged for me to go on a trip for six weeks among the colleges of the South in order to acquaint them with our plans for the Summer Quarter, which as a part of the regular university year was a novelty. The first Summer Quarter session had been held in 1894, but President Harper wished to get larger publicity throughout the South. Hence my pilgrimage. For a thorough New Englander born during the Civil War, who had never been west of the Mississippi and never South, this trip proved illuminating. I came to a better appreciation of the South and of theological inertia. I delivered addresses in a number of Southern colleges, never speaking about the Summer Quarter but getting lists of names of professors and students to whom the proper literature could be sent. The University authorities were good enough to say that the increase in attendance in the Summer Quarter of 1895 was partly due to this type of publicity work. Whether or not that was true I began an acquaintance with the representatives of religious and educational interests in the South which was to develop through the years. This spring as I visited the magnificent buildings of Duke University at Durham and the University of North Carolina at Chapel Hill, I could not help contrasting conditions with those I found forty years before. Chapel Hill was then reached over roads that were so poor that in one place we had to ford a shallow stream. It is wonderful what progress has been made in North Carolina during the past generation. No small credit is due to such forward-looking institutions as the University of North Carolina and Wake Forest College where my friend President W. L. Poteat has been for half a century, a veritable Atlas of liberalism and sane religious thinking. The same contrast is to be seen all over the South. Wherever the influence of institutions like these three and Vanderbilt University, Richmond College, and Emory University in Atlanta has been felt there has been progress both in religious thought and in social adjustment. I would not have it inferred that I think that the other colleges have had no part in the development of the South, but circumstances have made me more aware of the influence of those particular institutions. Some of the denominational colleges, I regret to say, have been too much under ecclesiastical control to become leaders in a new world. I well remember how during this early visitation of mine one professor took me into an empty room, locked the door and then proceeded to ask me about evolution and to disclose his own sympathy with modern thought. Subsequently he was forced from his position, but has acquired an international fame as an educator. I judge he feels no need of such caution nowadays.

IV

It was not long before new interest in Bible study began to receive attention by the directors of various denominational undertakings. Conferences and Ministers' Institutes were founded where instruction was given by lectures and classes. The Southern Methodists were leaders in this educational revival. They held Ministers' Institutes in connection with many of their colleges. Lectures in these Institutes were all but invariably given by men who were either committed to the new methods of Bible study or at least were not opposed to them. I began to attend them in 1903, first with Central College, Fayette, Missouri, then with Southwestern College, Georgetown, Texas, Southern Methodist

University at Dallas, Texas, Hendrix College, Crawfordsville, Arkansas, Vanderbilt University, Nashville, Tennessee, and several others. I also attended conferences held in various summer resorts as Biloxi, Mississippi and Lake Junaluska, North Carolina. Some of these I visited repeatedly.

Thanks to the liberal attitude of the faculty of the School of Theology later (under the momentary example of Yale) the School of Religion, of Vanderbilt University, there was a considerable group of ministers in Southern Methodism who were sympathetic with the new tendency in biblical study. I had rather a pride in this fact, as several of the Vanderbilt faculty had studied at Chicago. In the North the Boston University School of Theology had great influence. But the great mass of Methodist clergy like those of other evangelical denominations were conventionally orthodox. Their influence in the North was sufficient to have Professor H. G. Mitchell dropped from the faculty of Boston University, although the action was camouflaged under a statement to the effect that Professor Mitchell had not been tactful in expressing his views. That, by the way, was a commonly published ground for similar action in other institutions. Teachers were permitted to be progressive, but they must change position tactfully!

In the first years those Institutes were cautious. At one time I had finished my assigned lectures, but as there remained a few hours before I could leave (this was before the days of automobiles), I proposed to conduct a sort of class. The ministers agreed and I began by asking the question as to whether the Bible was a single book or a collection of books. Naturally they replied that it was a collection.

"What," I asked, "do we call the discipline that seeks to discover the time of writing, the construction and integrity of these books?"

There was absolute silence. Nor could I get any response by repeating the question. So at length I answered it myself:

"It is the Higher Criticism." Whereupon a college professor in the audience cried out, "We knew it, but we didn't dare to say it." There would be no such timidity in that Institute nowadays.

What was true of the Southern Methodists to a less degree was true of the other religious parties. Various summer resorts throughout the country had meetings modeled after the Chautauqua Institution, and established "schools of religion." A list of such institutions would be long. In those years they were about the only contact which the pastors of small towns could have with other than local speakers and students. In Winfield, Kansas, Ottawa, Kansas, Boulder, Colorado, and Madison, Wisconsin, were a few of such institutions that became points of contact between the new Bible study and the people at large.

Doubtless this educational extension was to a large extent responsible for the growing impatience with current Sunday school lessons and the new activities which were to develop in the field of religious education. They were also of great service in breaking down the provincialism of lecturers. One got to know little groups of people in small towns who were interested in literature and philosophic thought. I recall a remarkable man, John L. Williams, originally a coal miner who had become one of the best read men in the field of philosophy I ever met. He was the backbone of a local Chautauqua in Streator, Illinois, where he had become not only a director of a bank but representative of a labor union. He became arbitrator for Hart Schaffner and Marx, and organized the Protocol in New York. His breadth of view and sympathy were extremely stimulating and his indisputable superiority to me in the field of philosophy was a constant reminder that academic circles have no monopoly of thought.

All the members of the Divinity School faculty had a share in the extension of new biblical and theological ideas. We lectured at ministers' meetings in the various cities of the

Middle West. Most of us preached in churches of various denominations. We have maintained for seventeen years in Chicago a Conference for Religious Workers which offers not only lectures but class instruction.

For many years I traveled from thirty to fifty thousand miles annually and averaged more than one hundred and fifty addresses of various sorts. There was danger that I should become a peripatetic loquacity, but I undertook to avoid this danger by building up new courses in the University and writing books. There was more at stake than mere lecturing. We were propagandists to the extent that we tried to bring religion to bear upon all phases of human interest. The wider circle of contact made more opportunities to induce men and women to see how education, economic relations and political life could be given moral inspiration and direction by an intelligent religious faith.

V

I recall more than one hundred and ninety colleges in which I have preached or lectured. It is hard to say how much college sermons accomplish especially when attendance upon chapel is compulsory. In the years I was responsible for selecting the preachers at the University of Chicago I discovered that the men acceptable as college preachers are not numerous. Probably the reason is that so few ministers realize just what the interests of college students actually are. One may optimistically hope that they are getting educated but acquaintance with college students tempts one to a cynical judgment that their dominant interests are athletics, campus affairs, and the opposite sex. Probably only a small fraction of them are troubled by philosophic questions and only another fraction of them are interested in social and political problems. The numerically negligible minority who organize socialist, communist and other rebellious organizations are not likely to go to voluntary religious services, or if they do most of them would probably go to Jewish synagogues. The college preacher soon learns that he must not treat his audience as if they were modern Platos or Darwins, but as immature, restless human beings subject to the tensions of our common lot. If he is wise he will not talk down to them or endeavor to win their favor by references to athletics. Often, to show his broadmindedness he will be tempted to criticize the church. I finally used to suggest to our preachers that they should be cautious in such criticism. I did this not because of any desire to avoid the criticism but repeated belittling of the church on the part of successive preachers grew monotonous, and not conducive to religious enthusiasm. The same tendency to repetitious dealing with other subjects is observable. In one church the assistant minister who conducted the service said to me that if another preacher said that God was not an old gentleman sitting up in Heaven he was "going to yell!"

When one comes to understand his audience nothing is more stimulating than university preaching. If the preacher be himself a teacher he unconsciously senses the field of common interest and even a common vocabulary. If, as it happened in a number of institutions in my own case, one serves annually, each college audience gains a character of its own. And I think that all those who preached at Vassar in the old days when attendance on chapel was required will never forget the view one got through the open chapel door, of girls hurrying across the campus to arrive before the last stroke of the bell. Nor will he forget the conflict with inattention and the rising spirit of rebellion in the last years of compulsory Sunday chapel at Yale.

Quite as interesting as college audiences are those other groups to which one did not preach, and which were not even formally religious. I spoke to almost every sort. Credit Men's associations, political clubs, associations of commerce, Rotary and Kiwanis Clubs, women's organizations, forums like those of Cooper Institute and Ford Hall, teachers' conventions, banquets, brought me, a theological professor, in touch with a cross-section of American life. One was expected to talk on serious matters, but if possible to sweeten an address with humor. I had no stock of anecdotes except some that might illustrate a point, but after all humor may be an unexpected application of common sense to discussion. Provided that one does it naturally and without professionalism one can always give an ethical turn to an address. It was this desire to set up straightforward relation with an audience that has always made me rather unwilling, as a chairman usually said, "to pronounce the invocation," at public banquets. The introduction of religion under the usual conditions of such gatherings seems a meaningless formality. Once I was called to speak at a banquet of several hundred graduates of Rush Medical College. The clergyman who was to say grace did not arrive and I was apparently the only one whom the President thought it was safe to call upon for that purpose. I think it is fair to say that usually the person called upon for this service delivers a sort of keynote address to his hearers in the form of a prayer. In this particular instance as the crowd stood, I used the conventional formula of a single sentence and sat down. The doctors who had braced themselves for something much more lengthy were so taken by surprise that they burst into a great peal of laughter and broke into applause. Thereafter I was somewhat in demand for similar service by bodies who still observe the custom.

VI

These varied contacts gave me clearer ideas as to preparing men to enter a religious profession. Theological education to be effective must recognize the new public mind and shifting social conditions. How to develop the needed training and insights was a problem the answer to which I constantly sought. To democratize a new understanding of Christianity required technical training in something more than strictly academic subjects. Important as is literary and historical criticism it is only a tool to be used by those who bring religion into touch with great currents of human life. Especially is this true when it is recognized that a religion is an aspect of group behavior.

Such conviction was deepened by participation in the various conferences held by the Young Men's Christian Associations both in colleges and in summer assemblies. No one could come in touch with the hundreds of students thus gathered without sensing the beginning of that shift of interest which long before the World War was beginning to show itself in the younger generation. For those who were unacquainted with student life, the changes in ideals and habits after 1918 seemed catastrophic, but those of us who were in touch with it as university professors and conference lecturers realized that a break with traditional religious thinking on the part of youth was inevitable. To some extent this was tempered by the Christian Associations and Student Volunteer Conventions, but these institutions were already beginning to show lack of primary interest in theology and were becoming conscious of economic and social problems. The decade preceding the World War was critical for them. The older officials had difficulty in recognizing the shift of interest and attempted to develop an emotional religion which sometimes reached the borders of pathological self-disclosure. I recall with almost a shudder attending one of their meetings in a room lighted only by candle, in which several hundred college students gave simultaneously confessions of all sorts and cried out in prayer to God. I was never able to trace the total effect of such high-voltage emotionalism, but the Association authorities saw its danger and abandoned the method. To my mind it was clear that what the college student needed in those early years of transition was not only intellectual assurance that God existed and that prayer was not futile, but also some sort of leadership in the development of the moral guidance of economic life. The competitive fervor for Bible study which swept through the colleges in the turn of the century doubtless contributed to some degree to moral direction, but I suspect in many cases it served to weaken the relations of student bodies to their religious past.

This danger was certainly felt by the denominational officials and as a result in many state universities denominational houses with student pastors were established. I came in contact with a number of these institutions and can testify to their value in maintaining denominational loyalties and *esprit de corps* among religiously minded students. In some of the state universities these houses play a considerable role in university life. They not only serve as social centers and opportunities for personnel work but also arrange study courses for which some university credit could be given. If all the efforts to adjust the rising generation to social transformation had been as effective as this movement among state universities, there would be a larger interest in the church on the part of those now middle aged who were among the first to feel the tension between it and social change.

Despite these efforts the atmosphere of universities is not usually conducive to religion. Sometimes, especially if they have rebelled from rigorous orthodoxy professors are avowedly opposed to it. It is not difficult to account for their attitude. In their psychological *bouleversement* they identify Christianity with doctrines which their intelligence has led them to abandon. Acquaintance with modern religious movements might have made them less antagonistic to religious faith. Historical and sociological courses, too, singularly belittle or ignore the significance of the churches in the development of western civilization. Such facts argue the need of attention. The Divinity School courses were open to the student body of the entire university, and as under-graduates would not be likely to take professional courses others were given particularly adapted to their needs. Until the recent reorganization of the University curriculum they were elected freely, especially those dealing with comparative religion and the history and social significance of Christianity. Interest in strictly biblical subjects waned. Probably this was due to a general lessening of attention paid the Bible in Sunday Schools and interest in other topics on the part of students who came from religious families. Such classes were always enjoyable. One could see that the subject matter studied was practically unknown and the scientific method of treatment was judged in accord with that adopted in other departments. For a number of years some of us, including President Harper, offered Sunday morning courses giving university credit. As we were not paid for the extra work, students were not charged for the courses and they became rather popular among under-graduates who had deficiencies of one sort or another to make up. There were always those who wanted to get credit to offset their failure to take physical culture and athletes who wished in an inexpensive way to remove deficiencies which prevented them from playing on some team. One young man, who subsequently became a considerable figure in the industrial world, told me quite frankly that he took a Sunday morning course because he was trying to get through the University in the shortest possible time. Of course others had more suitable reasons. We tried to prevent the courses from being "snaps" and judging from withdrawals I think we were fairly successful. Such classes gave opportunity to apply Christian principles to various problems which young people face. It was with real regret that because of my out-of-town engagements, I found myself forced to abandon them. I now meet their members in almost every city I visit. Others who have offered courses for under-graduates have had the same experience. At all events in these classes religion was treated frankly as a legitimate social and philosophical field of inquiry. In some cases, I dare say, such treatment jarred the ideas which the under-graduates had brought from home. But we had no ambition to emulate ministers who introduce religion surreptitiously between stereopticon slides during a Sunday evening illustrated lecture on a non-religious subject.

CHAPTER VII

DISCOVERING THE REAL WORLD

ONE DAY in the winter of 1903 President Harper summoned me to his office. With his customary directness he said: "Burton and I have made up our minds that you can do two jobs better than one." He then proposed that I become editor of a magazine which a group of men associated with him was preparing to found. I had known nothing of the plan but promptly accepted the offer and so in addition to my work at the University I became an editor. For more than eight years I spent my afternoons in an office in the "Loop."

I

The motives which led to this adventure were really religious. Several years before Dr. W. D. Mackenzie, at that time a member of the faculty of the Chicago Theological Seminary, Dr. J. M. Campbell, and a number of business men had undertaken to establish the *American Weekly* patterned after the *British Weekly*. It was an attempt to do especially for the Middle West what *The Outlook* and *The Independent* were doing for New York—interpret current events from the point of view of Christian idealism. The undertaking was having financial difficulties and Dr. Harper was approached as a saviour. The proposal was quite in accord with his purposes and he went about the work with his customary vigor. A company was to be formed to take over the *American Weekly* and replace it with a journal more after the style of *The Outlook*. I never knew just how the group was formed. It could not be suspected of being obtrusively religious to say the least. John R. Thompson,

90

World Today, while claiming circulation of 100,000, was no rival of these two magazines, which like ours were to be a few years later submerged by the rising tide of weeklies. Muckraking was popular but dangerous. Our only experience in that field led to a libel suit which we settled out of court. But contact with corporations was invaluable for one who believed that the church faced the duty of developing new social ideals. In preparing an article on the packing industry, I discovered in ten days' investigation how far the reforms that followed the publication of Upton Sinclair's *The Jungle* had been carried out. Acquaintance with a vast business operation made me realize anew how complicated is the task of so organizing economic life as to further personal values, and how much a social gospel needed to be realistic. Fourteen years later I again visited the Stock Yards to find a decided advance in the relations of the employer and employee and the establishment of not a few forms of welfare work. As later during my activities as Executive Secretary of War Savings for the state of Illinois I came to realize the difficulties in social readjustments which so many clerical reformers who have never had experience in the nonecclesiastical world minimize or denounce. The academic idealist is unconsciously driven toward a world of abstractions and grows impatient with the world in which he actually lives and upon which he is dependent. It is one thing to organize the social teaching of Jesus and quite another to find ways by which the exigencies of economic struggle can be progressively faced.

In 1911 our financial adventure closed with heavy loss and the sale of the magazine to William Randolph Hearst. I was asked to continue in the editorial position but as it would involve the abandonment of my University connections and moving to New York, I wisely declined.

II

Editorial work has one important result. It is a constant discipline in appreciating the point of view of the general public and in the discovery of ways in which a social mind may be affected. Any good editor will constantly have before him either consciously or unconsciously the people who will buy and read his publications. It is this constant recognition of the human element that stirs the academic mind to contempt of the popularizer. In fact, it seems to be all but universally true that whoever can write interestingly enough to gain a circle of readers will be judged unscientific!

There is enough truth in this judgment to suggest caution to one who undertakes to make his professional interests contribute to a social mind. But if any one is ready to pay the penalty inflicted by specialists upon a "popularizer" and develops the editorial sense of an audience in his writing, he needs no dual personality to carry on scientific work. At least this has always been my conviction.

This attempt to serve a variety of interests raised the question as to just which of them should be central. It is a decision which every busy person has to make. However circumstances combine to direct one's life there must be a choice between passively submitting to their influence and following some principle of unity. I have often been tempted to envy the man who is temperamentally able to concentrate upon a single interest. In a university this naturally is research, the writing of articles and books adding to the stock of human knowledge. Especially does the historian who is concerned only with the publication of accurate, well-documented investigations seem admirable. I have always been ready to bow down at the shrine of the footnote. But movements of human interests, the organization of some cause, the intelligent shaping of group opinion are also indispensable. The world of scholarship, however, seems to be convinced that an administrator cannot be a genuine scholar. Such opinion was a challenge. I answered with the enthusiasm of inexperience and in accord with my temperament. As best I could I would combine the two fields of interest. I realized that such a decision would lay me open to the damning charge of versatility, but somebody must be a middle man in social movements and if intelligent and ethical views of religion were to find their way into human life rather than into theological libraries, some of us needed to deal with Christianity as a concrete social movement.

During the years that I edited *Christendom* and *The World Today* I was also carrying on my full work as dean and professor, and writing a volume on *The Messianic Hope in the New Testament,* for the Decennial Publications of the University of Chicago. If being uninteresting is a proof of scientific accomplishment I think I may be very well said to have succeeded in being scientific. The book was the outgrowth of a growing perception of the real meaning of the history of New Testament times as the history of ideas and social attitudes. My study included the examination of all material at our disposal from which one can judge the popular expectation during the period of Messianic ferment from the Maccabees to Akiba. In this study certain elements of Messianic expectation were found to be constant. It required no particular insight to see that these same elements were the pattern of the Messianic expectation of the early Christians. This study, so far as American scholarship was concerned, might be called a pioneer, and is open to the criticism which pioneering experiments evoke. But it was a step forward in the application of historical method to an understandng of Christian attitudes and doctrines. During the years of my relation with *The World Today* I also published a volume, *The Church and the Changing Order,* and expanded a series of lectures I gave at Haverford College into *The Gospel and the Modern Man*. Both volumes attempted to bring the results of a developing science of religion to bear upon social conditions with which I had come in contact.

III

After the passing of *The World Today* my editorial work continued in several ways. I became editor of the *Biblical World* already mentioned as our organ of popularizing biblical study. I was contributing editor to the *Constructive Quarterly*, which Silas McBee founded despite my rather discouraging advice given him when first he planned the work. He believed that there was room for a quarterly that would represent the different aspects of religious life, positively rather than critically. That is to say, in its pages a man could express his views freely but was not supposed to enter into theological polemics. My editorial connection was rather tenuous, hardly more than that of contributing articles.

For several months I wrote editorials for the *Independent* edited by Hamilton Holt. I also assumed editorial management of a series of books known as the *Woman's Citizen's Library*. The idea was not mine but that of W. E. Ernst who had been the business manager of *The World Today*. The volumes were to be used as textbooks for study by women's clubs and specially formed classes. Although the undertaking did not prove financially successful, it was a pioneer in the educational approach to women's political education. This editorial contact made me more than ever believe that politics offered a new field for women. It was natural in those days to say that their participation in politics would elevate our national life and lead to legislation of particular benefit to women and children and all domestic relations. Although it is easy to become cynical as to these hopes, I have no shadow of doubt that much of the social legislation of recent years has been due to the influence of women through women's clubs, the League of Women Voters, Parent-Teacher Associations and similar organizations. It is through such bodies that the influence of churches has been extended into social affairs. Indeed any one who would bring religion to bear upon group life must be in contact with service organizations like Rotary and Kiwanis clubs which represent group interests. To hold one's self aloof from such attempts is to detach religion from a real world and make it a matter of literary discussion.

The conviction that the discussion of social questions needed to take into account the assets as well as liabilities led me to become editor of a Social Betterment series published by Appleton. The publishers were not ready to adopt my rather ambitious plans, but two volumes of the series were published.

With the Macmillan Company my relations have been constant. Professor Francis G. Peabody had encouraged me to believe that my articles on "Christian Sociology" in *The American Journal of Sociology* were worth publication. I sent them to Macmillan and on my way to a six months' visit to Europe and the Near East I called on George P. Brett, president of the company, to discover the fate of the manuscript. This was before the erection of the splendid building in which the corporation is now housed, and I found Mr. Brett in a little office cut off from a stockroom. I was immediately drawn to him. He represented an adventurous but far-sighted philosophy of business which appealed to me. A friendship sprang up which continues to this day. I edited for him a series of *New Testament Handbooks* and one of popular commentaries, *The Bible for Home and School*.

During nearly forty years I have passed on manuscripts in the religious field for the Macmillan Company and have taken pride in the fact that in some years their list of new religious publications had hardly a title with which I was not concerned as author, editor or adviser. As reader of manuscripts I was kept in touch with the trend of theological thought. Of the hundreds of manuscripts which I examined only a few could be recommended for publication, but they gave me first-hand contact with religious thought in its successive stages. A reader like an editor gets an almost instinctive feeling for contemporary interests. Forty years ago the social application of Christianity was predominant. As one publisher said, "It makes little difference what the title of a book is provided it has the word 'social' in it." This was followed by interest in the psychology of religion and religious education, and this in turn by interest in the discussion of fundamental religious questions concerning God and the history of religion. If one could make a survey of all the manuscripts both published and unpublished of the present century, it would show that religious thought was being extended into the new areas which were being opened by the various sciences. When at the suggestion of the Macmillan Company I undertook to edit the series *The Bible for Home and School,* I had a feeling that interest in that field was passing, except among those who preferred the more conventional type of commentaries already on the market. My suspicions were justified for only fifteen numbers of the series were published.

My friend and colleague George S. Goodspeed and I had planned a one-volume dictionary of the Bible. Publishers, however, did not judge the plan practicable, and it was not until several years later that they awoke to the fact that there was a widespread demand for such publication. By that time I had become American editor of Hastings' one-volume Dictionary. Later I felt that there was a similar demand for a single volume dictionary dealing with the general field of religion and ethics. Ultimately the Macmillan Company undertook the publication and in 1921 with the co-operation of my colleague George Birney Smith, I edited a one-volume *Dictionary of Religion and Ethics,* which combined the definitions of a dictionary with the discussions of an encyclopaedia.

IV

This contact with business and current opinion in a way offset that withdrawal from the interests of the common man which threatens a person professionally engaged in religion. In the case of ministers the causes for such withdrawal lie sometimes in the minister himself, but quite as often in the attitude of the people with whom he associates. They expect him to embody the virtues which they themselves may not possess. However much he may want to be taken as a man first and a minister second he will always be taken as a man who is a minister. Frequently in his endeavor to escape the temptation of hypocrisy which lies in such an estimate of himself a minister cheapens himself and his calling by endeavoring to act as if he were not a minister. I remember one young fellow who thought he might achieve pastoral success by owning a horse that could beat his deacon's. It did not take long for him to discover that his congregation had no enthusiasm for supporting a racing parson.

I soon found that it was impossible for me to cease to be in business what I was at the University. It was an illustration of a general law that any one engaged in a religious work is wise to remember. Whatever his non-religious relations may be, he will always be taken as a representative of religion. I know what it is to chafe under the process of idealization. I used to feel a little more human when some one used profanity in my presence without apologizing for his language. It seemed to argue that I was being taken as a man.

In light of the changes which have taken place since 1918 those of the years from 1904 to 1914 seem tentative, but there was a new spirit abroad. In 1912 it was to find expression in the Progressive party. The cure of the evils of democracy we believed, was more democracy, and we turned to the direct primaries, the referendum and recall as infallible agents of reconstruction.

The control of affairs was passing from the men of the generation that had fought the Civil War and had wallowed in the conscienceless period that followed, and the new economic life was rapidly developing in the direction of organized labor and capital. The laws which had been sufficient for the earlier type of competitive commercialism were proving to be quite insufficient for the development of vast corporations due to the control of natural resources and the railroads. Inexperience in dealing with the social change was even more pronounced then than today, but there were no lack of critics in the social order. During the decade preceding the outbreak of the World War political liberalism was rapidly developing. The influence of President Theodore Roosevelt was paramount among those who felt that democracy must choose between self-government and the autocracy of corporations. In the editorials which I wrote for *The World Today* thirty years ago, I find this sense of change constantly present.

The past few years in the United States have closed one epoch and have begun anew. Even more than we have been aware democracy itself has been on trial. The plain American citizen was losing faith in the ability of the Republic to grow rich and remain democratic.

Such words sound familiar nowadays but these editorials have one characteristic which is often lacking in similar pronouncements today. They were hopeful. As liberals we believed not only that the individual had rights of initiative which should be recognized, but that it was possible to make economic laws that would establish more justice in our economic life. And in retrospect such hopefulness seems justified. We were really making progress. That we did not accomplish more was due to the fact that we were drawn into a war which sprang from conditions which were neither liberal nor democratic.

But the moral instability of this period of social change was apparent. Our ignorance as to how to adjust the individual's initiative to corporate action was even greater then than that of today. President Theodore Roosevelt's almost revolutionary extension of executive powers and the development of new legal procedure on the basis of the power granted to Congress to regulate the inter-state commerce were accustoming the nation to a sense of national solidarity and to a reliance upon government which would have scandalized the fathers of the republic. But the ruthlessness of competition still persisted. Business was business. Collective bargaining was beginning to assume real importance, but the attitude of labor and capital was too often that of war. Economic views which today would be regarded as conservative were treated as radical. Socialism and communism were little known and the American Federation of Labor under the guidance of Samuel Gompers was the most successful attempt at organizing wage earners. Political life was spasmodically aware of its threatened control by dishonest and vicious men, but the Progressive movement was unsuccessful in organizing a political party although its influence is still felt. The various attempts at social readjustments like those of William J. Bryan and Senator LaFollette had back of them no unifying philosophy like Socialism or Fascism.

One fact became clear—the real world was composed of real people. It was in the process of transformation but change was not algebraic but human. The closer one got to the social order the more one felt not only the pressure of the rapidly increasing group life but also the importance of imponderables. Among these imponderables was the need of establishing relations with persons of all sorts. Only an intellectual snob or one living in a detached world could fail to see that human relations are really human. In all my contacts I have never found any person who was not my superior in some activity. Such a discovery made for friendships.

When the real world is seen to be composed of real people, and not mere gadgets in a mechanistic society submerged in statistical averages, religion ceases to be a philosophy. Facing perplexing disappointment as well as success, men need whatever assistance to actual life religious faith can render. I came to see why men and women want their pastor to preach something beyond sociology. They are ready to admit that the social order needs to be improved but they do not want mere denunciation of social evils and championship of speculative reforms. Even men and women thoroughly committed to reforms wish to find a source of strength more powerful than a call to duty. Those who want ministers to preach about Heaven are not always indifferent to the new moral problems set by capitalism but they all are impatient with amateur prophetism. They want ministers to be experts in the field of religion. They themselves feel quite capable of managing their business affairs. What troubles them mostly are personal matters—family relations, their own shortcomings and ideals, their discouragements and fears, their experience of repeated frustration, economic anxieties, sickness and the threat of old age.

How genuinely interested people are in religion as a means of getting superhuman help to meet the exigencies of life can be seen in the spread of Christian Science, Unity, the Oxford Movement. In 1931 the *American Magazine* published a long interview in which I stressed the practical significance of prayer and the other elements of religion. I spoke of the efforts which we were making in the Divinity School to make a psychological study of religion and so develop methods of gaining help from God. I was surprised at the response. For weeks my mail was full of letters from men and women of whom I had never heard describing their religious experiences and proposing methods of getting divine help. Many of these letters, I suppose, were from cranks, but taken as a whole this mass of correspondence showed clearly that if the church and its ministry are to fulfill their own particular functions they must do something more than preach duties and discuss theology.

Humanity I found no more standardized in religion than in any other aspect of life. Nor is sublimated defeatism a description of this attitude. The emotional reactions are as varied as individuals. A man once came into my office and after seating himself said in the most matter of fact way, "I am the Holy Ghost." I said I was glad to meet him and asked him to come out and see the clerks in the outer office. I had no desire to be alone in a room with one who considered himself a member of the Trinity.

There are men who take their religion so seriously as to be indifferent to conventions. I remember a man whom I had never seen before or since met me on the street and said that in his office in the city he had thought of me and my various responsibilities and felt that he ought to come out and pray with me. As he had met me on the street he said we would pray then and there. This he proceeded to do in a rather loud tone of voice. I was in terror lest some of my neighbors might meet us, but I have always felt grateful to him because of his sincerity and evident desire to be helpful.

William James somewhere comments on the avidity with which men under almost any condition will want to discuss philosophy. I have found the same thing true in the matter of religion. The only requisite is that men must be convinced that you are sincere.

Men of sanity and ability want to talk about religion in something more than a speculative way. I remember one day a man holding an important business position asked me to take lunch with him. We went to a restaurant which I suspect was not accustomed to religious conversation and he proceeded to ask my advice. He said that when he was a young man he had been a member of a church but for years had had nothing to do with religion. A few nights before he had lain awake impressed with the fact that he was going to die. He had no disease and as a matter of fact he lived for years afterwards, but the thought of death had fastened upon him. He had made up his mind he would be religious and wanted to know what to do. I told him as best I could. Although he never came very close to orthodoxy he devoted himself and his money to the cause of the church in a way which was almost prodigal. When I once mentioned the matter to him he said that for so many years he had been indifferent to religion he thought he ought to make up for lost time.

I remember a discussion which I had on a train with one of the most outstanding men of the country, a man who was not only a great lawyer but a great citizen and later rendered his country an important service as ambassador. He had heard me speak the night before at the banquet of the League to Enforce Peace in Washington and he wanted to discuss something I had said. I had never thought of him as a particularly religious man but in the course of our conversation it appeared that he conducted family prayers every day and he disclosed to me a depth of religious belief that was really inspiring.

It may be that a vein of superstition underlies a person's piety. Sometimes it finds expression in social acts like charity, at other times in irrational inhibitions. I have known men who were otherwise sane and resourceful who would not begin a journey on Friday. Sometimes also there is a refusal to believe that religion has any connection with business or politics. Private virtues may serve as a sort of bridge between the two fields of interest but it is not difficult to train one's conscience so that it will approve of that which one wants to do. To deal with this real world intelligence and sympathy are more needed than denunciation and anti-social piety. The elements of a complicated social life are as easily disarranged as those of the human body. Whoever would wish to make religion an influence within it certainly should bring to his task something more than tradition. Above all he must realize that he has to deal with human nature never quite free from the control of the past, slow to adopt changes which threaten inherited privileges, and acting more from emotion than from logic.

In this real world composed of real people I came to see need of constant readjustment to conditions set by the introduction of labor saving machinery and the constant reshaping of economic procedure in general. Few of these changes can be foreseen and the necessary reorganizations are often haphazard. But one fact is plain, every readjustment involves a choice between values. Self-interest makes this inevitable. But this choice is not between definitions. The fate of a man's business or of a labor organization may depend upon it. The immediate bearing of these decisions upon life makes business a factor in the development of morals. The welfare of human beings involves the possibility of loss on the part of those who seek it. But economic life, in the interest of efficiency has been forced to give it increased recognition. Only an irreconcilable dogmatist can doubt the fact. The redefinition of honesty, the right of co-operative bargaining with labor on the part of employers and wage earners, the new freedom and personal rights of women, are only a few of the changes which have resulted from the new conditions given industrial progress by science.

It is the opportunity and indeed the duty of the churches to suggest the values which should be chosen whenever decision has to be made. They are in position to help men of affairs see the significance of economic change in the development of customs and relations of life. They ought to make it plain that any decision which does not subordinate economic efficiency to human welfare is contrary to the creative forces in the universe itself. In any intelligent observation of a social process antisocial and anti-personal action will be seen to result in depressions and wars as inevitably as the defeat of the Amalekites depended upon the prowess of Jehovah.

CHAPTER VIII

THE RECONSTRUCTION OF A DENOMINATION

Most critics and defenders of Christianity apparently regard Christianity as a body of doctrines and expect it to act as an independent force, like electricity. Such misapprehension is due in large measure to the failure to perceive that Christianity like every religion is a form of social behavior and that doctrines rationalize the attitudes and *mores* of social groups. Formulas tend to become slogans which conserve group solidarity and enmities, but they are emotional rather than rational. A religious group is always affected by other than religious motives and a religion to be understood must be treated as an aspect of a culture. Its permanent values will be disclosed only as its institutions and influence direct the social process to moral ends.

This failure to regard Christianity like all religions as a social behavior rather than as a body of doctrines also explains the mistakes in forecast of its future. Professional ecclesiastics often fail to see that Christian institutions are projections of social minds and practices. It is unhistorical to attempt to discover an "essence" of Christianity which exists as something distinct from Christians. Strictly speaking Christianity is the religion of people who call themselves Christians and organize groups professing loyalty to and faith in Jesus as Savior. It will always be misleading to identify Christianity with abstract truth, or with formulas which in their turn are projections of socialized presupposition. The conduct of these groups must be studied quite as much as the formulas which they have adopted as a sort of banner around which to gather.

I

The actual expansion of American religion has been that of groups. Both from its origin and because of formative influences, Christianity on the American continent took on a great variety of institutional forms. State churches, persecuted minorities and indigenous variations of each so multiplied that anything like a state church was impossible. Religious liberty came by the way of denominational rivalry. Practically without exception all persons of significance in the religious life of America have participated in the life of the denomination to which they belong. Such participation distinguishes the religious leader from the critic of religion. Even the leaders in movements for church federation and church union have been active in denominational affairs.

Among these various denominations the Baptists have represented radical democracy. There never has been a Baptist church in the sense of the Church of Rome or the Church of England. By virtue of its congregational polity the Baptist denomination now numbering several millions of members, is composed of independent churches which may meet in Associations or Conventions. Such organizations, however, have no authority although they do possess considerable influence. Baptist churches have been composed of those who belong to what used to be known as the middle class and share in its virtues and inhibitions. Except in the South they have not generally had the social position enjoyed by members of churches that once were state churches.

Theologically speaking the Baptists represent orthodoxy as found in Calvinism. While various Associations have Confessions as a basis of membership the Baptists have no authoritative formulas like that of the Presbyterian church. To them the New Testament is the supreme rule of faith and practice. Their insistence upon immersion as the form of baptism prerequisite to participation in the Lord's Supper is the outcome of this belief. They have always stood for complete separation of church and state. They have reached joint action in the mission field through the organization of missionary societies.

Their very looseness of organization and the absolute independence of each local church has given Baptists a certain flexibility which has made them less exposed to heresy trials than more closely organized Christian bodies. Yet their literal interpretation of the New Testament has developed a theological conservatism which is quite the equal of that of denominations with centralized authority. Southern Baptists decline to be called Protestants and are developing a near-Catholicism of their own. The Baptist movement has always favored education and there are few states in which they have not established colleges. They have furnished some of the leading theologians of America, among them leaders in progressive religious thought. This may seem contradictory to other characteristics of the denomination. And so it is. There are two tendencies within the denomination. A religious democracy like any other must cherish inner inconsistencies.

My family on both sides, so far as I know, have always been Baptists. It was all but inevitable, therefore, that I should have joined a Baptist church. I went to a Baptist college and to a Baptist theological seminary. Again as a matter of course, I was licensed, though never ordained, as a Baptist preacher. What theological questions I may have had did not affect the basic evangelical position for which the denomination stood, although fortunately I inherited none of that unfriendly attitude toward other denominations which characterized the early theological struggles over baptism and "close" communion. These denominational relations I have always kept not only because of circumstances and an ineradicable fear of religious authority, but also from a conviction that in America at least, whoever would be active religiously must share in denominational life. The liberal who stands outside church relations has had little opportunity for more than authorship and lectures. However important the contributions of such persons may be, the religious leaders of America have known how to organize. So far is it from being true that the final test of religion is one of solitariness. The religious development of America has been due to denominations in which there were opportunity and machinery for individuals and minorities to socialize their ideals.

In the case of Northern Baptists this expansion was begun by those who had come to see the inefficiency of existing denominational organization. A more or less non-conformist minority within the denomination may be said to have appeared when the Baptist Congress was organized in 1882. This Congress was an unofficial body composed of individuals who met for the discussion of vital topics both theological and social. Its published Reports show an interest in trends of modern thought sufficient to create considerable suspicion on the part of the more conservative members of the denomination. The Congress continued effectively for a dozen years but finally ceased to exist in 1907. Its demise was due largely to the rise of a movement within the denomination which looked to action as well as to discussion.

Many of us who had grown up since the Civil War came to feel by the beginning of the twentieth century that the Baptist denomination of the North numbering more than a million members was inefficiently organized. We did not wish to establish any authoritative body, but the lack of interest at annual meetings of the Missionary and Publication Societies was apparent. More than that, the denomination as such had very little share in forming the policies and overseeing the actions of these Societies.

The new movement was inaugurated in the Chicago Baptist Association in 1907, when a committee of three members, of which I was one, was appointed to confer with the Secretaries and Boards of the various Societies to see if there might not be organized a Convention in which the denomination as such might express its opinions. The first step in such a movement was to draw up a petition to these Boards signed by members in attendance at a Baptist Congress held in St. Louis, and by a large number of leaders in the denomination. After considerable hesitation the Societies agreed to some sort of action and the original committee was enlarged to draw up a program. This committee held a number of meetings and finally proposed a constitution which I drew up and published in the *Standard,* at that time the leading Baptist journal in the North. The matter was brought to the meeting of the Societies held in Washington in 1908. The meeting was marked by considerable tension. On the one side the representatives of the Societies feared the loss of their independence; on the other side there were those who believed that the denomination should be organized after the fashion of the Southern Baptists and the Societies reduced to the position of Boards of the Convention. The committee of which I was a member believed this latter condition impracticable on legal and other grounds. We chose as the chairman of the mass meeting the pastor of the First Baptist Church of Boston. His confessed ignorance of parliamentary procedure led to some rather difficult moments in the meeting. The assembly finally voted to appoint a committee who should bring in on the next day a constitution which could be discussed during the coming year. It was voted also that it should be appointed by the chair, whereupon the presiding officer pulled out the list of names which our committee had drawn up, and proceeded to say that "he had been handed the following list of names." There was much excitement. It was finally decided, however, that he had the power to appoint whatever names he saw fit, and as he saw fit to use those on the list, the committee was appointed and the meeting adjourned. The committee met at something after ten o'clock, having before it two proposals, one representing the establishment of the Convention with the Societies changed to Boards, the other that which our committee had drawn up. I proposed that we should use as a basis of discussion the tentative constitution already published in the *Standard* which began with the express recognition of the independence of the Baptist churches. Our committee remained in session until five o'clock next morning. At nine o'clock I proposed the constitution which should be submitted to the denomination, and the plan was all but unanimously adopted. Governor Charles E. Hughes was elected President. Surmising that he would be unable to serve, I nominated President Harry Pratt Judson of Chicago as the first Vice-President. As it turned out my surmise was correct and the denomination owes much to the administrative skill of President Judson in developing a scheme for the organization of the Northern Baptist Convention and its relation with the existing Societies. The constitution adopted the next year at Oklahoma City followed his general line of organization and from that day its broad lines have never been changed. The members of the individual churches appoint members of the Convention and they are also members of the Societies. The same body meets in its various capacities under different Presidents. The actions of the Convention have no authority but they are none the less of great influence. Each local church is perfectly free to differ with the findings of the Convention or of the Societies and is not thereby made subject to discipline. It is, in fact a rather striking illustration of how a democracy can express itself without powers of coercion through finding common expression of policy.

I was a member of the Executive Committee of the Convention from its inception. In 1915 I was elected its President. I was chairman of its committees in charge of its Three Million Dollar Campaign, its Five Year Program, missionary education, and of various other committees.

In the organization of so large a body as a denomination the
question of method is of primary importance. A temptation is
always present to adopt resolutions and policies which are too
much in advance of the body as a whole. Such a danger is
especially great when the body adopting a resolution is without
authority to put it into effect. But there can be no leaders without followers. Indeed the very conception of leadership involves a following. A boss drives rather than leads. Many would-
be leaders are so far in advance that those who would follow
them must send out exploring parties to discover where their
leaders are. There is, of course, a certain satisfaction in feeling
that others are out of step with one's own self, but such superiority is fatal to leadership. It is easy, and oftentimes pictur-
esque to be a radical, but radicalism is seldom constructive. It
may develop a needed discontent, but it ignores process. It is
one thing to get people to hate together and another to get
them to work together in the interests of social reconstruction.
Such generalizations as these are illustrated in the attempts at
hurrying denominations and churches toward more intelligent
self-expression. The zeal of reformers has often consolidated
opposition to reforms. It is difficult for those who are devoted
to social and religious ideals to realize that they may be out of
touch with the rank and file of the bodies to which they belong.

The early years of the reorganization of the Baptist denomination show how realistic its leaders were. It would have been
easy to propose radical programs and indeed such programs
were proposed. But those of us who were put in places of
responsibility endeavored to work from the point of view of
the denomination as a whole rather than from that of ideals
divorced from the existing situation. And after all an ideal
works when it directs social action toward itself. It is one thing
to be a prophet and another to embody prophetic ideals in
community action. The human element must be constantly taken
into account in any attempt to induce hundreds of thousands of

persons to break from accustomed action. Conventional attitudes may be disturbed by those who are indifferent to historical process, but such discontent can become socially constructive only by successive steps.

Transformation of the Baptist denomination in the North was in fact a problem of the socialization of democracy. It soon became apparent that the real issue was between those who relied upon an educational process and those who wished to rely upon overhead authority. It was natural that the latter policy should have been favored by those who wished conformity. Their devotion to what was the traditional position of the denomination led them to attempt to formulate denominational orthodoxy enforced by a central body. This was one purpose of the Fundamentalist movement. Its champions wished to consolidate and maintain the past and to prevent changes which looked toward the development of co-operative and social action on the part of the denomination. On the other hand there were those of us who sought by gradual and educational process to lead the denomination into larger sympathy with the modern world. Our method was largely that of committees which set up agencies for gradual expansion of the interests of the Baptist churches in other than the defense of strictly denominational characteristics. In other words, we had to develop a socialized religious attitude as far as possible without arousing controversy. In the first years of our attempts theological differences had not become pronounced and it was possible for us to set up committees on social service and city missions, to organize a pension system, a Board of Education, to adopt new policies for the Societies, and co-operate with the newly established Federal Council of the Churches of Christ in America.

In 1916 I was president of the Northern Baptist Convention which met at Minneapolis. Tension within the denomination then was already evident. A theological seminary had been founded in Chicago to offset the influence of our Divinity

School. An effort had been made to organize an anti-convention movement which, while it amounted to nothing, was none the less symtomatic of increasing opposition to the very moderate progressive policy of the denomination. In fact, one of its leaders wrote me that this would be the last Northern Baptist Convention ever held. In addition there were some difficult questions to be answered relative to the relationship of the Publication Society and the Home Mission Society. Between these two there was an increasing rivalry which, I was to discover, was not altogether marked by Christian forebearance. I had been unsuccessful in my attempts to induce the leaders of the pre-millennarian group to co-operate in maintaining peace. It needed only a war to develop a psychology which raised enmity to the plane of conscience!

There seemed to be only one possible way of preventing serious disturbance within our denomination and that was to have the Convention carried on in the atmosphere of religion. Ordinarily this quality was supposed to be given to the Convention by so-called devotional exercises and meetings. The first were purely formal and the delegates seldom came in until they had closed. The attendance upon devotional meetings which were held after the adjournment of each session was largely dependent upon the popularity of the speaker. Such a divorce of business and religion seemed unworthy of a religious gathering. I therefore had a great sign painted and hung up over the platform which read, "Let us get together by working together and praying together." I had the doors closed during the opening period of devotion and whenever we faced important business I would ask the Convention to pause for a brief season of prayer that we might proceed wisely. To pray in advance of a discussion is very different from what so often happens when a chairman undertakes to soften acrimonious discussion by calling upon people to pray. Such prayers are very generally *ex parte*. The deity is told rather explicitly what the outcome of his co-operation ought to be. The Minneapolis Convention, I find, is recalled by those who were in attendance as having furnished religious inspiration. The difficult matter of the relation of the Societies was referred to a committee of which I was made chairman, and the other business of the Convention was carried on so expeditiously that we were able to adjourn a day earlier than the program had provided.

I have always felt that one has no right to involve institutions in struggles which might be aroused by one's own individual views. The freedom of thought and teaching which was allowed in the University of Chicago could not well be expected from strictly denominational bodies. After the outbreak of the Fundamentalist controversy the theological seminaries were investigated by a committee of the Northern Baptist Convention. In a report creditable to the impartiality of the committee, some of whose members were sincerely opposed to any concessions to modernism, the seminaries were given a pretty clean bill of health. It seemed to me that it was unfair to the denomination to introduce technical theological questions into what was clearly a test of denominational solidarity. I therefore advised the representatives of other schools to withdraw from any active participation in controversy and give attention to matters with which they were immediately concerned leaving the Convention free to adjust matters within itself. I practiced what I advised lest the criticism directed against my views should intensify the controversial spirit within the denomination itself. I had made my contribution toward developing denominational efficiency and I believed it was possible for all parties to co-operate in active work despite theological differences. With real regret I saw the denomination pass into the control of men who were more concerned to maintain the machinery of the denomination than to lead it toward the ever-expanding horizon of a new era. In the course of a few years, however, younger men who had grown up in the new religious climate once more aroused the denomination to wider conceptions of the task of the churches. Such a renaissance of interest would have been impossible if theological controversy had been allowed to proceed to what might have been a more serious split in the denomination than has actually occurred. That such a misfortune did not befall a great religious body was in large measure due to the conciliatory policy of the modernist group, and the sagacity of Dr. William C. Bitting, Secretary of the Convention, my incomparable friend, Dr. Cornelius Woelfkin, and Dr. Wallace C. Petty.

II

What was true of the denomination as a whole was true of various local groups of Baptist churches. About their only unifying group was the Association. But in the course of years this had lost most of its significance and had little influence on the religious life of its constituent churches. It had no funds and no authority. It was impossible to plan collectively in a body whose number was very considerable. Nor could plans be made by which churches could follow trends in population. In fact, that was a weakness of all Protestantism, except those highly developed bodies which had found it possible to endow churches like St. George's in New York, and make them independent of the changes within their community. In some cases City Mission Societies or Church Extension Societies were sufficiently well organized to found new churches in new areas. Occasionally this was accomplished by individual churches. In the case of the Baptists in Chicago, however, at the beginning of the present century there was no such vigorous planning and most churches in the heart of the city had either been abandoned or united or moved to regions better fitted financially for their support. Long before the establishment of formal surveys any student of the trend in churches of congregational polity could see that they were growing more inefficient and futureless. So evident did this appear in Chicago that a committee was appointed to present the facts. We frankly said we planned to make the denomination nervous. Our report had the desired effect and from the sense of crisis emerged an organization which gave unity to what had been formerly hardly more than competitive independent bodies. Dr. Johnston Meyers, pastor of the Immanuel Baptist Church, an institution which was particularly suffering from the changes of population, is to be credited with the plan of the organization of a body known as the Baptist Executive Council which undertook to give new unity of action to the churches. At the start the organizers of the Council were more or less influenced by the organization of Roman Catholic bishoprics and made an ambitious attempt to take over the property of weak churches, protect them from dissolution, and at the same time develop a capital which could be used as a basis for church extension. The plan when put into effect in the case of a few churches was soon found impracticable and the titles which the Council had taken were given back to the churches themselves. But this after all was but an incident.

For something like ten years I was President of the Council, and with the hearty co-operation of its Superintendent Dr. Frank L. Anderson, as well as a group of successful business men, we were able to raise a revolving fund for the purpose of helping church building. At the same time there was developed a unity of action on the part of the denomination in the Chicago area. Fortunately theological differences did not interfere and we were able to establish a number of churches in strategic positions and to help support those that were suffering from changes of population. It was an interesting experiment in the range of institutional organization, for outside its financial aid the Council had no ecclesiastical authority. As in the case of the Northern Baptist Convention it was an example of how democracies can develop a unity of program through voluntary co-operation. The Council absorbed the old City Mission Society and in

1934 it united with the Chicago Baptist Association so that there is now a genuine institutional unity. There has always been difference of opinion both theologically and otherwise among its members, but it has never suffered from theological controversy. The years have not been without their critical moments, but the fact that those of us who were representatives of the more progressive trend refused to engage in anything that looked like controversy saved the denomination from what might easily have become schism.

I was warned that the publication of my views on the Second Coming of Christ would arouse bitter opposition but naturally I had expected it. I declined to seek re-election as the President of the Baptist Executive Council of Chicago, although I remained one of its members.

This participation in denominational life was not due to ecclesiastical chauvinism. Any less intimate effort may become a grandstand criticism. In my mind a denomination was one aspect of the total Christian movement. I have never shared in the rigorous logic of ecclesiasticism which would condition participation in church life upon rites. In the words of Phillips Brooks—"I cannot live truly with the men of my own church unless I also have a consciousness of common life with all Christian believers, with all religious men, with all mankind."

CHAPTER IX

THE SOCIAL GOSPEL

IT SEEMS to be difficult for the generation of religious leaders who are now in middle life to realize that it was not until the last years of the nineteenth century that churches began to take serious interest in the extension of the teachings of Jesus to society. The credit for arousing such interest must as usual be given to individuals who broke away from the individualistic interests of the evangelical churches and undertook to arouse the conscience of Christians to economic injustice. Washington Gladden, Josiah Strong, and Lyman Abbott were outstanding among these earlier leaders. But others like George D. Herron, professor in Grinnell, Iowa; David J. Hill, afterward Ambassador to Germany, then President of Bucknell University; Leighton Williams and Walter Rauschenbusch, who together organized the short-lived Brotherhood of the Kingdom; Richard T. Ely, the economist, who published some lectures on the social aspects of Christianity; William D. Hyde, President of Bowdoin College, who published a volume, *Social Theology;* Graham Taylor and Charles R. Henderson, who in 1892 were called from their pastorates to take up work in the Chicago Theological Seminary and the Divinity School of the University of Chicago, respectively; Francis G. Peabody, who developed social ethics in Harvard Divinity School; the faculty of Andover Theological Seminary, through the *Andover Review*—were among these pioneers.

I

There was lacking, however, a systematic study of the social significance of the teaching of Jesus. Shortly after I came to

Chicago, at the suggestion of Professor Albion W. Small, who was editing the *American Journal of Sociology,* I began a series of articles in that journal which I called "Christian Sociology." When published these articles had the title of *The Social Teaching of Jesus.* In them my interest in sociology and in biblical theology were united. So far as I know this book was the first volume in English in its field. It represented what might be called a transitional view of the kingdom of God as a social order to be reached progressively. In later years I came to see that this term was really eschatological and I rewrote the volume, publishing it under the title *Jesus on Social Institutions.* The original volume represented the type of biblical interpretation which was not yet responsive to a historical exegesis but, if its continued life would argue anything, served a useful purpose. Professor Peabody wrote his admirable volume *Jesus Christ and the Social Question* as one of a series of New Testament Handbooks which I was editing for the Macmillan Company. When his manuscript reached us, however, it seemed advisable to publish it as an independent volume and it has become almost a classic in its field. I might add that Professor Peabody, again on my invitation, wrote a volume on *Jesus Christ and the Christian Character* which likewise seemed to the publishers and me to be better as an independent volume than as one of the series of handbooks. Professor Peabody likes to say that I am responsible for his getting into the field of authorship. If this be the case I am proud of my success.

The early years of the twentieth century were marked by a very widespread interest in social affairs, due largely to the development of sociology and socialist writings. A large number of volumes were published during these years and served to stimulate the social interest of the ministry. Among them were Walter Rauschenbusch's exceedingly stimulating volumes *Christianity and the Social Crisis* and *Christianizing the Social Order,* and several volumes by me, *The Church and the Changing*

Order, The Social Gospel, a study book for the Baptist Young People's Union, and The Individual and the Social Gospel, a textbook for the Missionary Education Movement. The American Institute of Sacred Literature issued a study course I wrote The Social and Ethical Teaching of Jesus (later revised under the title The Message of Jesus to Our Modern Life). There was a constant demand for lectures in this field and the social gospel became a familiar term. Nor was the interest wholly confined to generalizations. One denomination after another organized its Social Service Commissions, the first of which, so far as I know, was that of the Protestant Episcopal Church. The Presbyterians appointed Charles Stelzle to deal with the relations of Christianity and the industrial world and Warren Wilson to deal with the work of rural churches. The Commission of the Northern Baptist Convention of which Walter Rauschenbusch, Charles R. Henderson, and I were members, issued a series of pamphlets and Samuel Zane Batten became its effective secretary. Other denominations began the discussion of social questions. Harry Ward became an influence in Methodism and Graham Taylor among the Congregational churches. The so-called Social Creed of the Churches drawn up by Frank Mason North was issued by the Federal Council of the Churches of Christ in America in 1908 and revised in 1912 and again in 1932. Beyond the criticism of President Eliot of Harvard it attracted little opposition except from the pre-millennarians. This group of earnest Christians vigorously and at times intemperately attacked the representatives of the movement, particularly Walter Rauschenbusch and me. To some of them we seemed atheists but to all of them the effort to bring in the kingdom of God by reforming society seemed akin to atheism. An extraordinary pronouncement was made by a group of English clergymen after the War, insisting that no plans for social reform should be made by the church pending the speedy return of Christ. The Federal Council was attacked in its efforts at introducing Christianity into social affairs, in emphatic and sometimes bitter pamphlets. I had the distinction of being called a member of a Trinity, the other two *personae* being the Pope and the Devil.

Another criticism of the social gospel was that it neglected the individual and attempted to convert the world *en masse*. The charge, while natural, was unjustifiable. I could quote from any number of books and articles which insist that there is only one gospel and that it is just as impossible to make a good society out of bad people as it is to build a marble house of mud bricks. But at the same time it has to be admitted that not a few ministers regarded pastoral work as drudgery and looked to some wholesale way of putting the principles of Jesus into operation. There was a tendency to deal more with the problems of society than with those of the individual. But there was really a more fundamental difficulty. The older evangelical orthodoxy regarded the gospel as the message of forgiveness of sins by virtue of belief in Jesus as the atoning sacrifice. Faith in him was of course to be followed by moral life but the good news of salvation was not primarily moral. It was the work of God in which men had no real part. The social gospel was aggressively ethical. It naturally produced moral discontent rather than spiritual complacency.

II

The attempt to make Christianity influential in human affairs is of course not novel. Churches and sects have repeatedly undertaken to abolish some social evil or to develop a social order. In a few cases like that of the Anabaptists of Münster these attempts have become revolutionary. Only the historically illiterate can think of Christianity as being concerned solely with *post mortem* salvation. The emphasis which the churches have placed on sin and repentance has evoked emotional response that has been a moral leaven. The very absoluteness of their ideals has stimulated criticism of the conditions recognized as evil and injurious to human welfare.

Such more or less unconscious criticism has been usually limited by a period's intelligence. As that has grown the influence of unrealized ideals has been felt in new criticism of existing conditions.

The new appreciation of Jesus was the immediate outcome of the scientific study of the gospels as the biography of the historical Jesus. Lives of Christ were numerous. Jesus stepped down from his theological pedestal and became a real character. Protestant Christians still worshiped the second person of the Trinity but they made new acquaintance with Jesus of Nazareth. At first he was clothed in a bizarre combination of piety, theology, and rabbinical exposition. Then, gradually, he emerged a mid-Victorian of the liberal type who could be counted upon to give his support to any idealism provided it was polite. The Jesus of history became distinct from the so-called Christ of experience. And then came the objective, untheological application of the historical method to the gospel, the better understanding of Judaism gained from the study of its own literature, a realization of the social psychology of early Christianity and its relationship to the Graeco-Roman world, and, most important, an appreciation of Jesus' teaching.

With the exception of various tangential and openly heretical groups the Christian religion developed for centuries with little reference to the teaching of Jesus. So far as the great creeds are concerned the Sermon on the Mount might as well never have been delivered. The Protestant Confessions are singularly silent as to the teaching of Jesus beyond a reference to his "new commandment." The pioneers of the social gospel seized upon this discovery of Jesus and his teaching. They took Jesus seriously. Most of them were members of evangelical churches and did not deny the Christ of the creeds, but they were more concerned with the Jesus of the gospels. Such a transfer of emphasis brought about a revolution in religious interests. Belief in the deity of Christ which had become hardly more than an unintelligible article of faith became a source of social courage, born of a pragmatic rather than a metaphysical theology. Whatever philosophical reservations were made, Jesus became a revelation of the divine will in human society. The great business of the church was to produce men and women who had the attitude and consequent behavior of Jesus Christ. Christology had to be social. Christ represented not only the way of individual salvation but also the will of God in social process. The duty of Christians was to order social relations in accordance with the basic principles which Jesus himself set forth. To do this demanded an understanding of group action and a conviction that since God is love, love is a practicable basis for a social order.

But what then was the teaching of Jesus? Was the Sermon on the Mount a new list of commandments? Or would it be permissible to select from his teaching some formulas and neglect others? If we were to be non-resistant, should we also give to every beggar? Or would the attempt to bring the spirit of Jesus into social affairs demand the intelligent understanding of his relationship to his own day and the distinction of the form from the content of his teaching? Such questions as these were evidently not to be settled by piety. No esoteric experience was demanded. Nor was Christianity to be merely adjusted to contemporary culture. Brotherliness was more than brotherhood. If the ideals of Jesus were to be a leaven of sacrificial social mindedness and his example was to be inspiration from the intelligent democratizing of privilege, it was not enough to save brands from the burning. We wanted to put out the fire. The amelioration of social evils might require good Samaritans but it was more imperative to clear the road from Jerusalem to Jericho of robbers.

It is not strange that our efforts should have been misrepresented as the substitution of sociology for the gospel. Many persons did make this substitution. Scientific philanthropy has very little use for religion, and the charities of the churches seem unscientific, as doubtless, to a considerable extent, they are. Some ministers seemed to think that it is easier to deal with political and economic generalizations than to strengthen men's faith in divine help. Some social prophets became common scolds. It is not strange, therefore, that in recent years it should become rather fashionable to allege the failure of the social gospel and to turn to worship as the supreme mission of the church. It is no accident that those who would thus retreat from the religious frontier should find peace in emotional excitement. Anything that can turn lives from frivolity to earnestness is, of course, to be commended, but there is nothing more deadening to moral life than "the enjoyment of religion." If there is anything inconsistent with the teaching of Jesus it is spiritual luxury. To make a congregation of prosperous and respectable middle-class people purr with religious content is no way to stimulate them to sacrificial Christian living. Nor is misery a thermometer of holiness. The New England puritanism of my youth made a choice between any two courses of action reasonably easy. God wanted you to do what you did not want to do. But the representatives of the social gospel tried to show that conscience was something more than a compound of prejudice and obstinacy, that scientific intelligence insures divine aid as truly as good intentions, and that however necessary a police power may be for protection against evil doers, a coerced idealism is dangerously like sin against the Holy Ghost.

III

It may seem strange that the presentation of the teaching of Jesus should have produced reaction, but acquaintance with the history of the church dispels such surprise. Jesus too much emphasized sacrificial social-mindedness to be popular with ecclesiastics. Organized Christianity has always championed the status quo. Whatever influence the church has had in the development of morals has been only incidentally based on the teaching of Jesus. Individuals and minorities who have raised its authority above orthodoxy have been treated as heretics.

Such facts account for the opposition to the social gospel. Orthodoxy was a presentation of how to get salvation in heaven. The social gospel proposed the teaching of Jesus as a call and a way to give salvation on earth. To orthodoxy the cross was a call to the enjoyment of divine grace. To those of us who were trying to bring the teaching of Jesus to bear on human affairs it was a symbol of the democratizing of privilege. It is not strange that many members of the Protestant churches should protest that they want the "good old gospel." They foresee that in the same proportion as the social interpretation of Christianity becomes dominant economic readjustments are bound to come. Praise of the old gospel is like praise of old-fashioned honesty. Men are to be virtuous by being like their grandfathers. But grandfathers' virtues like grandfathers' clocks are in our own day not always in good running order. Old-fashioned honesty gave sixteen ounces to the pound, condemned wooden nutmegs, paid its debts, told no lies, kept five or six of the commandments. But its limits were set by the individualism which had broken down political absolutism and thrown the bones of kings into lime pits. It goes without saying that we need this individualistic honesty. But the champions of the social gospel insisted that we need a very much bigger sort of honesty. Obligation is set not only by our relations with indivdiuals but by our relations with the groups of which we are members and by the relations of the groups themselves. We pioneers were optimistic enough to believe that it was possible to develop a social conscience but we did not suffer from the illusions with which we have been charged. Certainly we were blinded by no sentimentalism, nor was our new emphasis on religion a form of wishful thinking. At any rate, we did not baptize a sociological formula and call it a new revelation. We actually believed, and in my opinion the course of events has justified that belief, that it is possible to educate moral sympathies and arouse a desire for economic justice by self-respecting propaganda. Charles Stelzle brought the churches into touch with organized labor, and in several cities ministers were given a sort of honorary membership in labor unions. I spoke to all sorts of economic groups, credit men's associations, the American Federation of Labor, managers of public utilities, farmers, and women's clubs, but I was only one of a group of men who were possessed of the same belief that the teaching of Jesus was applicable to group action. If our participation with economic struggles were not as intimate as those in less academic and ecclesiastical groups, it was none the less actual. We were liberals of the ante-questionnaire period but we were not unpractical romanticists. One has only to compare the state of mind in the church today with that of evangelical circles in which most of us were brought up, to see that our labors were not in vain in the Lord. We may have been too sanguine in our expectations, and undoubtedly in the last years before the War felt that we had gone farther than the undercurrent of life later showed. Despite the unsupportable charge that we were blind believers in evolution, we did believe that it is possible not only to direct but to hasten progress. If we were too sanguine we paid the penalty in the disillusionment and agony of soul which came to those of us who suddenly found that we had mistaken what we thought ought to be for what really was. If any persons were justified in growing cynical it was those of us who were the champions of the social gospel. Had we been living in a dream world and was our message that of a bourgeois ideology—to use the jargon of modern days—which had been the rationalization of capitalism?

Such questions really threw one back upon the basic question as to whether in social action there is only economic determinism. Does history warrant the appeal of Jesus for adventurous sacrifice in the interests of a common good? When I was invited to give the Noble lectures at Harvard University, for the sake of my own peace of mind I chose as the subject *The Spiritual Interpretation of History.* I had seen that historical facts could be used to support some philosophical interpretation of history as something more than a mass of isolated facts, but was the philosophy itself correct? I felt that if one could see what actually took place in the past, compare *mores* and evaluate the ability of institutions to meet social tensions which they themselves had helped develop, it should be possible to say whether individuals were more than peripatetic chemical laboratories driven about by hunger and sex. In preparing these lectures I tried, by taking a long view of history, to see just what sort of trends made toward permanency and personal welfare. The influence of geographical and economic forces evidently had to be taken into account, but the real question was as to whether the resultant of the interplay of all such forces was in the direction of personal values or was simply a repetition of human experiences. So examined, I found history showing a substitution of moral for physical control, a growth in the worth of the individual, and the transformation of rights into justice. If that discovery be the recognition of progress, critics of so-called liberalism can make the most of it! It certainly furnished me with a basis for the presentation of values which were preserved in the Christian movement. A further study of the psychology of revolutionary epochs necessitated by a revision of my volume on the French Revolution made plain the dangers which lay in the treatment of these values as social absolutes and in the attempt to put them in operation without due regard to a social process. I remember saying in 1915, at a banquet in New York, "Sow the gospel in China and you will reap a revolution." I meant by the gospel, the principles which the teaching of Jesus represented rather than the theology of the West, and events have justified the forecast. The more I have had opportunity to observe the impact of Christianity as a phase of western civilization upon the Asiatic world, the clearer becomes the necessity of the recognition of process in any reform. I can understand why those who do not have patience or historical-mindedness turn to revolution. It is easier to arouse men to get justice than to give justice.

IV

Such a view carries one straight into the field of social techniques. One needs to discover just how various groups cross-fertilize themselves. The moment one ceases to think of the church as a supernatural body and regards it as a social group one needs to discover just what the function of a religion in a culture may be. I made this the subject of my Barrows lectures in India in 1933-34. They were published under the title *Christianity and Social Process*. In them I took the only position that can be historically justified, that Christianity as an organized religion is one aspect of western civilization. But it is an aspect, not merely a result. It is a movement which carries values which, with varied success, have been embodied in the social process from which our civilization has come. In such a study one may unconsciously yield to prejudice and predilection, but when one sees impartially what has been the relation of Christianity as a religious form of social behavior to political and economic development, one can intelligently discuss its function in our own time. I endeavored to follow out the practical results of such an investigation in the Cole lectures of 1934 which were published as *Creative Christianity*. I suspect that such a reading of history with its corollaries of practical policies may not appeal strongly to many Christians. It is much easier to adopt an absolutist position and to talk about truth rather than duties, to urge Christian coercion rather than Christian education, and to champion theological formula rather than participate in social change.

And it must be admitted that there is something attractive in a strictly logical theory of social reconstruction. But its attractiveness seems to be almost in exact proportion to its *a priori* quality. Revolutions are not caused by administrators but by undefined generalities like liberty, equality, fraternity, in which the underprivileged see a promise of new rights. The difficulty always comes when men try to translate abstractions into political action. Marxian socialism claims an historical basis but in reality it is a sociological syllogism with a major premise that is in the best sense of the word speculative. The term "kingdom of God" so long as it was left as a generalization had the same stimulating power as other undefined ideals. The practical difficulty was how to take the first step toward the ideal it represented. To those under the control of dogmatic communism there is no hope except in revolution. This certainly could not be derived from the teaching of Jesus. The dealers in Christian absolutism are therefore caught between two difficulties. On the one side they wish to adopt a social theory and on the other side they cannot appeal to violence. Their very Christian position serves to weaken their revolutionary efficiency.

If some step must be taken, the champion of the social gospel must recognize social process. The direction in which Christian social efforts should move is not a matter of good intentions but of intelligence, much like that of the engineer who embodies in materials the formulas of mathematics.

The discussions of social questions during the early stage of the social gospel were carried on by those who were members of the *bourgeois* group, although a few, like Rauschenbusch, were Christian socialists. Occasionally ministers with socialist sympathies became interested in party politics but as a rule, either their socialism remained theoretical, or like the most distinguished of their number, Norman Thomas, they broke with the church. It is somewhat remarkable that barring the sound redefinition of the kingdom of God as eschatological, the general discussion of the second generation of writers has added little to the views set forth by our pioneering literature. Many of them are, however, more or less under the influence of socialism and communism and the confused and pessimistic theology of Barth which, with all its emphasis upon faith, is a denial of the help of God in social process. In fact, there are in this second generation of liberals two trends of thought. There are those who ignore and those who recognize social process. The former group makes liberalism the object of criticism. They attribute to the nineteenth century a blind faith in progress and the minimizing of sin. I once tried to get from one of our critics the names of those he had in mind, but could get only general statements. Any examination of the literature of the first period of social awakening in the churches will show that it not only recognized the evils of society but treated sin as something more than a theological term. As a matter of fact, the ideas of the early movement have become a part of religious thought. Views which seemed radical in those early days are now the presuppositions of intelligent Christians. Church bodies now confront the question as to how these ideals can be implemented. In some cases this involves the paradox of opposing international war and of justifying class war. Such inconsistency is to be expected in those who deal with absolutes rather than processes, but the working leadership of the churches is more concerned with taking the next step in organizing the morality of group action. A study of the deliverances made by various denominations both national and state will show how far this new movement in moral education has gone. The Social Service Commission of the Federal Council investigated a number of strikes. However, its chief influence is educational. The Council publishes a valuable Bulletin of Information and serves by conferences and publications to spread the interest in the social gospel. It does not hesitate to point out evils in our economic life and to mark out the fields within which the church could have influence. The report of the Inter-church World Movement on the steel industry can be said to have influenced the policy of the United Steel Corporation. John D. Rockefeller Jr.'s brochure *Brotherhood* set forth a program as well as a moral attitude for capitalism. An outstanding illustration of the social interest is to be seen in the organization of the Committee on Social Action by the National Council of the Congregational and Christian Churches. Other denominations have passed resolutions more or less reproducing the Federal Council's Social Creed of the Churches. The Baptist Convention of Illinois without a dissenting vote referred to the churches for study a series of propositions defining the social service of the church which I drew up for the Commission on Social Service. The Methodist General Conference under the influence of Professor Harry Ward and Bishop McConnell has committed itself in a great variety of ways to the social application of Christian principles to economic life. The Anti-Saloon League was distinctly representative of membership of the evangelical churches. The collapse of the prohibition movement is a commentary on the position taken by those who would organize a Christian *bloc* and coerce people into adopting what it regards as Christian principles. It also clearly indicates the futility inherent in the habit of idealists to abandon the inculcation of their idealism whenever they get political power. Policemen and federal agents are no substitute for the minister and the teacher. It is no accident that the great terrorists have been idealists who got control of an army.

V

The complications in our modern world which hinder the application of Christian ideals were plain from the study of economics, but were made more evident by my association with the Western Economic Society of which I was the only President. The society was founded by the economists J. Lawrence Laughlin and Leon C. Marshall for the purpose of intelligent and impartial study of imminent economic problems. Professor Marshall was secretary for a number of years and Harold G. Moulton was his successor. To them rather than to me was due whatever success the society attained. Its first meeting was ambitious. We had President Taft deliver an address on "Reciprocity with Canada" at a largely attended public meeting. For a number of years we held conferences in which many of the leading economists and men of affairs of the nation took part. I was rather a figurehead as a presiding officer but contact with outstanding men of affairs increased my conviction that moral idealism must face actual conditions rather than rhetorical generalizations. It is easy to speak about "service motive" replacing the "profit motive" in industry, but its advocates are singularly indifferent to the facts of economic life. An out-and-out socialist or communist using such a slogan is really a propagandist. It has become fashionable to talk about the end of capitalism, but a realistic view of the world in which we live does not yield support to such rhetoric. The world cannot be saved by epigrams. A would-be reformer cannot safely ignore our social and economic heritage. If obsessed with the evils of the world he awaits a social deluge which will eliminate the past—he would do well to remember the experience of Noah. Economic institutions must be changed and made more conducive to human welfare, but the experience of the race cannot be ignored. No revolution has succeeded in exterminating economic motives.

VI

The last decades of the nineteenth century saw the beginning of new social trends. The influence of Toynbee Hall, London, was to be seen in the founding of social settlements like Andover House in Boston, Hull House in Chicago, Chicago Commons, and those of the University of Chicago and Northwestern University. Indeed, most of the settlements now in existence were founded during these years. The movement, which was avowedly distinct from the churches, was really the outcome of Christian sympathy, and probably most of the workers were products of church life. Unlike the Christian Associations the settlements, while in some cases associated with some church, as a rule did not hold religious services. They were, in fact, an expression of a new conception of Christianity which made service superior to theological orthodoxy.

Most of those interested in the social gospel sought to cooperate with institutions that were making toward better social conditions. However much we might be inspired by a belief that Christian principles involved more than they could accomplish we were not so doctrinaire as not to support institutions that looked toward the amelioration of underprivileged life. If we could not bring his father's home to the prodigal in a far country we could at least bring him food.

We had no sooner begun our life in Chicago than my wife and I went to see the University of Chicago Settlement. A few years before we had visited Toynbee Hall and we pictured the settlement behind the stockyards as on the same scale as the English institution. We were promptly disillusioned. Mary MacDowell, that magnetic champion of justice and neighborliness, was living in the upper story of a little two-flat building in an atmosphere redolent with odors of a glue factory. Not even the personality of Miss MacDowell could hide the fact that the rooms were bare and unattractive. I became a member of the Board of the Christian Union of the University, which was then responsible for the management of the settlement, and for a year or more I was its president. Indeed, I have been almost continuously on the Board of the Settlement. During these forty years the institution has developed until it is one

of the outstanding settlements of the country, with a fine building, playgrounds, and summer camp. A large group of women
more or less associated with the University have organized the
University Settlement League, which supplements and sup-
ports the work of the Settlement Board. With the development of professional social service the character of the Settlement has somewhat changed in that its resident staff is almost
entirely composed of professional workers on salary. But it is
still a center for the expression of voluntary philanthropic
interests like that of the Student's Settlement Committee. If
ever there were a genuinely religious person it is Mary Mac-
Dowell, but neither she nor the Board judged it practicable to
introduce religious services into the program of the Settlement. It would have been impossible for the Settlement to
carry on its work effectively in a community which was either
definitely Roman Catholic or anti-religious if it gave any
appearance of proselytism or sectarianism.

At the start it was hard for the rank and file of churches
to see why, if they were to be supported by the church people,
settlements should not become centers of evangelism. The
Chicago Commons to some degree was associated with a local
church and there are a number of other forms of Christian social
work such as those of the Salvation Army and Good Will
Institute. It became increasingly evident not only that the
Settlement was not to be identified with an institutional church
but that it really was the first step in the extension of ideals
which while certainly advocated by the churches were not explicitly Christian. As school teaching has become a profession quite distinct from the clergy, so social service is becoming a non-religious vocation. The relation of the churches to
this new development was a matter of first importance and I
was asked to speak upon it at the annual meeting of the Conference of Charities and Corrections held in Washington. The
purpose of this address was not to condemn the separation of

charitable work from that of the churches. Protestants were ready to pass over the responsibility for the care of the poor and unfortunate to the community itself. At the same time the churches were bound to express their impulses in charities, hospitals, and institutional churches. More than that, the new vocation itself needed religious faith in order to protect its workers from depression and pessimism. Such considerations still seem to me to be sound. It is hard to see why the vocation of social service is religious in any other way than that of the physician. It will get efficiency as our case work grows more scientific, and its efficiency will not be born of emotions but of technique. One great service of the church will be to stimulate young persons to commit themselves to this type of vicarious living and help them to feel that they can be brotherly because they are children of a heavenly father.

VII

It is always discouraging to discover the indifference of church people to conditions which threaten the well-being of their own communities. This seems to be true not only of great cities but of small towns. A spirit of moral *laissez faire* prevents serious effort for social reform. The city of Chicago is so accustomed to publishing its crime that the public has taken vice as a matter of course. Dean Sumner, however, headed a commission for investigating vice which undoubtedly had good results, at least in calling attention to the need of better policemen and judges. But it was hard to induce the average church person to do much more than vote the prohibition ticket. Even the heroic service of Phillip Yarrow in the Illinois Vigilance Association is poorly supported.

At the time when the Panama-Pacific Exposition was being organized in San Francisco there was a justifiable attack made upon the vice conditions in the city on the part of certain local clergymen and institutions. The Federal Council was also concerned about the matter because of the danger which threatened visitors to the Exposition. As President of the Council I was asked to co-operate with reforming elements in San Francisco and went to that city. The directors of the Exposition gave me a luncheon and when replying to their address of welcome I intimated that unless the Barbary Coast, which was on the way from the heart of the city to the fair grounds, was cleaned up, church organizations might declare a quarantine on the fair. At a banquet given by the Church Federation I pledged whatever support the Federal Council could give to efforts at making the city safe for prospective visitors. I do not know how influential such declarations were but the Barbary Coast was abolished.

This experience led me to feel that steps should be taken to prevent the development of vice in Chicago at the time of the Century of Progress Exposition. More than a year before the opening of the Exposition I invited a number of persons interested in municipal affairs to confer on the matter. After I had told them of my San Francisco experience they were unanimous that something should be done to forestall the exploitation of visitors. Consequently a body was formed and a method was developed by which it was hoped the various churches on the South Side of Chicago might report to a central group any development of vice conditions in their immediate vicinity. Prominent negro churches promised to co-operate in the undertaking, and Mrs. G. M. Mathes, of whose influence in arousing civic interest among women of the churches I shall speak later, and I undertook to develop district committees composed of delegates of various churches.

While this agitation was being carried on I also asked the representatives of the social service organizations of the city to meet and discuss the same matter. It was finally decided by this body that it would be better to refer the whole matter to the Council of Social Agencies. As a result, the Council appointed a committee, of which I was a member, to co-operate with committees appointed by the churches and the Association of Commerce. The interest of this committee was largely centered on the conditions within the fair grounds themselves. Considerable success was gained in the control of pickpockets and small thieves, but not in preventing questionable amusements.

Practically no results followed from our efforts among the churches. The ministers were sympathetic but inactive, and the church members even when members of committees were indifferent. The Committee from the Council of Social Agencies was able to bring the matter to the attention of Mayor Cermak and the Chief of Police, and as a consequence prostitution was somewhat kept under cover. Gambling, however, was carried on by those who were supposed to enjoy political favor. A number of raids were made upon gambling houses, but there was always the suspicion that they were due less to a desire for a clean city than to the internecine struggles between gambling over-lords.

These efforts to bring the influence of the churches to bear upon the activities of the police have convinced me that when properly developed and carried on through promises of co-operation rather than wholesale denunciation, religious forces will be respected by local governments. There are always in a great city organizations like the Crime Commission, the Juvenile Protective League, the Committee of Fifteen in Chicago that can act as agents for churchmen. Too often, however, the spirit of reform is short-lived and the initial success in the repression of various forms of vice is followed by indifference. The real difficulty is the unwillingness and ineptitude of the laity. It is much easier to arouse interest among church people in evangelistic services than in the maintenance of a militant social reform. The financial interests of laymen make them hesitate to take action which might subject them to the retaliation of those who directly or indirectly profit from the so-called "open town." If effort were to be concentrated upon decency rather than upon impracticable reforms results would be more promising. But we have yet to convince the churches that they can furnish a moral reserve for citizenship.

When the plans for A Century of Progress Exposition in Chicago were made they included some recognition of religion. As soon as this was announced I approached Mr. George W. Dixon who was the member of the Board of Directors responsible for this aspect of the Exposition and proposed that we set up a plan which would give religion a recognition comparable with other elements of the undertaking. To this end Mr. Dixon appointed a small committee which should not be composed of official representatives of different religious bodies but of their individual members. In this committee were an outstanding Roman Catholic clergyman, two Jewish rabbis, and members of several Protestant groups. The Roman Catholic later withdrew but the committee for several years devoted a large amount of time to planning. I drew up a general program which was adopted by the committee and approved by the President of the Century of Progress. At the start it was believed that we could have a considerable space in a proposed Social Science building. Such an arrangement had the advantage of intimately connecting the work of religious bodies with other social groups working for human betterment. In the course of time, however, the elaborate plans for the social science exhibition were abandoned and the religious exhibit was left without financial backing. It was necessary for the committee, therefore, to raise funds for the building as well as the expenses of the undertaking. This necessitated restriction of the participants in the exhibition to those who could pay for space in the building and ended our hopes that we could gain the co-operation of the representatives of Asiatic religions. It was soon apparent, also, that participation even among

American religious bodies would be impossible with the Hall of Religions the center of denominational propaganda. With the recollection of my experience in the World Conference for International Peace through Religion I proposed that each exhibitor should be asked to show what contributions its bodies had made to the progress of the century, thus carrying forward the fundamental purpose of the Exposition itself.

It was necessary that we should raise something like one hundred thousand dollars. The difficulty of so doing in a period of depression is obvious, but despite the initial indifference of some of the religious bodies, the plans succeeded. The building was erected by the sale of space and the religious bodies made striking exhibitions of their contributions to human welfare. Much of the success of the exhibition was due to the energy of Dr. Hugh McGill who took on the duties of the General Manager in addition to his work as General Secretary of the International Council of Religious Education.

If anything were needed to show the interest in the American people in religion this Hall of Religion supplied it. The attendance was enormous, I believe second only to that in the Hall of Science. The exhibits were very effective and the assembling of the evidences of the contributions to American life of such variant groups as the Lutherans, Jews, Mormons and the various Protestant denominations showed the social significance of religion.

My experience in conferences at the expositions in Buffalo and St. Louis had shown that visitors to an exhibition were not interested in public meetings, but we built a small assembly hall in the Hall of Religion in which it was proposed that addresses without any proselyting might describe the work of the various religious bodies. It soon appeared, however, that there was little interest in that sort of undertaking. Financial limitations made impracticable our ambitious plans to hold international conferences on such matters as concerned all religious orders like international peace, religious education and youth movements. The real influence of the Hall of Religion lay in the interesting and striking quality of the exhibits themselves. No visitor could fail to be impressed with the extent and variety of contributions which religious bodies had made to the cultural and social history of the country.

VIII

Advocates of social Christianity too often confuse the task and obligations of the churches with those of the individual Christians. I have caught myself many times in such a careless use of terms. If the word "church" is used as a sort of synonym of Christians its significance as a social group is lost. Christians can do many things that a church to which they belong cannot do. That is to say the function of the church as an organized social group is not as extensive as that of its members who necessarily belong to many other groups.

Failure to bear in mind this distinction has caused advocates of the social gospel both to minimize the importance of the church and to make upon it unreasonable demands. It is easy to say that if the church had done its duty there would be no slums or war or social evil or any other condition that we lament. Such a formula is all too easily drawn. A far more correct statement would be that if all people implemented the principles of Jesus with faultless economic, political, esthetic, and recreational techniques, society would be in a very much better condition than it is. It is mere rhetoric to lay the responsibility of human foolishness, ignorance and willfulness upon the church. Social science in the last ten or fifteen years has given us altogether too much information as to our social institutions, inheritances and trends in our economic life to leave us contented with the generalizations of a generation ago. The development of huge corporations has made our economic life a dictatorship tempered by strikes. No sensible person can deny that it is the business of the churches to direct the morals of the society that results. It is a hopeful sign that leaders of religious progress aim at being realistic. Even if, as it sometimes seems, the realism is academic rather than the outcome of contact with the world outside university or seminary walls, it will enable churches to see more clearly just what their relationship to society is.

The function of a church, whether it be local or denominational, is that of persuading men who believe in God's presence in social process to organize their individual and group life in accordance with the principles of love—that is to say, the treatment of others as persons entitled to enjoy any privilege which membership in a group offers. In a democracy the individual belongs to a great many groups, which have different functions. He himself contributes to and is conditioned by their efficiency. In consequence social life is not in compartments. Not only do members of groups carry over the attitudes of one to another but this cross-fertilization is supplemented by the attitudes of these groups themselves. My experience in various co-operative undertakings has made the need of co-ordinating these two facts perfectly plain. Officials of missionary societies in a joint session once took quite a different course of action from that which they took in their respective societies. A member of a political party in a non-partisan organization more or less unconsciously acts in accordance with his party affiliations. On the other hand organized groups in dealing with each other will often enter upon courses of action which some of their individual members could never take and in fact may disapprove.

These facts lead to action, not mere exhortation and criticism. A church, just as any organized group, must both educate and reinforce the moral attitudes of its members and so prepare them to affect the action of other groups to which they belong, and also by its own corporate action it must give moral direction to the action of groups themselves. As members of a group having such double function it is clear that Christians must give their loyalty to such economic and political programs as seem best able to further progress toward those ends which are consistent with their Christian ideals. That means, of course, that churches and individual Christians have a part to play in politics and other means of giving sanction to justifiable programs.

If a church is to be treated as a social group it clearly can use methods calculated to give it efficiency. It will not only unconsciously express the temper which characterizes a social order but it will consciously appropriate methods which are adopted by dominant elements comprising that order. In the history of Christianity it is easy to trace the emergence of these changes in the attitude and methods of the church as it participates in social process. Imperialism, feudalism, nationalism, democracy have all been embodied in types and methods of churches. There has been no actual unity in the transformation of Christian groups but rather a differentiation of new methods and institutions in response to the conditioning forces of society. In Graeco-Roman society in which political discussion and organization were forbidden it was natural that there should be especial concern with the metaphysical questions proposed by the elements of the Christian faith. Just as natural was it that decisions of Councils should assume the quality of law and that group solidarity should be maintained by the same methods as those by which the state maintained a respect for government. The separation of church and state in American religious life has not prevented the emergence of the same type of questions in church organization as have appeared in the political history. In the third volume of *The Outline of Christianity*, which I edited, I traced the participation of the various denominations in a social process. The Presbyterians, for example, in their denominational controversies, reproduced the constitutional struggles between the strict and loose interpretations of the Constitution of the United States. The different attitudes toward slavery which were largely dependent upon economic forces, led to the divisions of great bodies like the Baptist, the Presbyterians and the Methodists. The new social conditions which affected democratic principles caused the reorganization of religious groups like the Congregationalists, the Baptists and Disciples. In all churches the principles of business found more or less expression, because of the increased share of the laymen in the conduct of denominational affairs. When the ideas of scientific management were first expressed I wrote a little brochure on the *Scientific Management in the Churches*. In this I endeavored to show how a church could be efficiently organized in the interests of group efficiency.

At the same time that Protestant churches were centering attention upon group efficiency in so-called spiritual matters, there was a remarkable development in the so-called service organizations such as the Rotary and Kiwanis. It is rather the fashion of those who are not engaged in commercial operations to treat such organizations contemptuously. But it would seem to me that they represent the extension of Christian ideals into commercial relations which is just as legitimate and inevitable as the extension of Christian interests into the field of philosophy. Certainly any study of morality will show the importance of economic life in developing the *mores* of social life. While these groups are not strictly speaking religious they illustrate the influence of Christianity as a social ferment. The numerous Codes adopted by various trades and professions indicate the same. Even in the case of those who oppose the participation of churches in economic discussion and reform there is a distinct advance, at least in theory, from the heartless competition of the early days of the industrial era.

IX

If there were any need of proving that a church is not over against the world but a religiously organized phase of society it would only be necessary to call attention to the changes in the Protestant churches since the middle of the nineteenth century. As Catholicism embodies the idea of imperial unity so Protestantism has embodied first nationalism and then the individualism of democracy. At the middle of the nineteenth century both movements carried with them a modified pessimism. Every member of the human race had been born doomed to hell but churches were composed of those who had been selected by God to escape that doom. But no one could be assured of such deliverance until the Judgment Day when the elect would be separated from the lost. It was, therefore, appropriate for the church to emphasize the future blessing of those to whom it ministered the saving grace of God. The Catholic church also held up as spiritual superiors those who abandoned the joys of this life and made misery a thermometer of holiness. It knew how to adjust such a position to actual human life and did not undertake to burden the rank and file of Christians with the masochism of the truly spiritual. There were certain minimum requirements of discomfort like fasting which they could assume but pleasure was not a thing to be avoided. If it led to wrong-doing the church had its technique of penance by which the believer could regain divine favor. Unless he was guilty of major sins the church could reduce the discipline of purgatory.

Non-conformist Protestantism was much less genial in its dealings with life. While it had no system of confession and penance it inherited from its Puritan ancestry a suspicion of happiness. Death was an entrance upon an eternal state which was not determined by morality but by the decree of God. The Christian community was therefore set over against the world and the joys of a Christian were to be of anticipation rather than participation. Worldly pleasures were to be avoided and the true Christian was to keep himself unspotted from the world, with life governed by prayer and self-control. Yet such control was not asceticism. The families of the most pious of church members were generally large. There was only a vestigial regard for an annual Fast Day, and thrift and the pursuit of wealth were sanctified by charity which gained no merit but was regarded as a legitimate outcome of Christian ideals. It would not be correct to say that the consequent life of Christians was sombre. But it certainly had none of the enjoyment of life which characterized the state churches of Lutheran countries and was distinctly critical of the habits of Episcopalians.

During my boyhood church suppers became a recognized element of the life of a church, but not without criticism. When the kitchens were established, some church leaders like Dr. A. J. Gordon of the Clarendon Street Baptist Church of Boston protested against "the cooking stove apostasy." But the discipline of church members was not greatly lessened. While church members did attend the theatres—at least when visiting other cities—the old idea that life was a thing to be endured rather than to be enjoyed still dominated theology. Occasionally a minister would use tobacco but generally, as I recall in at least two cases, by physicians' advice. No minister would smoke in public. There was an underlying fear that happiness would be offset by misfortune.

The younger generation, while still subject to parental control, sought to enjoy life itself. Gradually the churches themselves came to feel obligation to meet the more liberal attitude which was due to a breaking down of Puritanism. A new philosophy began to emerge in churches as the older generation passed on their control to its successor. The Young Peo-

ple's Society of Christian Endeavor and similar organizations of
the various denominations, while strictly evangelical in their
published theology, tended toward normal enjoyment on the
part of the young. The theory of the church itself changed and
parish houses began to be built not only by Episcopalians but
by other denominations. Institutional churches appeared in
which recreational and social agencies were established to serve
community needs. They were still something of a novelty in
my youth. For two years I was associated with the Ruggles
Street Baptist Church of Boston which was one of the leaders
in this new type of church work, but even churches that did not
have its elaborate equipment found themselves less concerned
with keeping their members in the attitude of hostility to the
world. In the early years of the twentieth century the gymnasium and swimming pool became means of grace. It required
only a few years, however, to disclose the difficulties in such
church activities, and at the present time the building of gymnasiums has markedly decreased and a church provides opportunities for the social life of its clubs and for religious education. There is also a new regard for architectural beauty. At
the same time the old inhibitions as to dancing and theatre-
going largely disappeared except in cases of certain very orthodox churches. The educational value of dramatics has been
recognized and few churches will not give organized pageants
illustrative of missions or incidents in Christian history. Sunday-school libraries which once had a literature consistent with
theology have taken on the character of other libraries and
have become adjuncts of religious education. Particularly in the
case of churches whose leadership has been affected by current
discussions there has been less emphasis, at least formally,
upon theology, and a transfer of interest to the share of the
church in social and economic changes. Even birth control has
come within the range of discussion.

X

Efforts to revitalize the religious life of the times have been sometimes described as the adjustment of religion to culture. There is truth in such a statement but it is at the same time due to misunderstanding. Undoubtedly there were those who tempered their gospel to the unshorn lambs of their flock but such subserviency was not the outcome of the new religious enthusiasm. As today's tendencies show, the danger to which it was exposed was that the energy of church life should be dissipated among interests which were not primarily religious. In the case of ministers who had lost the fervor of evangelical Christianity, literary and various other cultural interests did masquerade as religion. In some cases ethical generalizations supplanted a sympathetic devotion to the Christian values which had come over from the past. In other cases the sense of economic injustice and the unhappy condition of wage earners in the less skilled branches of industry made pulpit utterances propaganda for class conflict. Moreover, the reaction from the severities of orthodoxy led to the exposition of God as love. He became a father rather than a judge. An obscurant optimism was in danger of degenerating into sentimentality, the American "daddy" becoming the pattern of the divine father. But it is a mistake to generalize these facts into a description of the new religious movement. What was actually taking place was not the sentimental adjustment of Christianity to culture but a sincere attempt to impregnate social process with the principles of Christ. It is not surprising that the use of the patterns of contemporary life should sometimes have appeared as a godless naturalism. To define religion as a search for the good life led to a neglect of the church as a social group through which the personality producing activities of the universe could strengthen and develop the personal worth of the individual. Solitariness became a philosophy of religion and the church ceased to be regarded as a channel of divine grace. But such discarding of historical Christianity seemed to me uncritical.

It was natural too that there should have been a reaction to what men called the mystical elements of religion and that the attempt to approach Christianity from the point of view of metaphysics should have tended toward the emotionalism of worship rather than the morality which Jesus made the condition of the experience of God. Undoubtedly the preaching of the love of God did at least for a time over-emphasize sweetness and light rather than sacrificial social-mindedness. The place of religion in a social order needed to be defined from the point of view of our expanding knowledge, of all aspects of human life. "If there is no hell, what are we saved from," was a natural question. If the Bible was not to be taken as a collection of inspired oracles, and if the church was not to be regarded as a phase of supernaturalism, if God was not to be thought of as a magnified individual with the habits of an unconstitutional monarch, just what was there left of our Christian faith? The answer to such question was simple. A man was not a liberal because he disbelieved what others believed, but because of a new perspective in his positive thinking. Our knowledge of social organization demanded that Protestants should give new attention to the significance of churches as elements in religion. The social gospel involved more than truth; it involved a new inventory of the function of churches as social groups. If they were to become simply other institutions devoted to charities, economic justice, international peace and cultural advance, they would be outmoded. If their doctrines were outgrown in Western society foreign missions would become a theological rummage sale.

XI

Efficiency in organization and moral influence does not exhaust the function of the church. As study and experience give one maturity of judgment, it becomes ever clearer that the function of the church is basically religious. Catholicism with its emphasis upon the supernatural has avoided the secularization which has followed the disintegration of evangelicalism in Protestantism. A church as a religious organization must be something more than an ethical group endeavoring to reform society. It can become in true sense a channel of grace. As a social group it can furnish motives and experiences impossible for the isolated individual. Such influence must be more than esthetic. However much Protestant services are enriched liturgically they must be genuinely religious. Otherwise they are mere pageants. At the present time there is danger that Protestantism shall become a lecture bureau to the exclusion of those experiences which the older evangelicalism as well as Catholicism have made central. If love is to become a practicable basis upon which to build human society it will be because men have come to feel that in recognizing the personal worth of others they are co-operating with those cosmic activities which find expression in persons.

One element of the social gospel has been too often overlooked; namely, its insistence that God is present in social process. We did not expect miracles, but neither did we believe in an absentee God. True, appeal to God is often an excuse for moral laziness or cowardice. Men have prayed when they ought to have increased wages. They have asked God to vouchsafe to keep them from sin when they ought to have gone to the polls. If there ever was an obscurant phrase it is that Jesus Christ can be trusted to abolish social injustice, economic exploitation, and international tension. If such a sentence meant that the principles which he enunciated are applicable to the adjustments of human relations it is the very basis of religious faith. But as it is commonly used it is the anesthetic for social change. Since Jesus and God can be trusted to bring about the reign of righteousness, Christians need only to prepare for heaven.

The proponents of the social gospel may sometimes have over-stated human responsibility and too often made it a call to duty, but what really separated them from other would-be reformers was the fact that they believed that intelligent attempts to base a social order on justice and love would be furthered by God. Religion is something more than ethics. There are super-human influences at work in efforts for a better social order. Just as it was in accordance with cosmic activities to develop techniques for the use of radio-activity, so one can count upon the co-operation of the personality-producing activity of the universe when a social order undertakes to develop the personal welfare of its members.

This genuinely religious attitude distinguished the social gospel from humanism. Indeed, humanism as it has appeared in the churches might almost be described as the social gospel minus reliance upon God. I share the impatience of my humanist friends with hypocrisy and moral cowardice. This is not the best possible world and it cannot be made a better world without intelligent human action. But we have a universe on our hands. It can help us or it can crush us. We representatives of the social gospel said that we could count on these cosmic activities in group action as truly as orthodoxy said they could be trusted for individual salvation. The church had not only a call to duty but a way of hope.

CHAPTER X

CHURCH UNITY THROUGH FEDERATION

THE HISTORY of the Christian movement has always shown the desire for church unity but until the rise of denominations the ideal has been that of Catholic unity. Political and economic changes rather than ecclesiastical reform initiated the development of national state churches and then free churches. The immediate result of such differentiation was naturally competition and controversy. Freedom to organize religious groups in the United States resulted in the multiplication of sects each convinced of its own importance and superiority. Prejudice was elevated into conscientiousness, and co-operation was hindered by theological suspicion.

The dangers which lie in this multiplicity of competitive religious groups have repeatedly been foreseen and there have been formed a number of organizations which disregarded the denominational affiliations of their individual members provided only they were evangelical. The bitter controversy resulting from the rise of Unitarian and Universalist churches continued well into the nineteenth century. Active membership in the Young Men's Christian Association demanded a confession of faith in the deity of Christ, and membership in evangelical churches was presupposed by membership in the Evangelical Alliance which was founded in the middle of the nineteenth century, and for half a century was the agency of the increasing sense of Christian unity. Indeed, the Disciples of Christ had made Christian union one of the main elements of their program. In their case, however, theological controversy worked against Christian co-operation and the movement became as genuinely denominational as other Protestant bodies.

There are two general theories as to how ecclesiastical divisions may be overcome. The one is that of Catholics whose ideal is that of a church organically unified, the other is that of the federation of denominations. The two programs are based on two social psychologies. Catholicism carried over from the Roman Empire and the Middle Ages the imperial idealism; the federation movement sprang from democratic experience like that of the United States. To one movement denominationalism is a matter of disloyalty to the Lord, to the other it is a datum to be recognized in all plans. On the one side are Catholic Christians, on the other are Protestants who do not want a single visible church, but seek to preserve themselves as independent denominations. They do not believe in the real presence of Christ in the Lord's Supper, or in baptismal regeneration. They do not believe in order, being convinced that all believers are priests.

From my understanding of social process my sympathies were and are with the second group of those who wish to get unity of action among Christians of different groups. My experience has convinced me that there is developing a genuine desire to carry forward co-operatively the Christian task, but I see no reason for asserting that God's unity necessarily implies ecclesiastical unity. Ancient issues which have separated Protestants are sinking back into their true perspective. We are getting together by working together. This co-operation in practical affairs is increasingly being shared by religious bodies that a generation ago would have had little or no commerce with each other. Such a change indicates a new appreciation of the moral power of religion.

It is a mistake to attribute desire for a united Christian movement to theological indifference. What we really see is a change within the Christian movement itself. Denominations are becoming agents of co-operation. Moral values are replacing theological shibboleths. In part this change is due to the new intellectual currents within evangelicalism, but quite as truly to practical programs which emphasize common tasks and common faith. Although it has been furthered by enthusiastic gatherings, it has been the outcome of undramatic work in committees and conferences. Sometimes it has been a heart-breaking task to get good people to rise above their inheritance of denominational Chauvinism. Repeatedly I have thought that Hell might be pictured as an everlasting committee meeting on a good cause that could not be brought to pass. But none the less the slow process of integration within the limits of Christian idealism has gone on. Christian groups have learned to co-operate without seeking to convert one another.

I

A desire to have some share in developing the efficiency of the denominational life led me to become a member of the Baptist City Mission Society of Chicago. It was a body composed of representative members of the denomination with a self-sacrificing and earnest superintendent who was financially able to bear more than his share of the relatively small financial burden of the society. The acquaintance with the Protestant life of the city which this membership gave disclosed the extent to which the religious effort of the various denominations was hindered by their indifference to a common cause. Denominations planted their churches without much consideration of the needs of a new community or any recognition of denominational comity. Oftentimes there would be almost a race between denominations to establish a church in some rapidly developing suburb or new section of the city. In consequence a community might become over-churched or monopolized to exclude the extension of other denominations. The steady migration of well-to-do families, upon whose support the city churches had depended, toward the suburbs, gave rise not only to the problems of maintaining old churches, but also the problem of new churches in new areas of population. If Protestantism was to maintain itself there was need of joint rather than competitive planning on the part of Boards and Societies that could adopt well-considered programs.

I asked that a committee be appointed by the Baptist City Mission Society to confer with committees to be appointed by similar bodies to work out some sort of co-operation. The Presbyterians, Congregationalists, Methodists and Disciples appointed such committees and finally organized the Co-operative Council of City Missions, of which I was President. This body did not represent the denominational organizations themselves but the Societies and Boards which were engaged in the extension of church life. To a considerable extent these bodies were independent of denominational control. In many ways the organization of this body was an adventure with few precedents for its guidance. It was pretty generally felt among the early advocates of denominational co-operation that any given church might regard an area as its own particular parish. Such a view was doubtless derived from the practice of the Catholic church and on paper looked desirable. A city was to be broken up into different parishes to be distributed among the various denominations. We soon found, however, that such *a priori* ideals were impracticable for Protestantism. The members of various denominations in any area, especially in the new suburban towns, were unwilling to lose their denominational affiliations, and, conversely, the denominations themselves disliked to lose their migrant members. The very existence and efficiency of a denomination depended upon its conserving the interest and support of those prosperous members that had moved into a suburban area. More than that, a community is more or less centered on an area in which railroad stations, shops and moving picture houses are gathered. A church, to be the geographical center of its denominational adherents, almost of necessity had to be located in the center of community life. Even in communities which had been served by a single church, the process of denominational segregation was inevitable. I recall in one rapidly growing suburb there had been such a Congregational church which, as the town developed, was joined by members of all denominations. But as the community grew, newcomers of the Presbyterian denomination wished to establish their own church. In the nature of the case this would have to be in the neighborhood of the Congregational church. A prosperous Methodist church had already been established before the organization of the Co-operative Council and the situation so often lamented by writers on church unity was in danger of developing. The Council became a court of appeal. It made a careful study of the situation and decided that the religious welfare of the community would be furthered by the organization of the Presbyterian church, even though it would involve the withdrawal of certain members from the Congregational church. The latter accepted the decision and invited the Presbyterian group to organize in its church building. Later the same was true in the case of the Baptists. As a result this community has a number of effective churches existing in the friendliest relations. Probably any student of the situation would say that such a process of religious differentiation was on the whole more effective in this particular community than could have been a single community church. On the other hand, in smaller communities, such differentiation has not been advised and an existing Protestant church—which I am inclined to think is seldom a Baptist church—has been maintained with an Episcopal church as its only ecclesiastical colleague.

Gradually the Co-operative Council developed a general plan for the location of new churches based upon surveys made by one of its committees. With only one or two exceptions the decisions of the Council were followed by the City Mission boards, and precedents were established for the later development of the Chicago Church Federation. The Episcopalian church never joined this Council and established its churches without consultation with the other Protestant bodies. The same is true of the Lutherans.

II

It marked a great advance in the development of co-operative Protestantism in Chicago when the Church Federation became really efficient. In the light of later events it is difficult to realize the early indifference on the part of the denominations to what was clearly a major problem of religious progress. There had been attempts at some sort of co-operation. I remember a meeting of which I was chairman held in the University Club. It was addressed by some of the great business men of Chicago including Cyrus H. McCormick and David R. Forgan. The latter made an especially telling speech. But nothing seemed to come of it. It was characteristic of unorganized Protestantism that at one time there were two movements toward organization of the Federation, neither aware of each other. But the persistence of Professor Hobson of McCormick Seminary and Dr. Herbert L. Willett of the University of Chicago brought form into the federation movement and with the coming of Mr. Walter R. Mee as Secretary the body became a real factor in the religious life of the city. The Cook County Sunday School Association became its Board of Religious Education and a series of committees were established which undertook to provide for the common interests of the co-operating churches. The membership is both lay and clerical, although as might be expected the clerical element is more in evidence. The Lutheran and Episcopalian bodies have never formally joined the Federation but individuals from both bodies have shared in its work. In 1935 the president of the Federation was a Lutheran. The Unitarians have not been represented. This is a matter of real regret to me, but I have long since come to feel that it is unwise to precipitate theological controversy in practical church work. To hurry a progressive process serves to consolidate opposition. Where a social movement is not dependent upon coercion or fear, concentration of effort on aims on which there is no division of opinion is certain to develop a unity which ignores differences in theology and ecclesiastical polity.

I served two terms as President of the Federation. During those years there was a growing realization of the need of participation on the part of church members in municipal politics. This became a phase of a larger effort which I describe in another chapter. I have to confess to a good deal of disappointment at the failure of the clergy to take interest in such work. Their hesitation is not difficult to understand because of the general lack of intelligence as to social ethics. We found the Federation would enter more enthusiastically into an evangelistic campaign than into any general participation in political reform. It is always easier to save men for Heaven than to induce them to take steps which threaten the *status quo* in economics or politics. Laymen, especially those having large interests in corporations and banks, are extremely hesitant to take any action which seems to criticize their existing policies. They want their ministers to devote themselves to such matters as are safely outside the area of economic practices. It is one thing to talk about the gospel and another thing to attempt to embody the ethical teachings of Jesus in a social order. On the whole, however, it seems to me that hesitancy is not without its values. It prevents hasty action. It should be regarded less as indifference to morality than to the lack of intelligence as to social and economic trends.

The financial stringency of the depression compelled my successors in the presidency of the Church Federation to center attention upon the maintenance of the Federation itself. That they were successful in so doing is greatly to their credit, for the maintenance of such an organization is itself an asset even though it does not undertake to help solve the larger tasks of a great city.

The Church Federation has organized evangelistic campaigns, but probably has been most significant in its work in public institutions, its Department of Religious Education and its Comity Commission.

Both of these latter bodies continued work of older institutions. The former, that of the Cook County Sunday School Association and the latter the work of the Co-operative Council of City Missions. The process by which change resulted in the latter case is a good illustration of the way in which we may hope to get a new Protestant unity of action. For several years the two bodies were composed of approximately the same men, and faced the same problems and made the same decisions. When it was evident that the work would be carried on by denominations as distinct from the City Mission Societies the Co-operative Council of City Missions transferred its various undertakings to the Comity Commission. The denominations themselves thus co-operated in the life of the city in ways which were born of experience rather than of theory. Repeatedly the co-operating bodies found themselves involved in difficult situations due to the persistence of that competitive spirit which came over from the days of denominational independence, but twenty years have shown that it is possible for patient and tactful leaders to develop a new community spirit among denominations.

What has been true of Chicago is true to a greater or less extent elsewhere. The New York Federation is especially effective, but in scores of other cities representatives of churches organized Federations which served to develop a unity of spirit even when not able to develop great efficiency in co-operative action. In several of these cities Federations have been able to make a study of population trends and thus develop policies which have at least had some influence in the establishment of churches.

III

Parallel with this development of city federations has been the rise of local federated and community churches. The former have been popular in small towns where denominational loyalties have gradually waned and the burden of supporting rival churches has been judged too heavy for the resources of the community. The general plan of federation which I have recommended in cases in which I have been consulted has maintained the organizations that have federated along with membership in the federated church itself. Such movement has not been as successful as one could wish. Practical difficulties are met when the federated body is composed of churches like the Baptist and Disciples which insist on adult immersion and Methodist and Presbyterian who practice pedobaptism. The professional representatives of the former denominations have sometimes been bitter in their opposition to federation, claiming that it means the end of their respective churches. Furthermore, in many cases there has been a persistence of institutional rivalry within the federated church. The provision that pastorates should alternate between the different denominations has given particular trouble to the Methodist ecclesiastical structure. The original bodies do not disappear and there has been something like politics in the selection of the officials of the federated church. The more aggressive denominational group gradually gets control of affairs. Yet in small towns the federated churches have been a success. When properly supported by the officials of the denominations concerned, such churches have developed the influence and often times the enthusiasm of a sensible movement. In view of these difficulties I have come to feel that it is probably better for a denominational church to become a community church and let the weaker church go out of existence after transferring its property under proper conditions to the surviving church.

I have seen non-denominational community churches often succeed. Such churches are likely to have interest in missions and sometimes divide their gifts between different denominational mission boards. Speaking generally, however, their interest is selective and they give their financial assistance to specific missionary undertakings and institutions. It is not surprising that having withdrawn from denominational affiliations these churches should tend to build up a form of organized association. The result might almost be described as a denomination of undenominational churches.

IV

In 1912 the Federal Council of the Churches of Christ in America held its quadrennial meeting in Chicago. The Baptist Convention was asked to nominate someone for the presidency and its Secretary, the great-souled W. C. Bitting, asked the Executive Committee to suggest my name. My experience of watching the federated movement in Chicago and other cities had aroused serious doubts as to the efficiency of the Federal Council. In fact, when I was asked to let my name be used I hesitated saying that I thought the Council was moribund. But the meeting of the Council held in Chicago, at which I was elected President, disabused my mind of any such apprehension. There was an enthusiasm and initiative in the body that were inspiring. The administration of its first President, Bishop E. R. Hendrix, faced many difficulties, not the least of which was to find a successor to his original secretary, Dr. E. B. Sanford, to whom much of the credit for the organization of the Federal Council must be attributed. It was largely due to the National Federation of Churches and Christian Workers which he had organized in 1900 that the Inter-Church Conference composed of delegates from thirty denominational bodies was held in 1905. This body had adopted a plan of federation and called a meeting of the Conference in Philadelphia in 1908. At that meeting the Federal Council of the Churches of Christ in America was organized. An evangelical basis was adopted which excluded the Unitarians, although that body had been represented in previous Conferences. It was probably a necessary though regrettable first step, for so theologically conscious were many of the denominations that it would have been impossible to establish the Council if some such test had not been adopted. As it was, the Southern Baptists did not join the Council, nor with one exception, did the various bodies of Lutherans join. The Episcopalians also, while many of the bishops shared in discussions, never joined the Federal Council, although they have co-operated in various commissions.

Particularly important was the attitude which the Council took at the start regarding the relation of the church to social affairs. It adopted a series of propositions which were drawn up by Dr. Frank Mason North which became well known as the Social Creed of the Churches. Dr. Charles S. Macfarland was made the secretary of the Commission on the Church and Social Service, making his entrance into a distinguished career as leader in federated movements. When Dr. Sanford's health made it impossible for him to continue as Secretary, Dr. Macfarland was selected as his successor. He brought to his work an energy and administrative ability which have made the entire movement of church unity his debtor.

It is a commentary on the bitterness of political feeling that although Theodore Roosevelt, who had just been defeated for President of the United States, was in the hotel in which the meeting of the Council was held, it was deemed inexpedient to ask him to attend the Council. Ernest Abbott, of the *Outlook,* however, insisted that I should see him and took me up to his room. He was in the midst of a conference and we were kept waiting for a considerable time in an anteroom. We were then taken into one of the bedrooms of his suite and Mr. Roosevelt came in. After greeting me with characteristic cordiality he exclaimed, "They are trying to get me to run politics as if it were a social settlement." I had heard Mr. Roosevelt described as rather overbearing in conversation, but found him quite the contrary. He discussed matters in which he thought I might be interested, and curiously enough the conversation finally closed in a tribute which he paid to Mrs. Roosevelt as a director of household affairs.

In my inaugural address I referred to the Nicene Council in a way which laid me open to later criticism on the part of Southern Presbyterians. What I had said was in effect that the results in European history might have been very different if the three hundred and eighteen members of the Council of Nicea—the same number as were at the Federal Council—had devoted themselves to the social crisis which was ruining the Roman Empire rather than to abstract theology. The comparison if true, was inept. Two years later the Southern Presbyterians held their General Assembly and threatened to withdraw from the Federal Council because of my theological position. At that time they failed in their attempt, although several years later they did withdraw.

The Federal Council offices in 1912 were modest, and the financial situation was difficult. Dr. Macfarland, however, not only proved himself self-sacrificing but remarkably efficient and in the course of a couple of years the Council moved to much larger quarters, established a number of Commissions and became a real factor in the religious life of America. Naturally I had some share in this development but it was small compared with that of Dr. Macfarland.

It is natural that religious like other organizations should have their headquarters in New York. Co-operation is furthered and financial resources are near at hand. I have noticed, however, an almost uniform psychological development in this centralization. America becomes a sort of foreign world. Executive committees are almost of necessity composed of those who live on the Atlantic Seaboard and are therefore subjected to influences which are not representative of the areas west of the Alleghenies. Particularly is this true in the case of co-operative movements in religion. It is only gradually that regions which have been the seat of Home Mission enterprises outgrow denominational rivalries and become able to express their attitudes in national organizations. The Boards of New York tend unconsciously to regard them as objects of ministration rather than co-operators in common tasks although to some extent this is offset by the co-operation of denominations and the great missionary Councils.

There have been some notable exceptions, but the churches of the South and of the Middle West have not shown active interest in interdenominational co-operation. There was distinct need that the Federal Council should come into closer relationship with the Middle West and that some of its secretaries should have their headquarters in Chicago where they could come in contact with a much wider range of religious interest than is to be found on the Atlantic Seaboard. Attempts were made by the Federal Council to meet the situation by the establishment of a Western Committee as a sort of adjunct of the Administrative Committee which was in charge of the Council's affairs. Two attempts were also made to have some of the secretaries have their headquarters in Chicago. It was hoped by this means to stimulate interest of the Middle West and enable its religious leaders to share in national programs. I was chairman for a number of years of this committee and I think it had some influence. The two secretaries who attempted to make Chicago their headquarters felt themselves somewhat isolated from the organization and returned to New York, but the Committee itself has continued. After the recent reorganization of the Federal Council's administration it seemed to be less needed and it has become little more than a point of contact with the traveling secretaries. It served, however, to bring the Council into closer touch with the churches of the Central West and has helped make the Federal Council more aware of the democratic and religiously conservative character of its churches. At the same time the Federal Council has had an appreciable influence in developing a sense of common tasks which face all the denominations.

The Federal Council of the Churches of Christ in America represents a definitely American conception of the way in which some form of unity can be developed among divergent Protestant denominations. Its basic principle is that of federation as distinct from that of church union. In this respect it represents the Protestant rather than the Catholic unity. The distinction is important and it is probably fortunate that the two conceptions should be developing simultaneously. In the minds of many federation is regarded as a step toward the idea of church union and various proposals have been made by some of the leaders of the Federal Council, notably among the Presbyterians, looking to what is called "organic union" of the churches. I have always regarded this attempt as at least premature. Bodies essentially the same can very wisely merge as the Cumberland Presbyterians and Presbyterians, Free Baptists and Baptists, and the three great branches of Methodism. Undoubtedly all churches will come closer together as they cooperate in practical Christian life but many denominations fear overhead control which anything like church union involves. I have always shared in this fear and believe that for American Christianity the federation, at least for the present, is the more effective way of inter-denominational action.

I heartily supported the participation of my own denomination in the Inter-church World Movement. I still believe that it was a wise move, although the financial prodigality of its management was to lay a heavy burden upon our churches. At the meeting of the Northern Baptist Convention in Denver, 1919, I endeavored to distinguish between co-operation through the Inter-church World Movement and the organic union proposed by the Presybterians. I was sure that the denomination would not go into the great co-operative effort until this distinction was made. Several leaders of the Baptist churches of the Middle West were opposed to both proposals. It seemed good strategy to clear the ground so far as organic union was concerned and then to take action as to the Inter-Church World Movement. To that end I offered a resolution setting forth the basic conception of the Baptist denomination relative to the independence of the local church. It was passed amid great enthusiasm. The Convention afterwards agreed to co-operate in the Inter-church World Movement.

Incidentally I had an opportunity to defend myself against the charge of insincerity. After the Convention had greeted the resolution with long-continued applause a clergyman friend of mine arose and said, "Now we can understand the definition of orthodoxy as that which Dr. Mathews expresses in the Northern Baptist Convention." Knowing the gentleman who made this remark I do not think that he meant to accuse me of hypocrisy, but I immediately arose and as a matter of personal privilege, protested against such a misrepresentation of my position.

The statement was born of a pleasantry of President Harper's. When I first entered the University of Chicago I was asked to read a paper at the Baptist Ministers' Meeting. Knowing the criticism which some of the pastors of the city were passing on the University, I determined to add no fuel to the flame, and read a rather technical paper on the teaching of the Apostolic Fathers. When I had finished, the presiding officer, Dr. P. S. Henson, one of the most outspoken and severe of our critics, said that he did not know exactly what I had said but he was very sure that it was entirely satisfactory. A short time after this Dr. Frank Gunsaulus was calling on Dr. Harper and the word "orthodoxy" was used. Dr. Gunsaulus asked, "What is orthodoxy?" Dr. Harper said, "It is what Shailer Mathews says at the Baptist Ministers' Meeting." The story got abroad and appeared in a great variety of forms, always with the unjustifiable intimation that I was double-faced. I have never said in public what I disbelieved in private.

V

The effort for unity among the churches has not been limited to America. In England the English church seeks a new Catholic unity which would include the Greek Orthodox and Roman as well as the English churches. The result is a new sense of corporate fellowship with the Greek churches, but, as might be expected, Rome has stood aloof. On the continent of Europe Protestantism has been weak except where there are state Lutheran churches and non-conformity has had to struggle for its existence in Lutheran states. It is only within comparatively recent years that denominations like the Methodist and Baptist have been able to develop.

The outstanding champion of church unity on the continent of Europe was Archbishop Soderbloom of Sweden, a man of exceptional ability and personal charm. While never breaking with conventional orthodoxy he undertook to restate its essence from the point of view of contemporary philosophy and science. It was his dream to bring the various Protestant bodies into some sort of fellowship and with this he found the Federal Council in sympathy. The Church Peace Union, of which I shall have more to say later, and the World Alliance for International Friendship of the Churches were also interested in the plans. A committee was appointed to prepare for holding a Conference of representatives of all Christian bodies in Stockholm in 1925.

The Church Peace Union undertook to help finance the meeting. There was no attempt at theological agreement for it was determined that this Conference should deal with Christian morals both individual and corporate. Commissions were appointed to make reports which should serve as a basis for the discussions of the proposed Conference. I was chairman of the American group that undertook to prepare material in the social and economic field. We worked faithfully over the report and it was delivered to the Executive Committee at the Conference in Stockholm. But so far as I could discover that was the end of it. The report which was finally adopted by the Conference was drawn up as an independent document.

The Universal Conference on Christian Life and Work was a remarkable gathering, not only because of its size and representative character but because for the first time in history there was a definite attempt to establish some sort of unity among the various Christian bodies based upon other than dogmatic grounds. The Roman church was not represented in the Conference but its representatives were present in the galleries and made full report of the proceedings to the Catholic journals. The Crown Prince of Sweden and his family were regular attendants at the meetings and a considerable number of members of the Conference were his dinner guests. Archbishop Soderbloom was the one around whom the proceedings of the Conference centered. He spoke the three official languages of discussion, English, German and French. If there happened to be a failure in the leading of the music he seated himself at the piano and led the singing. He was approachable but at the same time insistent. In every way a progressive leader.

It fell to my lot to give an address on the opening evening of the Conference upon the "Relation of the Church to Economic Life." I climbed up to the high pulpit on a level with the gallery of the great church, and saw the delegates below me arranged according to nations. On the right was a large group of

Germans composed, with only one Baptist exception, of able and distinguished Lutherans. On the other side of the church was the French delegation, much smaller and much less representative of political power. In the middle of the church were the representatives of other churches. Our American delegation was rather extemporized. In America there was not such interest in the Conference as there was in Europe, but there were a number of outstanding American churchmen who were particularly influential in committee work.

My address was listened to politely, but I doubt if it had any effect. It was of necessity general in character. To continental Christians religion had then little social significance and economic matters were not regarded as falling within its field.

The procedure of the Conference soon showed how far the American churches were in advance of those of the Continent in realizing their responsibility for social reforms. The Conference was in fact an experiment. Naturally its deliverances were cautious, and to American delegates, often platitudinous. The report of the Commission on Prohibition for instance, was so lukewarm that a little group of American representatives who each evening met to discuss policies, appointed Fred B. Smith and me to ask Archbishop Soderbloom to have the report merely read and not acted upon. One Scotch clergyman had argued that as our Lord had made water into wine the Scotch were justified in making whiskey in view of their climate!

The Conference was taken seriously by European churches and a Continuation Committee was appointed which established a secretariat and published a journal, *Stockholm*.

The Lausanne Conference on Faith and Order had quite a different purpose. I believed it anachronistic to seek unity along the line of creed and order. The proceedings of the Conference justified my belief that the real points of union among Christian bodies are in the field of service rather than in that of formula and organization. The Lausanne Conference closed about where that of Stockholm began. American Protestantism is too much the creature of democracy to accept the imperialistic conception of Catholicism, be it never so tolerant. The more the unity of the churches is seen to depend upon the Nicene Creed and sacraments the more will the divisions within Protestantism be emphasized. Tolerance will grow by co-operation in bringing Christian principles to bear upon the actual world in which we live. It need not wait upon ecclesiastical unity. The crisis which has come in Germany is a natural outcome of a conception of religion which makes the church a creature of the state and elevates orthodoxy and individual piety above the application of Christian morality to group action.

CHAPTER XI

BUILDING A MORAL RESERVE FOR CITIZENSHIP

To BELIEVE that love is a practicable basis upon which to build society is not to praise sentimentality. Nor is it to deny that the policeman is needed. Even the most myopic optimist can see that a community, be it large or small, local or national, cannot assume that all its members will act intelligently or unselfishly. Decisions to be effective must have sanctions. Even good people need sometimes to feel the weight of social control. If Milton and the churches are to be believed some angels had to be disciplined.

The point at which love meets a realistic view of the world is clearly that of human behavior. Ideals must be so implemented as not to commit moral suicide. If love is to be the determining factor in group action the methods of such action must be in accord with the extension of justice, the recognition of personal rights, and the protection of moral advance. To make coercion and fear a basis for a social order is more than the exercise of police power. The safe choice between courses of action will be determined by a decision as to which is most clearly in the direction toward conditions which intelligent love seeks to establish. This may be opportunism but it is not deductive politics. After speaking at Carleton College at Northfield, Minnesota, I had to go to the neighboring town of Randolph to get a train. The friend who drove me over was not well acquainted with the country and when we came to a crossroads was not sure which led to Randolph. In the dark we saw a road sign and went up to it. One of its arms read "Minneapolis" the

171

other "New Orleans." For a moment it seemed like many ideal-
istic programs, useless in an emergency, but then we recalled
that Randolph was on the way to Minneapolis and we con-
fidently proceeded. This parable teaches that any next step in
the field of social progress should be determined by the direction in which we wish to go.

It is inevitable that any attempt on the part of a church to
give moral direction to a social process will encounter the question as to its political action. Sometimes the church has decided
to control the state and sometimes the state has endeavored to
control the church. When once the church and state were
separated and religious liberty assured, the problem took on the
form with which the churches of America are acquainted. If
love is to be dominant in a social order the churches cannot be
indifferent to politics. But just what that relation should be is
a matter for intelligent decision.

I

There are at least three distinct theories as to the relation of
churches to the state in addition to that of the totalitarian state.
One is that of complete withdrawal from all civic responsibilities, another is the view that churches stand over against the
world and should separate from it, and the third that a church
as a social group with other social groups constituting society
has a function of its own. The first of these views is held by
certain sects of Christians and would probably never become
general. The second view has attractiveness. It enables its pos-
sessors to criticize severely those who hold the third view and
at the same time permits them to hold to some social program
like socialism or communism. The third view is not a child of
logic but of a realistic attitude which regards both the principles
of Christianity and the lessons of history.

For some of these realists the theory easiest to hold is that

the Christians should organize themselves into a political *bloc*.
It is not quite clear just what such a proposal means. In a country like India suffrage can be communalized and religious
groups can be assigned proportionate representation in a Legislative Assembly. Indian Christians, however, have refused to be
treated communally and prefer to act as citizens rather than as
religionists. In the United States such communalism is not con-
ceivable. It would mean the alignment of Protestants, Catholics
and Jews. Such an introduction of ecclesiastical differences into
politics no intelligent persons can for a moment approve. While
it might not result in the horrors of the religious wars of the
seventeenth century or of Ireland, it would make anything like
free democracy impossible. To make religious affiliation a
reason for the support of a political candidate has not been
avoided in the United States but it is always like playing with
fire.

None the less the obligation rests upon organized Christianity
to treat politics as a field for moral direction. It is one thing
to make Christians into a political party or *bloc* and another
thing for them to exercise a moral influence upon politics.

Discussion as to the relation of the church and the state is
apt to illustrate the all but universal habit of personifying institutions and generalizations. Strictly speaking there is no "the
church" in America. In a country in which there is a state
church one may really speak less metaphorically. The church
there is a legal institution which is either an aspect of or is
controlled by the government. In several countries the Roman
Catholic church is a body with which a nation has organized
relations. But none of these conditions exist in the United
States. Here there is no church, there are churches. These are
organized in accordance with legislative provisions and are
granted certain privileges like exemption of taxes, and their
ministers can perform legal marriages. Such conditions make

clear thinking necessary. If there is danger in thinking of churches as political *blocs,* there is also danger that no sharp distinction is made between the function of the churches as religious bodies and the duties of their members as citizens. The relation of churches to political action is limited by their function as religious bodies. Because their members must act in political groups no more justifies the churches becoming political units than the fact that their members must go to school justifies them in becoming school boards. A real obligation, however, rests upon the churches to regard politics as a field for moral action and citizenship as demanding moral education. In all political action there are elements of coercion, but the enforcement of laws which represent public opinion is not the same as programs superimposed upon citizens by terror. Therein lies one obvious difference between any form of dictatorship and democracy. It is time to stop talking about the relation of "the church" and "the state" and consider the relation of Christian citizens to political action.

It sometimes seems as if interest in political matters was inversely to their nearness. International disputes and policies can be discussed without arousing any immediate responsibility. The individual citizen does not feel impotent when confronted with matters of sanctions and treaties, although national action is in the hands of a government. As a result his interest is acute. On the other hand the same citizen is likely to be indifferent to local politics. The sense of futility becomes a defense technique against meeting civic responsibility. The individual bulks larger in a mayoralty campaign than in international tension but his readiness to act is sometimes irritatingly small.

In both cases citizens neglect the moral responsibility which democracy lays upon the individual. If good citizens do not perform their political duties, bad citizens will. On the whole I am inclined to believe that American communities get about the sort of governments they deserve.

II

Such considerations as these have led me to what political action I have taken. Decent respect for the obligations of citizenship seems a Christian's duty. Whatever share one may have in opposing war he has an inescapable duty in local politics. I did some campaigning on behalf of the League of Nations and more for some of my friends who were candidates for mayor of Chicago or membership in the Board of Aldermen. My candidates were invariably defeated. It may be we did not know how to play the game of politics or were too high-minded to resort to "practical" measures. We did not have patronage to distribute, and in many cases the persons whom we were seeking to dislodge had plenty. We neglected to realize that we were dealing with many people who had no high sense of honor and less civic idealism. We once held a meeting of Republicans for organizing a precinct. Our reforming compatriots were out in force. The Chairman and the Secretary of the Republican organization did not appear. We waited for an hour or more and then the two officials calmly entered the room and declared they had been holding a meeting and transacting all the business in a room upstairs. As we had not held a formal meeting there was nothing for us to do short of assassinating the officials but to disperse into individual innocuousness. Generally, too, it seems easier to start an independent movement than to work within political parties. But I have become convinced that except in very rare instances, when a community is thoroughly disgusted or horrified with existing conditions, independent movements are ineffective. If the so-called "better element of society" wants to have a share in local government it must follow the lines of practical politics. It must attend ward meetings and become sufficiently interested in precinct affairs to make the party organization take notice. Resolutions passed by ministers' meetings and addresses made by reformers who have no organized support are not much feared by politicians.

When the direct primary was first proposed I was one of its enthusiastic supporters. But in the course of time I became skeptical as to its efficiency. It has been so hedged around by legislation as to make free selection of nominees all but impossible. Candidates are still named by party organizations and the public has to bear the expense of two campaigns instead of one. The big and little bosses control the mass voting in the primaries. After that it is a choice between politicians. And the result has been the undue prominence of mediocre but ambitious men and a most unfortunate lowering of the judiciary.

There have been in Chicago several eruptions of good citizenship which in some cases have been able to bring about the nomination and election of good officials. But after a little while the zeal of good people has waned, and they are content to lament rather than to vote. The Better Government Association which frankly represents the Christian group has attempted to bring about the nomination of desirable candidates through the primaries but it has been efficient only in moments when there has been an upheaval of good citizenship. Sometimes its policies have been open to serious criticism. It has, however, undoubtedly rendered service in making the public acquainted with the misdoings of political candidates.

III

During the terms of my presidency the Church Federation of Chicago undertook to present the political situation of the city as something which appealed to the moral judgment of the churches. We raised some money to meet expenses in building up a "moral reserve for citizenship." In one day we had over twenty meetings in which we endeavored to arouse the Christian people to indignation over the subserviency of officials and the police to organized vice and crime. The American Institute of Sacred Literature prepared series of lessons for classes and the Department of Religious Education of the Federation undertook to introduce the study of civic duties to adult classes. Some interest was aroused but there was no general concern on the part of religious forces of the city. Yet we attracted the attention of the politicians and for a time at least there was a little more concern over the religious forces as possible elements in municipal politics. As effective as any agency was the Christian Citizenship Council, an organization for women founded and directed for a number of years by Mrs. G. M. Mathes, a woman of great earnestness and organizing power. Under her leadership there were groups of women formed in a number of churches for the purpose of studying municipal affairs and devoting themselves to the cause of good government. There was no similar organization among men, although some men's groups became interested in political decency. There resulted an appreciable growth in civic conscience, but it was not evenly felt in the churches.

The failure of reforming organizations to co-operate became a matter of real importance. The Better Government Association and various other groups became violently opposed to each other and reform was really hindered by its friends. After the municipal election in 1930 had resulted in the complete discomfiture of political reform I undertook to get some sort of unity among the various reform groups. It did not seem to me to be wise to attempt to do this expressly through the Church Federation, but I have no doubt that my official position was an advantage. I called a meeting of the representatives of all groups that were appealing to the better citizens for a luncheon at the City Club. There was a good deal of bitterness to be expected. In fact, the chairman of one reform group asked a friend to pull him back into his seat if he undertook to hit the representative of another body with whom he had quarreled. During the luncheon I kept the conversations non-political. If the Kingdom of God is not eating and drinking, luncheons and dinners may become means of grace. By refusing to discuss points at which we differed we concentrated attention wholly upon the question as to whether we should appoint a committee to bring in some plan for common action. Without dissent the committee was appointed, and the meeting was adjourned. It was another illustration of the fact that when people differ in their attempts to accomplish the same purpose, wisdom dictates the centering of attention upon that in which all are agreed. The committee reported and there was formed the Voters' Clearing House, of which I was made chairman. This Clearing House was composed of members of various organizations, and had for its purpose the making of a ticket composed of less objectionable (in some cases we could hardly say the better) candidates nominated in the direct primaries. It appointed a committee consisting of persons not officials of the co-operating organizations who were selected unanimously from a list of those with recognized standing in the city. The various bodies agreed to adopt the findings of this committee in making recommendations or giving publicity to candidates. The ticket was issued over the names of the committee of which I was chairman. The members of the Clearing House lived up to their agreements and this ticket was given wide circulation, and was sent through the Christian Citizenship Council and the Better Government Association to committees in various churches. I wish I could say that the results were commensurate with our hopes. As it turned out, there was a political tidal wave which elected a straight Democratic ticket and all our Republican nominations were defeated. A study of the returns, however, made it appear that our efforts were worth thirty-five thousand votes. In any ordinary election such a group would have been an important factor. At any rate it attracted the attention of the politicians and for a while at least there was new respect for the Christian citizen.

We were able to capitalize somewhat this interest. We knew only too well that any extreme demand would have had small effect, but we did bring some influence into the office of the County Attorney. I doubt if it did much good, but it showed that church people were interested in politics.

In the next mayoralty election we were faced with a choice between William Hale Thompson and Anton Cermak. Our one hope of clearing the city from the control of Thompson lay in the election of his opponent. It seemed imperative therefore that Mr. Cermak should be committed to at least a modicum of reform. We decided to get his promise to institute very moderate reorganization of the police department along lines recommended by a group of the University of Chicago professors who had made a study of the police administration. Rush Butler, one of our Clearing House committee, Henry Stewart, a representative of the Association of Commerce and I had an interview with Melvin Traylor who had influence with Mr. Cermak and asked him to make it plain to Mr. Cermak that the support of our group would be dependent upon his promise of instituting these reforms. This he did and there was an improvement in the police department.

The Voters' Clearing House in succeeding elections found it difficult to find a committee whose members were not already committed to one or more of the candidates and it lost much of its influence. I think it was partly due to the confusion within the Republican party and the inability to find satisfactory Republican candidates. Whatever hope the city had of political reform lay largely in a committee composed of business men and bankers who had some influence in freeing the city from the financial tangle into which Mayor Thompson's administration had brought it.

IV

These attempts to arouse a sense of civic responsibility on the part of church members brought me into touch with some prominent political leaders. I realized the practical difficulty which lies in municipal politics is that which is inherent in democracy itself. The party leader has to win the support of masses of people who have little interest in the government beyond the enjoyment of political patronage and who have no permanent relation with the particular locality in which they live. Democracy historically is rooted in property as contrasted with class privileges. Great cities weaken the sense of political responsibility. Democracy has not yet assimilated the apartment house. In older days men could be urged to fight to protect their hearths and homes, but it would be difficult to arouse patriotic enthusiasm by appeals for the protection of radiators and janitors. Protestant churches have found the same difficulty in serving the procession of men and women who have no connection with a community except payment of rent in an apartment house. They do not care to support the institutions in the neighborhood in which they may for a short time live. It is inevitable that the churches should follow the trend of population and abandon regions that have ceased to be those of homes. The Protestant churches which remain in such communities must become churches of ministration supported by non-residents. They become representative of a quasi-class interest determined by race and economic conditions. Persons unaffected by a Protestant conception of democracy are consolidated into party groups under the control of men who are in politics to further their personal interests. It is all the more reason, therefore, that churches in communities where *bourgeois* Protestantism exists should be concerned with developing civic morality. Such efforts, however, will almost certainly be interpreted as party politics unless ministers and church leaders are exceedingly wise. The requisite wisdom, however, is not hard to find if men really look for it. It amounts to education in group morals. In the present struggle between government by force and government by co-operation the churches should be educating citizens to have a part in the political life of their community first of all. For if the experience of European nations means anything, peoples who by temperament or religious subservience lose confidence in their ability to find economic and political security through democratic methods will turn to some type of dictatorship and one-party government which seems to promise the desired security. If both churches and communities are to lose a sense of civic responsibility or submit to the overlords of a local body it will follow ultimately that the same political incapacity will find expression in national affairs. The separation of church and state does not mean the separation of Christians and citizenship. But citizenship in America means participation in party politics and party politics involves the dependence upon the vote of great bodies of men and women who are citizens without any sense of responsibility. As I have seen how the political fortunes of men of high personal character depend upon alliances with those whose schemes and character they condemned, I have realized that the churches' share in political life must be something more than the passage of resolutions by ministers' meetings. They must lead in the organization of political idealism and a civic conscience. The politician will pay attention to them in about the same proportion as there are Christian voters. So far as great cities are concerned the fate of Protestantism is indissolubly connected with that of democracy.

It is not hard to see why the so-called respectable classes of society take little part in the political life. To be a candidate for an office is to expose one's self to misunderstandings and to endless annoyance. The immediate results of reform movements are sometimes so short-lived that it is much easier to move into the suburbs than to continue in performing uninteresting duties. More than that one has the feeling of being a pawn moved by party overlords whose professions of good citizenship are little more than bids for votes.

Yet it is cowardly to withdraw from the moral obligations which citizenship involves. The struggle must be continued against those who exploit politics and make office a source of profit rather than a public service. No institution has the opportunity for developing a sense of social responsibility on the part of individuals comparable with that of the churches. They need not become partisans but they should make their members sensitive to the moral implications of political life. It is too much to expect that the rank and file of people will become zealous for ideals that may cost them time and possibly money, but that is no reason why the churches should not develop the vicarious tenth of society—that is, a dynamic minority that serves others without expecting gain for itself. The readiness of professional idealists to limit their efforts to platform addresses, as well as disgust with methods of political parties prompt one to cynicism, but neither that nor pessimism is excusable in those who would make religion a moral ferment in the social process.

> *"Charge again, then, and be dumb!*
> *Let the victors, when they come,*
> *When the forts of folly fall,*
> *Find thy body by the wall!"*

CHAPTER XII

THE CHURCHES AND INTER-RACIAL RELATIONS

THOSE OF US who grew up in the New England of the nineteenth century find it difficult to realize that the oratory of New England societies and Mayflower descendants is not identical with the American spirit. In my boyhood immigrants were mostly French Canadians and Irish, and they were Roman Catholic. Then came Lutherans from Germany and Scandinavia. It was only in the latter part of the nineteenth century that the tide of immigration from northern European countries was exceeded by that from southern European countries and Russia. A new task was set for Protestantism. The millions of new immigrants were Roman Catholics and Jews unaccustomed to democracy. The various ethnic groups organized churches of their own and preserved the religious habits and attitudes of the different sections of Europe. Religion thus served to develop national *blocs*. Foreign governments endeavored to conserve the loyalty of their emigrant nationals, but the second generation was introduced to American life through the public schools. They were thus alienated from the older generation.

It was natural that the first reaction of American Protestantism to these newcomers should be a combination of missionary zeal and denominational ambition. Strange as it may seem, in the minds of zealous evangelicals like the Baptists, the Lutherans occupied much the same position as the Roman Catholics. Nor is such a condition quite so anarchic as it may seem. To the inhabitants of the Atlantic Seaboard the West, into which these new citizens were pouring, was as truly foreign as if it were across the Pacific. Practically the only forms of Protestant Christianity with which they were acquainted were more or less of Calvinist descent.

It is always difficult to determine just where legitimate religious activity ends and proselytism begins, and it is not strange that the Lutheran and Catholic bodies regarded the missionary activities of the eastern Protestants as proselytism. It must be admitted that there was some truth in this charge although there entered with it also the sincere desire to establish churches in new towns as a contribution to human needs. That there should have been a duplication of effort and the founding of too many churches in communities that were never to be large must be charged to denominational zeal and the hopes of becoming a metropolis which illuminated every unpaved Main Street. In recent years, however, there have been marked changes in the methods and ideas of Home Mission Boards. Both they and the Christian Associations have endeavored to serve the immigrants in the spirit of co-operation and helpfulness. The older motives for religious work in new areas have become decreasingly imperative and the church organizations have come to realize not only that immigrants should be helped as newcomers but that they have valuable contributions to make to the developing American life. Study courses were organized for the various church groups and the need of what was called Americanization was emphasized. It may have been that in these efforts there lingered still a certain superiority which members of an established society are apt to feel toward those who cannot speak their language and are unacquainted with their customs, but a decidedly more intelligent attitude was to be seen. America was evidently not going to be a second New England. America, men said, was a melting pot. As a matter of fact this was not the case. As President Faunce said, America resembles a garden in which there is cross-fertilization. Ethnic *blocs* have maintained their identity even in the third generation. Until their numbers made it impossible, each nationality maintained a neighborhood of its own within a certain definite area of a city. Even when their numbers increased and the ethnic group extended into new territory it maintained its solidarity. Any map showing the population trends of a great city will indicate this. The development of religious interest among these people was of necessity complicated by social conditions. The foreign-speaking churches especially ministered to the older generation but the second and third generations partook of American spirit without sharing extensively in the religious life of their communities. To quote Dr. Charles H. Sears whose experience in these matters is the most complete of any man I know:

The second generation young people of whatever race are now forming new codes for youth, new civic codes, new political codes, primarily to govern their own conduct. They are destined to stamp these on the generations to follow, thereby displacing in no small degree the culture patterns under which former generations have lived and worked.

I

No one can have had any part in the religious life of a city like Chicago without coming in contact with the foreign-speaking churches. My experience has been largely with the Scandinavians and the Bohemians.

For a number of years the Divinity School maintained two theological seminaries, one for the Swedes and another for the Danes and Norwegians. Because of my official relations as well as personal friendship I became pretty well acquainted with the Baptist churches of these peoples. The Swedish churches have grown in numbers and have been able to adjust relations of the two generations with considerable success. I could foresee that the need of using the Swedish language was likely to pass with the older generation and used such influence as I had to make the churches in a Swedish area of the city prepare for becoming the only churches of the denomination in that area. Unfortunately this plan has not proved satisfactory because a community continues to regard such a church as the property of the ethnic group.

The contributions of Germans to music were always clear, but I gained a new appreciation of what a European group could bring to American life at a meeting of Hungarians which was held in a hall over a saloon. I had gone there to speak for my colleague, Charles E. Merriam, in his campaign for the mayoralty of Chicago. I don't know what influence my speech had, but the skill of a young man who was playing some strange musical instrument filled me with admiration. I found that he ran an elevator in one of the office buildings of the city.

My interest in the Bohemians was first attracted by reports that they maintained a number of schools in which atheism and opposition to the churches were taught. In Chicago a Baptist minister with a university education, Rev. M. Kralicek, undertook to stem the tide. A number of us at the University of Chicago tried to help him and in consequence we gained acquaintance with Bohemian churches and Bohemian groups in general. I spoke at the great meeting celebrating the five-hundredth anniversary of the death of John Huss, and was impressed with the difference between the spirit of the Bohemians and that of the Poles, among whom neither Protestantism nor free thinking had made any great impression.

Acquaintance with these ethnic groups brings the inevitable conclusion that Protestantism is needed if for nothing else than its power to arouse a pride in American democracy. I would not belittle the services of the Roman Catholic Church nor do I approve proselyting, but if statistics mean anything the vast mass of New Americans are indifferent to religion and never attend church except possibly on some feast day. And this seems to be true whatever may have been the religious affiliation of the immigrants in Europe. There is an obvious need for religious and moral instruction if the great masses of the second and third generations of the New Americans are to be led by men who are loyal to ideas and institutions on which our nation has been founded. It is no mere coincidence that men and women who have abandoned the customs and churches of their parents should be responsive to anti-democratic propaganda.

During the last generation the leaders of Home Mission work have come increasingly to see that the task of the churches is not that of proselyting or of dissociating individuals from their national culture. The study courses which have been adopted by the Home Mission Boards have shown a gratifying appreciation of contributions which the immigrant can make to American life. Many churches in foreign-speaking sections of a metropolis have been made into centers of community uplift and neighborliness. The immigrant question will be answered within the course of another generation—because of laws limiting immigration. Men of European descent will be native American citizens having only such connections with the home of their ancestors as may arise from sentiment or political propaganda. One can well hope that the churches may have become centers of such moral influence as to offset the injurious influence which such relations may possess. We cannot afford to have European enmities impregnate American politics.

The relation of the Protestant churches and the Jews is marked by two distinct tendencies. The first is that which establishes "missions to Jews" and endeavors to convert individuals by biblical arguments as to the Messiahship of Jesus. This effort is due to a sincere desire to bring religious services to the great number of Jews who have broken free from the synagogue, but in many cases it is also an extension of a theological conviction that the conversion of the Jews is a precondition to the second coming of Christ. Whatever the motive such proselytism is bitterly opposed by Jewish leaders. I had a rather unfortunate experience in the case of a converted Jew who undertook to establish a social center in a well-to-do Jewish community. It was not long before I found that some of my Jewish friends in the vicinity regarded the organization as a means for alienating young people from their parents' religion. Despite my best endeavors I was unable to understand the situation, but I suspected that proselyting might have been carried on surreptitiously and it may have been unconsciously. On the other hand I could not approve all of the methods adopted to undermine the influence of the institution.

The emergence of anti-religious movements in American society has made it clear that all religions face much the same problems and must co-operate in combating trends toward sensuality, selfishness and the loss of moral authority because of a loss of faith in God. In consequence there has developed a well-charted movement of co-operation between the more far-sighted Jews, Catholics and Protestants. The Federal Council of Churches of Christ in America has set up a Commission which is undertaking the education of its churches through the proper literature and the establishment of conferences in which there is less attention paid to tolerance than to the need of common effort to give spiritual guidance to life in America. It would be difficult to know just how far such views have permeated the rank and file of the various bodies involved, but at least a beginning has been made in co-operation.

The difficulty is by no means on the side of the Christian churches alone. Anti-Semitism in Europe has evoked from certain Jewish leaders in America what may become a dangerous method of defense. Judaism, according to this school, is not merely a religion but also a civilization. While such a view is not held by all leaders of Judaism it is being propagated in such a way as would give religious sanction to the exclusiveness of an ethnic *bloc*. Such a policy may well cause anxiety and is as much the enemy of religious co-operation as the proselyting zeal of Christians. Judaism as a religion is clearly the property of a definite people and reform Jews are often as race conscious as the orthodox. But so to a less degree are Roman Catholic Poles and Protestant Anglo-Americans.

The extraordinary influence Jews have gained in the industrial and recreational life of America should not become, as in Germany, a source of jealousy and fear. Nor is brotherhood an excuse for acquiring something belonging to newly discovered brothers.

I have found not only friendship but community of ideas and hopes with many religious leaders of Judaism. Not a few of them have been members of my classes. I have spoken in Jewish temples and in meetings of protest against the action of Nazis. I have found leaders of Reform Judaism always ready to support any social or political reform having a well-defined aim. This spirit of co-operation is more than that of mutual tolerance. Co-operation between Jews and Christians of similar outlook and religious faith is something more than a polite gesture. It is an intelligent facing of moral tasks common to all religions in our modern world.

II

The relation of the negroes and the whites presents its own difficulties. Problems which were formerly confined to the South now appear in the North. But the situation is not quite the same. The negroes in the North are to be found rarely in the country and entire quarters of cities like New York and Chicago have been taken over by them. Negro immigration from the South became marked as the result of the War when negroes were needed to do the rough work in various industries. The migration aroused bitter feeling not only among those whose property greatly depreciated in value because of the spread of the negro population, but among the laborers whose places the negroes had taken. The psychology of the negro in the North is different from what it had been in the South. The restraints which there existed are no longer felt and the negro sections, which included some of the finest residential districts, became attractive to criminals and vice. The fact that they could vote exposed negroes also to political corruption.

But these newcomers were not indifferent to the churches. In many cases those from a certain community would organize a religious body, hire a vacant store and a minister of their own choosing, and set up religious worship. Innumerable religious groups of this sporadic nature, some of them undoubtedly existing for the purpose of supporting the preacher, could be found throughout the negro areas of Chicago. They very seldom developed into churches of any size and they were by no means the only expression of religious interest of the negroes. Some of the most effective pastors and the largest Protestant churches of the city are negro. The ministers of these churches are educated, fully alive to the problems which their people face, and are a leaven of righteousness. Most of them are Baptist or Methodist, although there are churches belonging to other denominations.

Among the negroes there are two schools of opinion as to what should be the relationship of the negroes and the whites. Highly educated leaders like Mordecai Johnson are severe in their criticism of the founding of independent negro churches. They hold that such segregation is an indication of the lack of brotherliness on the part of white churches. Other leaders see in the actual organization of negro churches and the rise of great denominational bodies an opportunity for development of self-respect and self-direction. It has always seemed to me that denunciation of the past for originating conditions which cannot be changed is apt to produce enmities. We have to face conditions in the present whether we like them or not. Churches whose membership includes negroes and whites seem practicable only in exceptional conditions. The real problem is how the churches of two races can co-operate for the good not only of the negro but of an entire community. The relations of individuals will contribute to the relations of the races. The successes of negro athletes, and of negro actors like those of *Green Pastures,* the new position which negroes are gaining in literature and music are all indications of a more intelligent conception of the relation of the races. Among college students there is a distinct movement toward racial co-operation on the part of more liberal minorities. I have had a number of negro students in my classes and cannot see any difference between them and the whites that could be regarded as biological. Without exception they have won my respect for the way in which they have carried themselves and for the quality of their work. I remember with great satisfaction an occasion in which the inferiority of the negro was being argued on the basis of an article in the *Journal of Sociology.* The critic was rather taken aback when I told him that the article was written by a negro. For several years I served as one of the judges who awarded the Harmon medals in appreciation of accomplishment of negroes in some field of literature or art. No one could examine the material which was submitted for my examination without being filled with admiration for the accomplishment of a race which in my own lifetime was in slavery.

Acquaintance with the negro churches has confirmed this respect. When I came in touch with the Baptist negroes they had nothing like the resources which they now possess. Their numbers were comparatively small and they had only begun to erect churches. They naturally came to their white brethren for aid and the City Mission Society lent them as much money as it could afford. I came to have great respect for some of these leaders although I regretted the divisions which sometimes sprang up among them. We found the churches financially trustworthy. When the great migration began, the membership of these negro churches increased by leaps and bounds. As the negro population swept into the old residential quarters their congregations proceeded to occupy some of the best church edifices in the city. In most cases they purchased them far below their cost but none the less they did purchase them. In one case a magnificent Jewish synagogue had been sold to negro Baptists at a very considerably lower sum than it would have brought if purchased to be put to secular uses. So confident were we of the reliability of the new church that some of us lent the pastor our own securities to enable him to turn a financial corner. We soon had them returned. Negro churches naturally suffered during the depression but their financial record is certainly as creditable as that of other religious bodies.

In the interest of helping these churches and developing some body that could represent them in their dealings with the representatives of the white church I suggested the organization of a body elected by negro Baptist churches which could furnish information and opinions upon which co-operation between the groups could be furthered. I was again impressed with the wisdom and ability of the representatives of the negro churches. And this was not lessened by the fact that the newly established body found it impossible to straighten out all the rivalries between the negro churches themselves.

In 1922 the Church Federation established an Inter-racial Commission for the purpose of furthering the relations between the churches of the two races. I was chairman of this Commission for a number of years until I became president of the Federation, and again am. We worked in co-operation with the similar Commission on the Federal Council but within more specifically religious limits. It soon appeared that this Inter-racial Commission might find itself involved in all sorts of social and economic problems. It is indeed a constant temptation for a religious organization interested in social matters to deal with such matters directly. But if churches be regarded as social groups having their own exclusive function it seems axiomatic that before attempting to solve all problems of our social order they should discover just what contribution they themselves as religious bodies can make. The need of facing this question of method was constantly before the Inter-racial Commission by virtue of the fact that various negro organizations wanted to use us to further their aims. In most cases the problems they proposed were such as deserved careful consideration but I saw plainly that our Commission would become simply one reform body among others unless we recognized clearly that our task consisted in helping establish closer relations between the negro and the white churches. In the abstract this looked easy. Practically it was hard. In many cases members of the white churches have suffered serious financial loss by virtue of the all but enforced sale of their property to negroes. On the other hand many negro pastors felt deeply social discrimination. To have made such issues central was not to arouse racial friendliness. When, at the suggestion of the Federal Council, we established an Inter-racial Sunday in which the pastors of the negro and white churches should exchange pulpits, our Commission, after careful discussion, decided that the best results of such an exchange would not be the discussion of racial problems but the delivery of sermons of the sort which would be preached in the respective churches. This inter-change of pulpits still continues. The chief difficulty at the present time is that the larger white churches do not cooperate heartily. Negro pastors accustomed to preaching to huge congregations find themselves assigned to small churches. It is hard for Christians to overcome their inherited social attitudes and a feeling of racial superiority. Social justice will be possible only when members of one race can treat those of another as human persons, and this Christian attitude will not be gained without surmounting the inherited prejudices of both races. The churches of America sooner or later must come to realize that racial enmities are as much their concern in America as in Germany.

CHAPTER XIII

INTERNATIONAL GOOD WILL AND WAR

UNTIL THE outbreak of the World War there was no widespread interest in the problem of peace among the leaders of the church. The Society of Friends, the Mennonites and other groups of Christians were committed to opposition to war, but the general position of even those interested in the social gospel was lukewarm. There had been the anti-imperialism movement after the war with Spain, and there was a slight stirring of interest over the Boer War of England. Individuals like Mr. Carnegie and Mr. Ginn gave huge sums of money to found bodies to work for international peace, but as a rule churches did not take the matter very seriously. Even the war between Russia and Japan did little more than arouse surprised admiration at the military achievement of Japan. Military service on the continent of Europe aroused no apprehension and even the feverish construction of navies was taken as a matter of course. We were incredibly optimistic, which is another way of saying we were incredibly blind.

I

There were various peace movements, some of which I joined but in rather a dilletante spirit. In the winter of 1914, however, at the instance of Andrew Carnegie there was founded the Church Peace Union. Mr. Carnegie endowed it with two million dollars and hoped that it would supplement the work of the great Carnegie Peace Foundation, by organizing the religious forces to oppose war. I remember distinctly his address to the Board at the luncheon in his home when he transferred

195

to us the funds. He read a paper on the evils of war to which I listened, but I recall thinking that his apprehensions were unfounded. And Mr. Carnegie himself showed most interest in the illustration given an article he had written for *Life*. Foundations were no novelty to him.

One of the first steps taken by the Church Peace Union was the organization of the World Alliance for International Friendship through the Churches. A number of persons from Europe and America met at Constance in the latter part of July, 1914, for the purpose of organizing this new body. At the very time it was meeting the World War broke out. Yet the Alliance was formed and the delegates made their way as best they could back to their respective countries. The new organization was to prove one of the most efficient agencies in turning the attention of churches to peace and to the condemnation of war. It established groups of peace-minded persons in practically every country. On its platform appear Jews, Roman Catholics and representatives of the Eastern churches. Until the rise of Naziism it had offices in Berlin, Geneva, London and New York. It has held both national and international conventions of religious workers. It by no means represents absolute pacifism. In the convention held in Prague in 1928 it refused to adopt a resolution proposed by Dutch delegates explicitly declaring that war is un-Christian. National enmities persist even in the midst of religious fellowship and the Germans repeatedly endeavored to get some sort of pronouncement as to war guilt and the Treaty of Versailles. The first meeting of representatives of the warring nations after the Armistice was held by the World Alliance for International Friendship through the Churches.

II

The outbreak of the war in 1914 shattered all optimism. Human nature was still untamed. A state could command the loyalty of its subjects in the face of interests that extended beyond the frontiers. It is easy now to be contemptuous of the optimism of pre-war liberalism but when one recalls the elements of the world situation it is not strange that we should have suffered from illusion. Socialism, international labor movements, international commerce, international science, the Roman Catholic Church, Protestant Christianity, peace societies, the mixture of populations, common culture, all seemed to insure the maintenance of peace. The outbreak of war did more than excite horror for itself. It argued a breakdown of forces which we believed were shaping up a new world order. During the period in which the United States was neutral there developed also a belief that democracy as a form of government was itself threatened. That such fears were well grounded the history of continental Europe makes plain, for Fascism, Naziism and Communism are even more opposed to democracy than constitutional monarchy. This legitimate apprehension was driven hysterical by propaganda full of apparently well-authenticated tales of atrocities. People on the Atlantic seaboard were definitely in favor of the Allies, but the Central West had too many associations with continental Europe to be equally sympathetic. There were, in fact, two general tendencies in our national psychology, the one urging unpreparedness and the other support of the Allies. Although President Wilson was elected on the ground that he had kept us out of war, clever evangelization in favor of participating in the war had its effect. Nothing is more unifying than a common hatred. When this hatred is focused by fear and a sense of injury it is incredibly efficient.

Before the fears and passions of their members had been aroused, Christian organizations were opposed to anything that looked like military preparation and favored neutrality. I shared in this attitude. In the summer of 1916 we organized at Chautauqua an entire week devoted to unpreparedness. Gen-

erally speaking our sympathies were not with Germany, but
it was not the sinking of the *Lusitania* and the development of
submarine warfare which threatened our rights upon the ocean
that brought us to feel that the war was really our concern.
Even in the case of the *Lusitania* I urged in an address at the
Sunday Evening Club in Chicago that we wait for more information before giving full scope to our indignation.

If it was incumbent upon Christian people to avoid war, it
was also incumbent upon them to avoid quixotic attempts to
end the war. That seemed undeniable, but when were attempts
quixotic? I declined an invitation to go on Mr. Ford's peace
ship. At the meeting of the Federal Council in St. Louis in the
fall of 1916 I was told that Wm. J. Bryan was going to
invite me as President of the Council to go to Europe with him
to stop the war. When the invitation came to me I pled engagements and so avoided it. Subsequently he wrote me in a
tentative way relative to our taking some action. In justice
to Mr. Bryan it should be said that the plan was not quite
so megalomaniacal as it might seem. Mr. Bryan was taken
seriously in foreign countries. This proposal showed his indifference to facts, but with the backing of the churches, while it
would have been futile, it would have been less absurd than
our pro-Ally sympathizers felt.

The opportunity of the American churches to develop international good will was made plain to me when as President of
the Federal Council I went with Dr. Sidney L. Gulick in a
so-called Christian Embassy to the churches of Japan. It will
be recalled that the anti-Japanese legislation of some of the
western states, particularly California, had aroused strong
anti-American feeling in Japan. It was one of a series of tensions which our American policy was to make successively
more critical. In 1914, after the outbreak of the war, missionaries in Japan felt that the churches of America ought to
take some step which would convince the Japanese govern-

ment that public sentiment in the United States was not anti-Japanese. They commissioned Dr. Gulick, at that time a missionary teacher in Doshisha College, to present their request to the Federal Council asking that action be taken to bring this fact home to the Japanese people. So the Christian Embassy was established and in the fall of 1914 Dr. Gulick and I went to Japan. Before going we had long interviews with President Wilson and Secretary Bryan, and carried from each of them a letter expressing the friendly spirit of America toward Japan. Our visit was therefore given a color which, while not official, indicated the government's attitude. This was to some extent confirmed by the attentions which we received from the American Ambassador. In fact, when Dr. Gulick and I left Japan for home Ambassador Guthrie and the various secretaries were at the railroad station to see us off. The Ambassador remarked to me that he was glad we were going because he was tired of going out to dinner with us!

The official Japanese attitude toward us at the start was cautious. Dr. Gulick could make public addresses in Japanese and he presented his theory of the immigration quota. Japanese public opinion, we found, favored it as a substitute for the Gentleman's Agreement which was a source of much of the misunderstanding. Doubtless because of my University connection as well as my official position in the Federal Council, I was given very wide hearing. I soon found that while Japanese Christians would be glad to have me speak about the kingdom of God, official Japan wanted me to speak about the United States. In consequence I had somewhat to modify my addresses and to use such material as I could remember from my college lectures on the constitutional history of the United States. I traveled from Morioka on the north to Kumamoto on the south, speaking not merely in churches and Christian groups but also in imperial universities and other colleges, and before large audiences which were arranged by unobtrusive governmental agencies. When Dr. Gulick and I arrived at a city we were met by the highest municipal and provincial authorities who also appeared at our public meetings and delivered addresses of welcome. Dr. Gulick had innumerable interviews with prominent Japanese in which he sought to discover the attitude of the Japanese toward his policy. We were entertained at dinners and luncheons by the Foreign Minister Baron Kato, former Premier Okuma, Baron Shibusawa, and leaders in the commercial world. The newspapers gave us extraordinary publicity.

One of the most interesting of our conferences was that arranged by Concordia, a literary group organized by Baron Shibusawa for the purpose of discovering some common basis among the various religions of Japan upon which the morality of the nation might rest. I had been asked to speak on the subject "What the United States Disapproved in the Policy of Japan." The audience included Baron Kato and a considerable number of the most prominent Japanese and, as I recall, the American Ambassador. I asked whether there was to be any newspaper report of what I said and was assured that there would not be. With some trepidation I proceeded to state every criticism of Japan I had heard in America, assuring my audience, of course, that I was simply acting as a reporter. One of the statements which I made was that the American people thought they had been assured that Japan was going to give Tsing Tao, which they had taken from the Germans, back to China. In fact, Count Okuma, then prime minister, had stated this explicitly in an article in *The Independent*. When I had finished this address, to my astonishment, Baron Kato proceeded to make a long speech in Japanese. I naturally was exceedingly apprehensive as to what he might have said. When it was translated it proved to be a discussion of the various points which I had made, in the course of which he especially denied that any promise had been made by Japan relative to Tsing Tao. After the meeting broke up Baron Kato came to me and said that he could not speak officially but that his personal opinion was that Tsing Tao would be given back to China. I never reported this in America as it seemed to me to be confidential, but later, when the matter was again under discussion, I passed the information to President Wilson, and received a non-committal note of thanks.

The next day, after this meeting of Concordia, *The Japanese Advertiser* issued a full report in English as a sort of broadside and the Japanese papers also gave it large attention. Editorial comment was on the whole favorable and I have no doubt that it was one cause of the reception which was accorded us in Japan.

When we left for home *The Japanese Advertiser* summarized the effect of our mission in a long editorial, part of which I venture to quote:

Dr. Shailer Mathews, "ambassador" from the Federal Council of the Churches of Christ in the United States to the Christians of Japan, and in a quite real though unofficial sense, an ambassador to the people of Japan from the people of America, leaves the land of the risen sun today after having enjoyed for a month the overflowing hospitality which Japan invariably extends to distinguished Americans. In the thirty days or so of his stay Dr. Mathews has delivered 85 addresses in public, has been banqueted to the limit of human endurance, has talked to the governors of twelve prefectures and been talked to by them, has met the mayors of Japan's principal cities, has been entertained by the heads of the government of the Empire and has talked to Baron Kato with the utmost frankness of certain big questions which underlie the relations of the two nations. In addition to this "ambassadorial" work he has preached on Sundays to eager audiences of Americans in the ports, has come into personal contact with a large number of the missionaries whom America has sent to Japan, and has even found time to read papers to various learned and literary societies. A wonderful record this for one month and it is well-rounded off by the fact that Dr. Mathews leaves Japan as fit as when he entered it.

Dr. Mathews did not interpret his mission as one of "kind words," alone. He addressed himself to the task like a statesman and faced difficulties which a small man would have evaded. He did not apologize for the California trouble but showed that it has two sides, that it is not a mere display of "race hatred" but part of a great and serious labor question which is making its presence felt all over the United States, and that relief from discrimination—the real sensitive point of Japan's objection—raises the large and difficult question of state and federal authority. He emphasized, with the public endorsement of Baron Kato, the essential smallness of the question as compared with the terrible possibilities which superficial observers are prone to attach to it. He told the Japanese with the utmost candor of the growing doubts regarding the drift of Japan's Asiatic policy which makes some Americans wonder if Japan has set herself to be the "Germany of the Pacific," and he reminded them that the argument of publicists who question Japan's intentions was "a simple presentation of modern history on the shores of the Pacific." By thus putting before the leading people of Japan with friendly frankness the underlying causes of the slow-growing spirit of doubt in the United States Dr. Mathews has given Japan an opportunity to show that her policy is really non-aggressive. We believe the best elements in Japan will welcome his frankness. The scathing and effective manner in which he exposed the bogey of American imperialism must be noted. It will surprise none who knows anything of American history or the spirit of American institutions to learn that Dr. Mathews could at first hardly believe that such a fear existed. The files of the vernacular press abound with evidence that the bogey has waved his turnip lantern frequently. If Dr. Mathews has given him the happy despatch, he will have laid Japan and Americans in Japan under a real debt of gratitude.

I remember telling one of the representatives of the Associated Press that in my opinion the agitation over the California legislation was really less significant than Japan's interest in China. He assured me that I was correct but that I was the first person he had heard say it. The recent events are a commentary upon my reading of the situation. At the very time of our visit, Japan was without any publicity presenting the twenty-one demands upon China. We were told of this as we were leaving Japan with the further statement that some of the demands were made in the interest of diplomatic bargaining.

I felt certain that in view of such facts as I had at my disposal the Japanese government was not seeking war with the United States and that it wanted the United States to be friendly. On our return from Japan in a number of public addresses Dr. Gulick and I emphasized this view, at the same time pointing out how serious was the irritation which anti-Japanese legislation was causing. It is one of the tragic inconsistencies of history that although Dr. Gulick's idea of quota-immigration was adopted by Congress the Japanese were excluded from its operation. The effect on prominent Japanese who were looking for international understanding was one of bewildered disappointment and of personal hurt.

When I revisited Japan in 1933 I had been for several years the President of Kobe College Corporation which had raised a large sum of money to provide that woman's college with new and beautiful buildings. I was regarded as a friend of Japan and the relations established in my former visit were renewed. Baron Sakatani, one of the choicest men I ever knew, arranged a luncheon for Mrs. Mathews and myself with the Assistant Minister of Foreign Affairs, at which time, however, little opportunity was given for discussion of Japanese-American relations. Baron Sakatani also arranged two luncheons with men representing large business interests for the sake of getting me to understand the attitude of Japan toward the United States. In both of these luncheons the same point of view was expressed. As men of large affairs they did not share popular misunderstandings, but they wished me to know that it was commonly believed that the United States was preparing to make war upon Japan and the presence of the fleet in the Pacific was interpreted to mean just that. They therefore asked me to use my influence to get the fleet recalled. (It will be remembered it was recalled!) It was not possible in these conferences to get any more than this reportorial expression of opinion. In 1915 we had discussed international peace repeatedly. In 1933 no discussion was even initiated. The nearest approach to it was this throwing the blame for the situation upon the United States. While I admitted the ineptitude of American legislation governing immigration I tried to make plain that sentiment in America had been swinging toward inclusion of the Japanese under the quota until it was checked by Japan's actions in Manchuria and Shanghai, and that the idea that the United States was planning war was absurd. Yet it is undeniable that expectation of attack from the United States has been made the subject of regimented propaganda in Japanese newspapers and schools. It looks as if Japan has suppressed if not cut loose from the liberalism which twenty years before could be seen developing and has entered upon an imperialistic program which will make her the mistress of Eastern Asia. Imperialistic nationalism has broken with liberal internationalism, fear and enmity deliberately being made a national fixation by virtue of which the military party can force the hand of the cabinet. To give, as it were, spiritual value to this imperialism there has been a marked development of interest in Shintoism and Buddhism. It is frankly stated that Christianity is a western religion too international in character, while Buddhism is regarded as more distinctly nationalistic. The fact that it should become an agent for the support of military imperialism is not surprising in view of certain periods in Japanese history.

It is impossible to say whether the development of Japan would have followed these lines had it not been for the confusion following the World War. In 1915 we were being assured that the democratic movement was gaining ground. In fact, suffrage was extended, yet it is hard not to believe that the policy which Japan has followed had already been adopted in 1915 and that the decline of liberalism was inevitable. Despite the fact that Japanese Christians have shown a readiness to fraternize with Chinese Christians, that Kagawa can establish co-operatives and that many Japanese high officials are Christians, the churches have had little observable effect in preventing military imperialism. But weakness in this regard is not limited to Japan!

III

Observation of a nation engaged in war gave impetus to my desire to share not only in the maintenance of the neutrality of the United States but also in efforts for the prevention of war. The newly organized League to Enforce Peace seemed an intelligent and hopeful step in the right direction. My contact with international affairs, slight as it has been, convinces me that there is no likelihood of the abandonment of war until a nation can act as a moral unity. But can a nation be moral? It never has been. International relations, except as modified by treaty, have practically invariably been based upon military efficiency. Holy Alliances even when using pious expressions have never been able to prevent war. The only peace which European civilization as a whole ever enjoyed was that of conquered and disarmed peoples under the control of Rome. Morality is a group product and a nation cannot be moral until there is a group of nations which can establish national *mores* and international relations less military than those established by treaties and *ententes*. The League to Enforce Peace looked toward the establishment of a group of nations within which there could be established non-military agencies for settling international disputes. The League was organized effectively and I became one of its representatives, although the University did not judge it wise to detach me for organization purposes. I spoke at a number of meetings, worked on committees and felt that we had at last found a way in which the beginnings of international morality could be organized and made effective. There was little opposition to our agitation. On May 27, 1916, a banquet was held by the League in Washington at which President Wilson made the first public announcement as to his position regarding a league of nations. As President of the Federal Council I was asked to represent the churches in one of a series of brief addresses. I doubt if I ever addressed a more distinguished audience. After stating the interest of religion in the organization of an agent of international morality, I said that while such a plan might seem Utopian I would rather prepare for Utopia than hell. When I sat down, Henry Cabot Lodge reached over and said: "That was a damned good talk." When his turn came to speak he argued for some sort of international league. The issue had not become political although his attitude toward President Wilson was clear in his whispered comments in the course of the President's address.

Our entrance into the war did not interfere with the activity of the League to Enforce Peace. In fact, it served to increase it. We believed that out from the war that was to make the world safe for democracy and end war, there might come a league, as indeed there did. I have always felt that if partisan and personal enmities had been more intelligently handled the United States would have become a member of the League of Nations.

IV

It would be a mistake to think that those of us who had worked for peace were victims of pro-Ally propaganda. We believed that while war is terrible it was a choice between two evils. It is doubtless indicative of moral advance that religious leaders should publicly repent their support of the war, but I have never shared in their remorse. I was convinced and I am still convinced that while we undoubtedly yielded to the psychology of war, our inability to maintain neutrality was due to conditions which threatened a reorganization of the world which would have been fatal to those democratic institutions which with all their imperfections promise most for the development of personal welfare. I shall never forget those days

in March 1918 when "England's back was against the wall."
It seemed that democracy was liable to be defeated. I left my
office and sat by the side of the lake to gain peace of mind.
At home I opened a prayer-book with something of my old-time
hope for a message. I found it in some of the imprecatory
psalms! I recovered my poise.

One cannot look back on such moments without feeling
that they were more than war hysteria. In the addresses which
I gave from New York to California I never used such mur-
derous eloquence as did some of my clerical friends. Patriotism is not sadism. I saw in the war a conflict of two conceptions of society. It was tragic that they should be forced into
arms, but I hoped that the new national feelings and the misery which war caused might lead nations to see the futility of
war and establish relations which would lead to international
morality. I embodied these hopes and interpretations in lectures which I gave in 1918 at the University of North Carolina,
and published in a volume entitled *Patriotism and Religion*. As
I look over these lectures I see that I was not untouched by
war psychology but it is not surprising in view of my own
convictions as to the significance of the conflict and the fact
that I went directly from Chapel Hill to say good-bye to my
son on the evening before he sailed for France.

V

My participation in the war was not limited to public
addresses. Mr. Martin A. Ryerson, a man for whom I had
boundless admiration, was made the Director of War Savings in
the state of Illinois, and I was released from my University
teaching to act as Executive Secretary of the organization. I did
not give up my work as Dean of the Divinity School but after
an office hour at the University went to the headquarters of War
Savings in the city. Thanks to the hearty co-operation of able
men, every county in the state was organized and kept in inti-

mate touch with the central organization. We held conferences of workers, published literature and established a complete system of reports of activities. We sold something like $100,-000,000 worth of War Saving certificates. No one could have had the intimate contact with the American spirit which my position gave without being impressed with the genuine patriotism of our citizens. I learned, too, a great deal as to the methods of efficient propaganda. We did not attempt to arouse hatred of Germans but loyalty to the ideals for which we believed we were fighting. Altogether it was instructive experience. For a little while it even made academic life seem remote. In fact, when I once more took up my teaching in the Divinity School my classes felt my new attitude and one of my colleagues with brotherly frankness called my attention to it. I recovered my interest in the history of Christian thought but dogma ceased to be abstract. It was the religious aspect of group solidarity. I drew also from this experience the overwhelming conviction, which subsequent events justified, that as a nation we were faced with critical social changes. That fact made it imperative that the churches should be more than champions of ancestral faith. I believed not only that we should enter the League of Nations as an indispensable prerequisite for the development of national morality, but that Christian leaders should face all problems set by group action of which politics is only a type. In giving the Bennett Lectures at Wesleyan University in 1921 I endeavored to formulate this conviction, freed from the emotional disturbances of war. They were published under the title, *The Validity of American Ideals*. I never was satisfied with them and I doubt if the volume had any wide influence.

My conviction that the national feeling aroused by our participation in the war should be turned from military preparedness to education in civic affairs led me to accept an invitation to join a committee composed of some of the prominent citizens of Chicago, including Victor Lawson of the *Chicago Daily News*. The Committee was endeavoring to bring about the establishment of training camps by the Federal Government by supporting a representative who would probably be called a lobbyist in Washington. In the light of my experience in the War Savings Department I urged that the proposed camps, while organized under military discipline, should give primary attention to training in citizenship. The Committee came to hold these same views, but the death of its representative in Washington ended its activities. The camps were established but it is to be regretted the civic and educational elements were minimized or disregarded. The CCC camps have, however, to some extent embodied these educational elements.

This intimate connection with national spirit served to deepen my sense of the opportunity confronting the church. The refusal of President Wilson to compromise his radical plans and the identification of membership in the League with partisan politics and personal enmities, while bitter disappointments, were new incentives to the extension of Christian principles into political action. It was no accident that so many church bodies urged membership of the United States in the League of Nations and the World Court. The growing suspicion of both indicates the need of showing that Christian morality must be something more than individualistic. Faith in the God of process must replace worship of the Lord of hosts.

VI

Since the World War the discussion of international peace has been somewhat confused with the question of individual attitude toward war. The Kellogg-Briand Treaty has been interpreted to mean the abandonment of war on the part of the various nations. This treaty, like all others, depends for its efficiency upon the attitudes of nations and has no power to enforce itself. Events since its adoption have sadly disappointed those who overlooked this fact. Public opinion and national policies must be developed before such a treaty can become more than a gesture.

Such public opinion is clearly in process of formation in countries where public opinion is possible. In both Great Britain and the United States religious forces have become outspoken in their opposition to war. Absolute pacifism has gained many followers and if the published results of questionnaires are to be trusted thousands of ministers have stated that they would neither participate in a future war personally, nor use their clerical position to bless it. Opposition has developed against ministers holding military chaplaincies on the ground that such a relation commits Christianity to an approval of war system. Various religious bodies in their national meetings have declared war to be un-Christian. The Federal Council of Churches of Christ in America has joined various peace societies in protesting against the enormous expenditure on the army and navy by the Federal Government. Evidently there is shaping a new international climate—unfriendly to militarism.

On the other hand, various patriotic bodies have not hesitated to brand the movement toward peace as due to communistic influences and to allege that foreign governments have financially supported some of the bodies and persons opposed to the development of military and naval strength of the nation. At the same time there has developed an almost hysterical fear of anti-American propaganda within the nation and an attempt to control the free discussion of economic and political theory.

That war, like theft and adultery, is contrary to the ideals of the Christian religion is too obvious to need discussion. This is not to say that a nation should neglect preparation for defense. My repeated visits to Europe and Asia have shown me an armed world unfriendly to the United States. Conditions might arise and, as I believe, did arise in 1917 in which one has to choose between two evils. A Christian is a citizen and cannot act as if he were not. As a good citizen he will oppose any action of his government that does injustice to another people. But he may have to sacrifice his absolute ideals in the interest of practical idealism. To give legal quality to the sayings of Jesus involves one in difficulties. If his words relative to non-resistance are to be made into law what shall be said about his directions to sell a coat and buy a sword? His sayings cannot be made into political legislation, but an intelligent opposition to war demands the application of the principles which they illustrate to international relations which otherwise might lead to war. A declaration that one will not engage in a hypothetical war does not relieve a citizen from an equally heroic determination to do his best to see that a nation does not adopt policies which are essentially selfish. I have wondered how many Englishmen who took the Oxford oath not to engage in any war would favor such a modification of the Treaty of Versailles as would restore the colonies taken from Germany. A thoroughgoing opposition to war is not merely negation. It involves such concrete matters as the control of territory where there are oil, iron and other natural resources, the adjustment of tariff and economic quotas, the recognition of the self-respect of other nations in laws regulating immigration, the rectification of boundaries and the giving of political rights to conquered and dependent people. For a citizen to refuse to engage in a war due to conditions for which he must share responsibility is not to be justified by abstract morality. Consistency would demand that such refusal to participate in a war be preceded by opposition to national policies which have led to the war. To apply the principles of Christianity to a social process is as much a moral imperative as to accept some form of martyrdom.

Any patriotism which is not a collective sadism will be concerned with the setting up of conditions in which a national morality can be developed. A nation like any other group can implement the ideals of its members only when those members are ready to act intelligently as members of the group itself. The maintenance of international peace is indissolubly connected with group morality. As in illness good intentions and love involve reliance upon medical skill, so group morality of all kinds involves economic and political skills. As the social desire to avoid smallpox and yellow fever led to the adoption of vaccination and the extermination of mosquitos, so Christian hostility to war must lead to international policies and national self-sacrifice which will remove the causes of war. Conscientious objection to sharing in a war may be a last resort, but it should be practiced by those who have shared in political action.

Such considerations lead inevitably to the conclusion that a part of the task of the Christian is to give quality to the collective emotion we call nationalism. Developments throughout the world make it plain that nothing is more futile than the denunciation of nationalism. Political grouping must be recognized as an element in a world situation. Nationalism must be made moral. Here is the opportunity for an intelligent application of the principles of Christianity. Christians should endeavor to do for nations what has been done for denominations, that is, to develop a group relationship in which national *mores* can be developed. Whether or not this should be the existing League of Nations may be left to the future. But a public opinion which will see in a nation not an end but an instrument of human welfare will make international relations something more than a reliance upon force. In the same proportion as a church can induce individuals to order their lives on the faith that love is a practicable basis for the social order will it contribute to that public mind which in time will make a nation a moral entity. Distrust of the efficiency of love in our social and individual relations lies back of international enmities.

VII

The possibility of utilizing religious organizations for the development of a public opinion and national attitudes which would make international peace practicable had been so ably argued by Frederick A. Lynch and others that Mr. Carnegie had founded the Church Peace Union. It was also one of the major fields of interest of the Federal Council. Its Commission, first on Relations with the Orient, and later on International Justice and Good Will, was established during my term as President of the Council, and became the center of influence under the leadership of Dr. Sidney L. Gulick. The World Alliance for International Friendship through the Churches has established centers in thirty-seven different countries and utilizes church organizations in carrying the principles of good will into political life. The Roman Catholic Church in the United States has established a Peace Commission which has had intelligent and broad-minded direction. The Pope by his Encyclicals has called upon all Christians to unite in the interests of peace. It was logical to extend such a movement beyond the limits of Christianity and Judaism. Dr. Henry A. Atkinson, Secretary of the Church Peace Union, proposed that there should be called a Conference of members of all religions to adopt some method by which their respective groups should undertake to shape up an attitude of international good will.

A committee was appointed by the Church Peace Union and I was made its chairman. A widespread inquiry was made as to the desirability of such a Conference and the replies were so unanimous in its favor that a call was sent out for a meeting of non-official representatives of various religions to be held in Geneva in 1928. Those of us who were present will never forget its sessions. Eleven major religions were represented in the body of more than two hundred delegates and the discussion was free and exceedingly earnest. As a result it was determined to hold the Conference, and a large committee in which all religions had membership was appointed, and I was elected the chairman.

This meeting was exceedingly encouraging and at the same time was an education in what may be called the technique of co-operation on the part of those who differ upon matters of primary importance. We Americans are accustomed to co-operation but it is by no means easy for us to realize that men may disagree on many points and yet unite in one course of action. How necessary it is to recognize the religious sensitiveness of others appeared in this first meeting. Professor Hume of Union Theological Seminary had prepared a beautiful liturgy which was an anthology of the noblest sentiments of all religions. It seemed most natural for the Conference at Geneva to use such a liturgy as an expression of its religious interests. It was, therefore, used in one session, a Parsee acting as leader. It seemed successful as well as impressive, but the next day it became manifest that there was some suspicion that the Christians had used the occasion for their own purposes. It therefore seemed wise to avoid all types of religious exercises during the Conference. When our business was over and we were ready to adjourn, the incongruity of a religious meeting not giving expression to religion moved me to call for silent prayer according to the custom of each religion. So impressive were the moments in this bidding prayer that when the Executive Committee met the next year at Frankfort, at the opening of each session I asked that we have a moment of silent prayer. One day I asked for silent meditation rather than prayer. Just as I said this a Hindu said, "Mr. Chairman," and then immediately said that since the chairman had said "meditation" he had nothing to say. He and his co-religionists could meditate but not pray. Americans have little interest in meditation. So thereafter I called for a moment of silent prayer and meditation. Peace prevailed in a peace conference.

The meetings of the Executive Committee illustrated how it is possible to get co-operation among people who have radical differences. Some of the German professors, notably Professor Rudolph Otto, in true academic fashion wanted first to decide what religion really is and in the light of that decision to discuss what religious people might do in the interests of international peace. The proposal of course was logical but we were dealing with something very much more human than logic. To get the representatives of the different religions to discuss religion would have called for a peace conference of its own. There was difficulty even in the use of the word. We originally planned to use the expression "Universal Religious Peace Conference" but at the first meeting of the Executive Committee the Roman Catholic members pointed out that some people seemed to think that it was a new Parliament of Religions. I therefore proposed and the Committee adopted the name which is now used.

The work of preparing for the World Conference on International Peace through Religion has been conducted under three commissions which endeavored to answer four fundamental questions: (1) What are the causes of war and the tendencies that make for war? (2) What are the spiritual forces with which these influences can be met? (3) What is being done by the religions and religious associations throughout the world in the cause of international peace? (4) How can we mobilize the spiritual forces of the world to do away with war and to ensure peace?

The first commission has prepared its report which was accepted and published in a volume, *The Causes of War*, a valuable brief treatment of its subject. Reports of progress have been made on the second and third commissions. The fourth commission, of which I am chairman, proposed a program of work, but the financial depression has limited our attempt to carry it out. We have, however, been able to establish committees in different countries. The one in Japan includes some outstanding religious leaders. Baron Sakatani is chairman. In India a committee was appointed with Professor Wadia of Bombay as chairman. We have also maintained an active co-operation with the International Fellowship of Faith which has a large number of chapters throughout India. We have been able to interest some individual representatives of Mohammedanism.

This approach to international matters through religion has disclosed two facts; first, the representatives of all religions declare that religion involves love; and second, national loyalties leave these protestations without practical expression. A nation like Japan would not permit religious persons to undertake to organize any movement which would involve national sacrifices and the Indians say somewhat bitterly that India is not a nation and that there is no use of talking about international peace. The Moslem world is so intent upon the development of independence in Turkey and Egypt that religion has become either something to be avoided or a servant of national ambitions. On the continent of Europe religious leaders who favor peace are liable to prosecution if not imprisonment. In Japan imperialism permits "no dangerous thoughts."

So far as my experience makes any conclusion possible it seems that religion is about the only field where all can talk about international peace. In not a few countries about the only course open is that of academic discussion which serves to keep alive the ideals which seemed so potential in the years immediately following the war. From 1929 to 1932 can be seen a weakening of those ideals in large measure, due to the Peace of Versailles and the development of national economies. The inspiration of religion would seem to be especially needed under these conditions, but religious enthusiasm that is an agent of nationalist ambition may become a curse rather than a blessing. For it to limit itself to unpreparedness or the outlawing of war may, it is true, develop attitudes which may ultimately be socialized, but it is more likely to promise God's help to the stronger battalions. What is really needed is that a religious movement should undertake the moral education both of individuals and of groups. Except in democracies, education in political matters has become regimented propaganda. All the greater, therefore, is the need of well-considered planning that will not allow the desire for immediate results to postpone the achievement of the desired end. Not the least important lesson which our work on this proposed World Conference has taught me is that a church that expects God to do what intelligent human action ought to do will become an indirect aid to revolution.

VIII

Sometimes a nightmare grips my imagination. I am again on a stormy night at Camp Upton, taking leave of my son who is just about to sail for France. And then I see him also in his turn taking leave of his son as he goes to war. The crowded cemeteries of France beckon new companions. The ruined cities grin across devastated fields and farms. I see young men and women disillusioned, cynical and reckless.

And then I know that it is not a dream but a prophecy of what may happen in a world where nations have not learned to give each other justice and to substitute reason for cupidity. Such forebodings make it hard to be hopeful. And yet, the smoking flax is not to be quenched. The efforts which are being made to substitute co-operative action for war, the growth of the will to peace in democratic lands, the discovery that true religion is not limited to visiting widows and orphans in their affliction, are all harbingers of a better day. How any one can think that Christians, both as individuals and organized groups should refuse to help in making these hopes come true is beyond my comprehension. To say that religion has nothing to do with politics and that national morality is outside its purpose, that one must wait for the return of a triumphant punitive Christ or the intervention of an unapproachable God in an expected crisis, seems too much like moral cowardice. For those who take the ideals of Jesus seriously and share in his confidence in the power of love, there can be no other way than that which the prophets showed Israel, a national life loyal to the righteous and loving will of a cosmic God.

CHAPTER XIV

RELIGION AND SCIENCE

IT IS yet to be seen how far intelligence is consonant with religion. As natural forces replace Divinity and bacteria replace devils, the area of fear within which religions have had control contracts. There is no use to offer sacrifice to a cosmic law or to attempt to make diseases merciful by flattery set to music. But is that the end of the story? The representatives of rebellious modernity say "Yes." If fear made the gods the conquest of fear means the unmaking of the gods. That was in effect the prophecy made to me by one of the world's greatest physicists. But is such a negative position justifiable? Certainly many intelligent men are religious and many religious men are intelligent.

I

One of the surprises of life is the reappearance in a younger generation of questions which an older generation supposed it had answered or at least comfortably neglected. In religion as in politics and business it is hard to capitalize experience. Instead of learning how to use parental experience to avoid duplicating parental mistakes a new generation apparently wishes to recapitulate foolishness before making new moral adventures. Such a reflection is certainly suggested by the recrudescence of the so-called struggle between science and religion. In my boyhood we had echoes of this struggle but it was largely confined to British areas. Huxley and Tyndal were good publicists. Probably few people remember the

"prayer gauge" debate. The representatives of science proposed
to put the power of religion to test experimentally. The patients
of a hospital were to be divided, one half of them would be
prayed for and the other half left to doctors. The religious
people would not accept the challenge and there sprang up a
considerable pamphlet literature over the matter. At the time it
seemed to me an irreligious proposal, but as I look back upon
it I cannot help feeling that the champions of religion were
afraid. Yet before psychology ceased to be "mental philosophy," and physiology and biology had contributed to medical
science, it may have been wise for the mid-Victorian Elijahs
to decline the challenge of mid-Victorian priests of Baal. After
all Mt. Carmel was not a hospital. Probably no one except
writers of doctors' theses now reads Gladstone's *Impregnable
Rock of Holy Scripture*. In my student days it was regarded
by good Christians as having quite demolished the assaults of
the agnostics. The arguments of Robert G. Ingersoll, which
seem today not a little like contemporary apologetics, were met
by denunciation, stories about his military career and heart-
breaking anecdotes of suicides which followed in the wake of
his lecture tours. It was all very confusing for those of us
whose sense of religious security had been jarred by the self-
assurance of the new school of agnosticism. Laboratory science did something more than lead to research. It undermined
habits of thought and substituted the tentativeness of experiment for authoritative formulas. True, there were some scientists like Asa Gray who championed Darwinian evolution while
holding to the Nicene Creed; John Fiske used evolution in setting forth a cosmic philosophy which included theism and
belief in immortality; LeConte did much the same. But these
men were not representative churchmen. When Beecher and
other liberal preachers accepted evolution their evangelical
brothers looked upon them with suspicion. Scientific method
had not touched religious thought. It was only when educa-

tional processes had ceased to be controlled by the study of classical literature and grew more contemporary, that orthodox theology was felt to be incompatible with intellectual integrity.

In the last years of the nineteenth century, also, "Christianity" ceased to be a synonym of "religion." Until then (and to this day in certain quarters) Christianity was the true religion and all others were false. The genuine Catholic even yet hesitates to speak of "religions." When the sacred books of the East began to appear something like a panic seized the champions of Christianity. There was so much in these religions that Christians had claimed as their own that it was impossible to think of them as wholly false. The Parliament of Religions held at the Columbian Exposition in 1893 made the study of comparative religion popular. Edwin Arnold's *Light of Asia* aided in the discomfiture of those who claimed a monopoly of truth for Christianity. Anthropologists became evangelists of a conception of religion which left little room for evangelical complacency. Yet at the same time interest in foreign missions born of the older convictions was sweeping across student life. It was only a question of time when these two attitudes would collide.

II

It is not strange that we who were growing up in the midst of this disintegration of religious self-satisfaction should have failed to draw the corollaries which we were later to champion. We knew little about scientific method for we had studied Greek and Latin and had hardly more than played with chemistry and physics. We believed that in some way the new facts could be appropriated by old beliefs but just how we did not know. Books which attempted this appropriation were sometimes eloquently written and while they did not demand a reconstruction of thought they did serve an emotional acceptance of evolution and the results of the new study of religions. My graduating address on leaving Newton Theological Institution dealt with the supremacy of Christianity over its rival religions. It must have been an amateurish discussion but it showed awareness of a trend of thought. When in 1909 the University of Chicago celebrated the centenary of Darwin's birth I gave a lecture which attempted to set forth the bearing of evolutionary thought upon religion. By that time my generation had come to feel that evolution was no longer an issue in intelligent religious circles. We gave it no such supreme position as today's critics of liberalism assert, but we accepted it as a datum in modern thinking. Who nowadays can say that we were mistaken?

The early literature dealing with the relations of science and religion gives one the feeling of another world. Men seemed to be thinking on two levels. The presuppositions which lay back of their religious ideas were those of contemporary orthodoxy. God was not thought of as a monarch but he was an entity working in a universe which he had created and sustains. Evolution was a way in which he worked. Men could therefore believe in him without seriously affecting their theology. They became religious romanticists. Such an appropriation of scientific facts in the interest of inherited belief was transitional and was to have results not foreseen by the authors of books like *Ad Fidem* which served to allay my fears as to religion while I was a student. The same was true of that influential book of Henry Drummond's *Natural Law in the Spiritual World*. The basic idea of this volume was indicated in the title. Although Professor Drummond in his later works changed his presentations of evolution, he never really abandoned a dualistic philosophy. But quite contrary to his intention he weakened the infallibility of evangelicalism by giving theological thought a new set of analogies and patterns. Biology took the place of politics, environment usurped sovereignty, organism replaced subject, and the dynamic relationship of organism and environment gave new content to religion. All religions could be seen to have the same function however different their techniques. The use of social experience in getting helpful relationship with the cosmic environment became a phase of the vital process. Supernaturalism followed magic into the limbo of history.

As one looks back over this period when natural science was made to support evangelical theology, one realizes the absence of those social sciences which had only begun to develop under the influence of Herbert Spencer and of Ward. The masters of laboratory technique and astronomy and geology were then as now rather intolerant of the extension of the term science to history, economics and other social studies which undertook to do more than observe the habits of mankind. It was natural, therefore, that defenders of the Christian belief should have constructed a new dualism in thought. Science, they said, dealt with material facts and religion with values. Therefore science could not hurt religion. Such a view is still held by those who approach religion through philosophy and are unacquainted with or indifferent to the social sciences and psychology. The difficulty, however, with such summary dealing with the undeniable conflict between scientists and theologians is that it does not deal with the real world. Values are the obverse of existence. An empty revolver will function only as long as the man at whom it is pointed believes it to be loaded. Sooner or later the discussion of values introduces one to questions of reality. Whether a man may become a metaphysician or a pragmatist or very likely both, he cannot overlook the fact that value involves the existence of something which is not the product of experience and cannot be tested by questionnaires. There is no finality in a complacent apologetics which solves a difficulty by ignoring it. Altogether too many theologians having brought their followers face to face with a real intellectual difficulty call upon them to pray.

When religion ceases to be an acceptance of a sanctified past and becomes a phase of life's adjustment to objective reality, a new pattern is needed. To determine what elements of the past are to be discarded and what, if any, are to be retained requires something more than ecclesiastical authority. Others than theologians become involved. The question as to whether one can be religious in the universe which the various sciences are disclosing demands answers which evangelicalism cannot give.

It seemed to me that it would be possible to issue a series of small volumes, each of which should show what the bearing of some particular science had upon religious faith. The investigation of Professor Leuba of Bryn Mawr College has shown that religious interests varied among leaders of different sciences. Those dealing with cosmic phenomena like the geologists and astronomers are more favorable to religion than the biologists and physicists. There may have been personal reasons for this difference but it seemed to me a series of such handbooks would be very serviceable. The publishers, however, did not think that such a series would be practicable, and instead commissioned me to prepare a single volume on *The Contributions of Science to Religion*. I therefore asked thirteen outstanding authorities in their respective fields to state briefly the findings of their various sciences and in the light of these I undertook to show what bearing such views had upon religious faith.

The method of the book still seems to me to be sound. While scientific method is not the same as the facts of science, a man has to be religious in the universe in which he is. He cannot select from it a little universe of his own. A religion as a factor of human life has always been relative to such scientific conceptions as its followers possess. Men have found in the world which they understood some justification for holding the faith which they inherited. The mental serenity derived from harmony between religious faith and current knowledge of the world has always been disturbed by new facts and new generalizations. The question of method in the consequent intellectual ferment grows paramount. If the appeal is to be made to an authoritative revelation sooner or later one reaches ecclesiastical authority. If one explores religion as a phase of human life the center of thought becomes not philosophical but practical. Every religion is obviously an attempt to adjust life to the environing universe. It must be justified or condemned by its efficiency to direct life in accordance with our expanding knowledge of the reality in the midst of which we live.

Can the experience born of social relations of persons legitimately be used in the setting up of relations of the cosmic activity? Does science give us a universe which warrants such behavior? Obviously we have outgrown the sovereignty pattern. Can our scientific knowledge furnish us patterns which can be equally effective for those who accept the findings of science? I attempted to deal with these questions in my volume, *The Growth of the Idea of God,* but in the earlier period of my thought I had not clearly seen the significance of conclusions which my historical study had enforced.

The attempt to show that religious faith was justified by our knowledge of the world given us by science demanded something more than academic discussion, and in the beginning of the struggle over evolution our American Institute published a tract I wrote entitled *How Science Helps Our Faith.* This was followed by a series of tracts written by outstanding scientists on evolution, astronomy and various biological processes, which circulated by the thousands. It is impossible to trace the effect of such literature but wide circulation would argue that it met the need felt by religious persons of finding something more in scientific findings than a support for romanticized orthodoxy.

III

The radically different methods of religious thought accounts in large measure for the struggle over evolution. Any one who is indifferent to religion will find it difficult to understand why there should have been such a new outbreak of the evolution controversy when apparently all scientists were accepting it as a presupposition for an understanding of the history of life on our planet. But evolution was no longer merely a matter over which the clergy and scientists could debate. It was becoming embedded in public school instruction. Teachers with any sort of scientific training could not avoid the evolutionary hypothesis in any account of the geological ages or in courses in biology and botany. It was inevitable that such instruction should cause apprehension among church people unaccustomed to scientific thought. The opponents of evolution were not interested in scientific questions. What they cared about was the implication which the scientific method, embodied in evolution, had for their religious faith and specifically for the infalliblity of the Bible upon which orthodoxy depended. They had no patience with the attempts to translate the first chapter of *Genesis* into scientific equivalents. Their line of argument was clear. If evolution was true the Bible was false. If the Bible was false Christianity itself was untrustworthy, and morality was endangered.

Those of us who had found our way through this apprehension were sometimes inclined to be impatient with those whose unfamiliarity with scientific thought and method left their religious thought unaffected. Not until the storm of controversy actually rose did we appreciate how far the public schools were unconsciously developing disaffection with the teaching of the church. But the fathers and mothers and ministers of many states were much better informed and more apprehensive. They argued that if public schools were supported by taxes they had no right to undermine the religion of the tax-payers. The legislatures of several states undertook to pass bills which made the teaching of evolution in tax-supported schools an offense before the law. It was only by great exertion that such legislation was prevented in a number of states, both north and south of the Mason and Dixon Line. In Tennessee such a bill was passed. In other states, school committees and state Boards of Education exercised an authority which led to the dismissal in certain states of teachers and the rewriting of textbooks. In a number of addresses and articles I pointed out the dangers which threatened education and medical training. In my opinion the teachers of science themselves were partially to blame because of sometimes a "smart Alec attitude" toward religion. Freedom of teaching certainly does not mean license to insult other people's convictions. The hostility of church people to evolution was not born of mere bigotry but of apprehension as to the dangers which threatened morals in the breaking down of the authority of the Bible. It is only from this point of view that one can understand the attitude of otherwise intelligent people.

On our return from Japan, President Wilson asked that any report Dr. Gulick and I wished to make should be made to Mr. Bryan, then Secretary of State. We had a long interview with the Secretary and found him rather indifferent to what we had to say about Japan but very much concerned about evolution. I had little interest in his scientific views, but it seemed to me that proper relations of Japan and the United States were vastly important. Accordingly, after listening to his disquisition for several minutes, I said to him that I sympathized with his concern about the religious life of the students but my experience had been different from his. I had found that when students were told that they had to choose between Christianity and evolution they chose evolution. Mr. Bryan proceeded to pace the floor and finally said to me that if any young man did not agree with him as to the falseness of evolution it was because of some secret sin. There was, of course, no arguing over such an issue and the interview came to an end.

It was no surprise, therefore, to find him engaged in the so-called "Scopes Case" in Dayton, Tennessee. In that little town a young man, who was a teacher of science and coach for the football team, deliberately disobeyed the law against the teaching of evolution and gave his classes information which is commonplace in scientific circles. In consequence he was tried for the violation of the state law. The trial gained widespread attention and the little town of Dayton became a center of extraordinary interest. Mr. Clarence Darrow undertook to defend Mr. Scopes in the interest of freedom of speech and religious tolerance. I was among those who were asked to serve as experts in the trial. Mr. Darrow hoped to have the relation of evolution and religion come into the trial and to be able to examine Mr. Bryan himself. As it turned out several of the so-called experts in education and science attended the trial but were not called as the judge ruled that the real issue was whether Mr. Scopes in teaching elements of the evolutionary hypothesis had violated the law. As the facts were admitted the decision against the young man was inevitable. I was not able to attend the trial because of my engagements in Chautauqua Institution but I had a conference with Mr. Darrow with whom I had struck up a friendship. While at Chautauqua I was asked to send a telegram as to the attitude of religious leaders relative to evolution. I had examined the writings of a good many conservative theologians and in this telegram I gave a list of several of them who accepted theistic evolution. Among them was my friend, Dr. E. Y. Mullins, President of the Southern Baptist Theological Seminary, and the outstanding theologian of the South. My justification was a statement in one of his books. When the telegram was published one of the anti-evolution champions immediately telegraphed President Mullins, stating that I had quoted him and asked him if he believed in theistic evolution. He replied that he did not believe in theistic or any other sort of evolution. Whereupon I was accused of misrepresenting his position. I did not quite understand President Mullins' answer and in the course of correspondence with him over another matter I incidentally mentioned my surprise and gave him the reference on which I had based my statement. His reply was to the effect that if there could be such a thing as a Christian theory of evolution he would accept it, but such a thing was impossible as evolution was mechanical and impersonal and could not be brought into line with the Christian doctrine of God.

Whatever may be thought of his explanation it at least made plain how difficult it is to adjust orthodox theism with scientific method of thought. There was in reality an issue far more fundamental than the question of whether or not God's creative acts were by the way of evolution. Underneath all such discussions was a question which increasingly came to the fore in the years following the controversy; that is, what is really involved in the conception of God? In orthodox Christianity this involved belief as to the Bible. When Mr. Bryan submitted voluntarily to the interrogations of Mr. Darrow he summed the matter up with characteristic clarity. When asked about the sun standing still, he replied in effect that he understood the difficulty which astronomy pointed out but that if the choice was between the findings of astronomy and the Bible he chose the Bible. Supernaturalism could not have been more unqualifiedly set in opposition to scientific method.

IV

Science has not been confined to those who are professional scientists. It has become a social mind-set. Not only does laboratory experimentation serve commercial ends but our civilization is being transformed by the application of orderly method to almost every phase of human life from the raising of children to the writing of advertisements. A religion as a form of social behavior faces a very different social mind from that of any period in the past.

The proponents of biblical orthodoxy were right in their general feeling as to the disintegrating effect of science upon belief. Anything under investigation will not have authority. Wherever there is the spirit of inquiry there is the weakening of theological security. The inertia of social life and vestigial fears may prevent outward break wth ecclesiastical practices but they lose their efficiency in the second generation. I once was asked by a young woman, member of the Roman Catholic church, what she should do in order to join a Protestant church. I had no particular interest in inducing her to make the change but gave her such directions as I could. She went away evidently unprepared to act. A few days later she returned and made the same inquiry. I happened to be busy and not wishing to prolong the interview I said bluntly, "If you want to leave the Catholic Church and join a Protestant church all you need do is pick out the Protestant body you prefer and join it." Whereupon she disclosed her real attitude. "I know all that," she said, "but the priest tells me that if I do so I shall go to hell. I don't believe him but I don't dare to take the risk."

The attitude of the members of evangelical churches who accepted scientific method was at the outset much the same. We were ready to go with the evolutionist as far as reasonable interpretation of facts warranted. We believed that the Bible should be studied historically and critically but we did not wish to break with organized Christianity. It was not that we deliberately refused to accept conclusions, we really did not see them. They were none the less inevitable and the questions which the experimental and tentative habit of thought developed gradually became dominant. Theological doctrines like the atonement, the deity of Christ, the personality of God and the worth of prayer were either outgrown or restated. The rapidity of the consequent changes varied according to the temperament and experience of different persons. Those who had suffered from ecclesiastical discipline were more interested in what they would call truth than organized religion. Honesty to them involved the abandonment of conceptions which seemed to be untrue. In the name of humanism they objected to the use of the word "God" and prayer became a meditation. This movement was particularly in evidence among the Unitarian clergy. Among more radical persons there developed organized propaganda for atheism.

The substitution of scientific method for ecclesiastical obedience was more than a change of emphasis in the presentation of Christianity. It was a phase of social psychology. The churches which had organized orthodoxy in an era of unconstitutional absolute monarchy had effectively utilized current political patterns. The change in the social mind resulting from education found the sovereignty of God a survival rather than a creative concept. Such a change was, of course, not universal. The rank and file of Protestant church members were not accustomed to scientific thought. Among younger persons the change was toward religious indifference, and even a contemptuous superiority to the church. The substitution of the teaching of Jesus for authoritative doctrines, the conception of Christianity as a movement which undertakes to reproduce his attitudes and consequent behavior in our own day, the softening of God's sovereignty into a divine paternity, the development of the social gospel and the substitution of Christian nurture for supernatural conversion of children suffering from a corrupt human nature inherited from Adam, the modification of doctrines of the atonement were the direct result of the substitution of scientific attitude for that of implicit reliance on the Bible, demanded by orthodoxy. Religious workers began to see the pathological significance of many things which were regarded as immoral. The Emanuel movement was a striking illustration of the new conception of religion as co-operating with and aiding the medical procedure. Psychiatric methods were adopted for the cure of souls. Where once the church had endeavored to correct evil practices by threats of hell, Christians who were thinking scientifically sought to discover complexes and removed diseased tonsils.

Moments in which one is conscious of religious change are likely to be those of distress. I well recall how in a four days' quarantine in the harbor of Beyrout I struggled with the question as to the place a god had in a universe of law. The tension of such moments is due largely to the fact that questions proposed by scientific methods of thought are being answered by methods derived from the older non-scientific thought. In religion as in everything else questions and answers must be on the same plane. The neglect of this elementary requirement weakens the thought of otherwise open-minded Protestant theologians. The inconsistency would not be so serious if the theologian were not obsessed with the notion that he is finding truth. As a matter of fact he is justifying religious attitudes in a romantic rather than scientific way. For a long time I unconsciously yielded to such wishful thinking. But if one regards a religion as a technique for progressively personal living through more or less perfect adjustment to social and cosmic environment, such transitional theology will not be so severely judged. For it may well be expected that inconsistencies in thought will be ironed out as one becomes more adept in the use of scientific method.

Such a view is realistic rather than speculative. It contemplates morality rather than "truth" as its end. The effort to define "religion" seems less important than the observation of that human behavior to which the religious label has been attached. But the label does not determine the sort of behavior to be studied. Choice depends upon function. Adam did not emerge in Eden with a dictionary under his arm. Behavior of human beings is not purposeless. Dependent upon nature, needing food and shelter, seeking security and happiness, men have sought superhuman aid in attaining these ends. They have treated environing forces which they could not control, as they treated superiors in their circles of life.

All this is very simple. "Religion" stands for the behavior that seeks superhuman, and as culture develops, what is regarded as cosmic aid. Its technique is that of personal and social relations. Impersonal techniques used in seeking proper adjustment to reality we call science. The effort to go beyond, interpret and justify such behavior we call philosophy. The three are inseparable but not identical.

The recognition of cosmic activities upon which humanity is dependent functions like the old conception of supernaturalism, but because of its philosophical implications it necessitates a reconstruction of one's ideas of religious faith, prayer, immortality and the church itself. In consequence, religious behavior without changing its function changes its techniques.

Such a view of religion has no room for miracles in the strict sense of the word. The unique will be recognized but it will not be treated as the momentary intrusion of the Divine into human relations. Even the apologists for miracles now try to show that they are consonant with our knowledge of nature. This is, of course, to make reason rather than revelation the final court of appeal. Miracles, instead of being the ground for faith, become its stumbling block, for the Bible abounds in miracles. Gradually those who were sympathetic with science came to feel the need of some new basis upon which their faith could rest. In some cases this was made Christian experience but the early books in this field like Stearns, *The Evidence of Christian Experience,* nowadays seem special pleading. They found in the experience they analyzed most of the content of evangelical orthodoxy. They did not realize that the approach to Christian experience had to be through psychology and social sciences, and that the ultimate test would be empirical.

A friend of mine was one day standing by the rim of the Grand Canyon when an automobile of tourists stopped near him. Like all those who look at that stupendous work of nature, the newcomers began to question how the canyon had been formed. Finally one of the women of the party declared that she knew how it had been done. "The pre-historic Indians dug it out." Her companions tried to argue with her but she declared it was her opinion and she had as much right to her opinion as any one else had to his.

The same type of argument is found among those who approach religion from an unscientific point of view. A view is accepted or rejected because of its proposed bearing upon an individual's faith. One of the most common types of argument is that "if such and such a view is to be accepted my faith would be destroyed." Such an argument grounds itself on that which has been everywhere, always and by all accepted as a form of revelation. Those who approached religion from a scientific point of view could only reply to such an argument that no one has any right to believe what is contrary to a well-substantiated fact. But the bearing of such a position upon the nature of a church and the body of beliefs which it may represent, is certainly disconcerting to those who do not share in the scientific treatment of religious experience.

From the scientific point of view immortality ceases to be an element of religious faith and takes its place among those hypotheses whose tenability depends upon available evidence. Heaven and hell have been repeatedly redefined but among intelligent persons they no longer bulk as the basis for morality. The appeal to be saved in the sense of escaping eternal torture and enjoying eternal bliss gains no response except from those who live in the atmosphere of pre-scientific fears. Yet, a new basis is given to the belief that death is not annihilation by our better knowledge of the universe and evolution. My thought as regards these matters has passed through a number of stages but despite the difficulties and mystery involved, the Christian conception of the survival of personality—not the physical body—after death seems more probable than that life is purely mechanistic. In my Ingersoll Lecture at Harvard, in 1933, with the rather ambitious title *Immortality and the Cosmic Process,* I summarized what seemed to be a scientific approach to the question. There was little original in the treatment except perhaps the frank acceptance of the results of the views of matter and the abandonment of the last vestiges of animism. Without a full knowledge of the conditions of life after death, it is possible to believe that the process of personalization of the individual may go on. Rewards and punishments after death are of less concern than the organization of behavior in accordance with an intelligent understanding of just what personality means and how its development is the outcome of our organic relations with the cosmic process from which humanity has emerged.

Thus, however tentative may be one's view as to the survival of a person after death, it becomes a corollary of a conception of God which grows more dynamic as one gains better understanding of the universe. It seems illogical to say that this universe with humanity in it must be interpreted from the analogy of the machine or that it is incapable of personal response to its personal product. In setting up such personal relations anthropomorphism is no more illegitimate than in the setting up of friendship between masses of matter we call human beings.

Prayer, therefore, is more than a defeatist technique. True, to conceive of God as a sovereign makes such prayer easy. It is the asking of favors from a definite personality who it is hoped can be induced to do favors to the petitioner. One has only to read any prayer book to realize how far religion has found expression in flattery and cries for mercy and security. But such an attitude is quite impossible for one who in any way is acquainted with the forces of the universe and the laws which describe their operation. One would not think of petitioning atmospheric pressure to be merciful and end a drought, or the law of gravitation to prevent earthquakes. The belief in cosmic reason and will does not yield itself to pleas for forgiveness. It is not strange therefore that many have felt little warmth in the scientific approach to religion. If prayer cannot effect changes in actual situations what is the use of praying? And if that to which we look as reality is cosmic activity what is the use of petitions?

So far as I have observed, the answer to such questions depends upon how far a person continues to share the activities and companionship of the Christian group. His views may be organized as scientifically as possible and his rejection of doctrinal formulas may have left him able to treat the creeds and hymns of an older faith as poetical expressions of what to him is of his own faith, but he practices religious behavior. He is convinced that the way to establish helpful relations with those activities of the universe which he can see have produced personalized humanity is to live personally. Such a faith grows normative for action. That is to say, just because he does believe that he is organically connected with personality producing cosmic activities capable of personal response, he knows that only action making personal values supreme—that is, love—will be supported by the universe itself. Prayer is not an attempt to win a sovereign's favor but the use of a technique by which personal relations are set up. He probably will not pray for anything contrary to what he knows is natural law, but on the other hand he will not hesitate by means of thoughts and words to place himself in help-gaining relationship with what the more conventional religion would call the will of God. Prayer must not be judged by so-called answers to prayer. The one legitimate test is whether by prayer one finds one's self more enabled to give justice to other people, to serve a common rather than a selfish good and to avoid such action and purpose as would do others harm. That such power does lie in prayer will not be denied by any one who prays. Enthusiasm and sacrifice are born of the conviction that love is not futile but a personal co-operation with cosmic activities.

All symbols must be consistent with the realities which they endeavor to enforce. One can never understand the relations of God and man by plucking a flower out from the crannied wall. It must be left in the wall. Without elevating the observed sequences of the past into an all-embracing evolutionary philosophy, it is unavoidable that we should think of humanity as the outcome of a definite process which is conditioned by what we know of the relations of an organism to its environment. So long as one recognizes something more than chemical or physical reactions in humanity, the belief grows more compelling that the principle of love which Jesus enunciated and for which he died is guaranteed by our understanding of the conditions under which we live as human persons. Whether one speaks of the ultimate force of the universe as integration or concretion or co-ordination or mutuality, the love which Jesus sets forth as the ultimate requirement for human welfare is the expression of that activity on the level of personality. Religion, therefore, becomes not a mere matter of convention or a more or less superstitious performance of inherited rites, but a behavior of human life both in its individual and its corporate expression seeking helpful relationship with that which is cosmic, or in its own language, with God. Any one with such conviction will grant others full freedom in the exposition and justification of the same belief. It is not likely that he will get much help from a theological system which is born of political rather than scientific patterns, but he will feel a kinship with all those who seek to treat Jesus seriously and believe that love is a practicable basis for human relations because it is the expression of that which is ultimate in the universe. Such a faith will not explain the presence of suffering and evil, but it will give one strength to endure them and a motive to intelligent effort to ameliorate or end them. For love can be implemented by science.

V

The scientific approach to religions has an unescapable influence upon one's conception of the relation of different religions and the significance of foreign missions. Any conviction that one's weal or woe for eternity depends on the acceptance of certain theological beliefs regarding Jesus is naturally abandoned. That is not to say that all religions are equally effective in forwarding human welfare, or that they equally maintain their efficiency when the social order in which they have developed is changed by contact with another. Such opportunity as I had enjoyed to observe the operations of religions in different countries had quite prepared me to admit that a religion must be adapted to the habits and culture of its possessor. In consequence I was able to approach the relations of Christianity to the religions of Asia with a detached point of view, when in 1933, after my retirement from teaching I went with my wife to India to give the Barrows Lectures. By the terms of its founder this lectureship was intended to develop sympathetic relations between Christians and followers of other religions and in that spirit to expound Christianity itself. Charles Cuthbert Hall and A. M. Fairbairn had given the lectureship a recognized standing in India, but their attitude was on the whole apologetic. Dr. Hall believed that the East had much to contribute to Christianity but he evidently looked at Christianity as the final religion for the world. My appointment was welcome, not alone because the months of travel it involved would serve to adjust my life to that of a professor *emeritus*, but also because it gave opportunity to present Christianity from a non-apologetic, historical, and social point of view. In my lectures on *Christianity and Social Process* I endeavored to show the actual relationship of the Christian religion to Western civilization and to express the hope that Indian scholars would make the similar study of the relationship of the various religions of India to its social life. The lectures were given in seven cities of India, but in addition I spoke many times before universities and met groups of those interested in religion philosophically. The temper of the Indian people and student bodies, I was told, was not that of a generation ago. In Bombay, for instance, while I was speaking to an audience of perhaps 150 persons in the chapel of Wilson College, thousands of men and women were gathered every evening on the beach just across the street from the college to listen to political discussions. Nationalism, with its corollary of interest in the effort on the part of Gandhi to win religious and political privileges for the non-caste millions deadened interest in the discussion of a religion that all Asia is increasingly coming to regard as of alien origin. I found in a number of colleges and especially in the person of Mr. K. Natarijan, the editor of *The Indian Social Reformer,* an interest akin to mine in the social approach to religion. But the Indian mind is essentially contemplative and separates sharply between social action and religion.

Any impartial observer of the missionary movement in Asia will be impressed with its magnitude. I had supposed that I was informed regarding its progress both from reading and from contact with missionary activities in the Near East and Japan. But I really had no adequate appreciation of the extent to which it had wrought itself into the life of Asia by its churches and hospitals and educational institutions. The missionary movement can best be described as Western civilization carrying its ideals and the basis of its morals to other civilizations. Among the leading missionaries there was a growing recognition of their undertaking as something more than that of proselyting from one religion to another.

While in Japan in 1915 I had endeavored to distinguish between Christianity and Western civilization. I now came to see that such a sharp antithesis is unwarranted. Western civilization itself has been affected by Christian principles and carries those principles into all its contacts. Even the earliest missionaries became carriers of Western customs. Their introduction of some of the elements of the life of the West into the simple social structures of the Pacific Islands have not always had the best results, but they have been handicapped by the conduct of sailors and traders who were indifferent to a morality which they had to respect at home. In highly organized civilizations like those of Japan, China and India, Western civilization has carried institutions and social ideals of great influence. One cannot visit any of the cities of Asia without being impressed by the universities established by the State. To an American observer these universities, dominated as they are by English conceptions of education, seem not altogether adapted to the needs of the hundreds of millions of people who live in villages and are largely farmers. Indeed, at a convocation at the University of Allahabad, I heard one of the most distinguished men of India, Sir Taj Bahadur Sapru, declare that India needed trained engineers more than an increase in the number of young men who had only a literary education and could find no employment except as lawyers and employees of the government. To some extent this is being rectified by agricultural training and experiment like that conducted by Higginbotham in Allahabad, and Case in Burma. The economic structure of the agricultural society and the laws governing land ownership make changes difficult, but progress is undoubtedly being made not only in the provinces under British government but in the areas governed by the more liberal native princes.

A striking illustration of the extension of social service is to be seen in the great Tata Foundation in Bombay which has appointed as Director Dr. Clifford G. Mansart who already, as a missionary, has had success in the establishment of a community house where something like six hundred persons are daily in attendance.

Two distinct movements are discernible in the extension of Christian ideals into the Asiatic society. On the one side are the work of the evangelistic missions and the foundation of churches. In Japan churches have attracted the educated group and many high officials are Christians. The work of Kagawa is being extended into agriculture and industrial fields by the organization of co-operative groups. In Burma the number of converts from Buddhism is relatively small. Missionary effort has had its success among primitive races like the Karens and the Kachins and in India proper among the depressed groups which have not yet shown much ability to conduct their churches except under direction of the missionaries. One can see the importance of the work. Not only do the churches become centers of moral influence, but a new self-respect is developed among individuals. Indeed, it would be difficult to see how a movement like that of Gandhi for the increase of political and religious rights of the outcaste people would have been so great had it not been for the century of work of Christian missionaries among these same people.

But Western civilization itself as a carrier of Christian ideals has had its influence outside of church statistics. Its expression in philanthropy, education, the elevation of women and the development of constitutional government is recognizable. But further than this, all over Asia one can see the emergence of groups, some of them of considerable size, in which the effort is made to organize religious movements within native religion. This is a trend not to be confounded with that absorption of religions into Hinduism of which the fate of Buddhism is an example. These groups, appearing among different nations, conserve elements of national culture which are not altogether consistent with the ideals which they represent. How far are they traceable to the influence of Christianity is a matter of opinion, but it seems clear that they are due to the evocative power both of Western civilization and of the impact of Christianity. In Japan is Tenrikyo, a movement founded not quite a hundred years ago by a woman. It has now several million adherents among the Japanese, but it is so allied to Shintoism that it has not appealed to members of other nations. The new development in Buddhism in Japan involves ideals and institutions which are like those of Christianity. The same is true of the New Life movement in China. In India there is a surprisingly large number of these groups among the educated classes. In talking with their representatives in many university centers I found an interest in basic moral and religious conceptions and an indifference to current religious practices. I found myself at home with their ethical idealism although I could not always agree with their philosophy.

Any scientific approach to such facts as these will certainly lead to the conclusion that in the Asiatic cultures Protestantism will be regarded as a Western faith until it has been modified into something more characteristic of the Asiatic mind and social structure. As long as the Christian religion is regarded as the property of the white race, it will be identified with political imperialism or economic exploitation. At the same time it will be regarded as alien to the rapidly developing spirit of nationalism. Forward-looking missionaries I found recognizing this fact. They are endeavoring, tentatively, to introduce into the Christian worship elements of Asiatic culture like music. The history of the Christian movement in the West will undoubtedly be duplicated as it develops in the East. If a religious movement founded in Judea by Jews became in the course of a few generations anti-Jewish and later was differentiated by new political and economic forces into still other forms, it seems inevitable that in Asia it will be composed of religious groups which maintain the cultural characteristics, thought forms and many religious practices of Asiatic peoples. It may be expected that there will appear a type of religion which will not be dominated by Semitic or European and American social experience. Whether such new religious forms will be called Christian seems to me less important than their ethical and religious kinship with Christianity of the West to whose influence, direct through missions and indirect through Western civilization, they owe so much.

CHAPTER XV

RELIGIOUS EDUCATION IN THE CHURCHES

In no field has the influence of a scientific point of view been more evident than in that of religious education. The church has always given instruction to the young and this instruction has always been an extension of the methods of contemporary education. The more common forms of such instruction have been the learning of the catechism and the committing to memory of passages of the Bible. Yet the Sunday schools are comparatively modern in origin and during my boyhood the first general uniform lessons were established. I remember distinctly the discussion as to whether they should be used instead of the lessons which the Sunday school of the church itself had selected. The Uniform Lessons were chosen altogether from the Bible and were arranged in six-year cycles. The same lesson was studied by all pupils but different ages had lesson helps of different sorts. The pupil was expected to memorize a golden text each Sunday. The lesson helps had questions which the teacher was supposed to ask and which could be answered from the chosen passage of scripture.

The spread of the Sunday schools was practically universal through the country and, as the public schools became increasingly secularized, were the chief means of moral and religious education of youth. It is undeniable that the organization of Sunday schools in the nation and the world served to maintain the churches. Despite the statistics given out by revivalists the overwhelming proportion of church members come from the Sunday schools.

The movement became well organized and the publishers of lesson helps soon had large financial interests at stake. The

244

fact that the editorial committee which selected the passages for the Uniform Lessons was supported by these denominational and private publishers made any change in the system difficult.

The methods of the training in the Sunday school were very simple, but so were the methods of teaching in the public schools. The science of education was itself undeveloped and the so-called normal schools were more concerned with methods to be followed by the teacher than with the study of the children. In the Sunday school the classes were gathered in pews or settees either in the audience room of the church or in a vestry which was usually the basement of the church. There were no classrooms. The confusion, however, of teaching was not as great as might be supposed, especially if the classes were separated by one or two pews. The Sunday school room of the church which I attended had settees, the backs of which could be turned over so that the members of the class faced each other during the half hour of instruction. The *esprit de corps* of the school was kept up by various devices such as Sunday school concerts, socials and picnics. There were teachers' meetings but I do not know much about them. My father was for years Superintendent of the Sunday school and I think that his interest in getting the children to join the church was probably shared by all the teachers. With present theories of education it is easy to criticize these Sunday schools but it should not be forgotten that they were then as now the chief agency of the churches, and that there was something inspiring in the knowledge that Sunday schools whether large or small were studying the same lesson on the same day throughout the world. But the development in educational philosophy and methods, the study of the psychology of childhood and adolescence, and the gradual shift of emphasis in the study of the Bible were felt in the Sunday school. Perhaps the first evidence of change was that of the development of the Akron plan for a Sunday school building devised by Lewis Miller, one of the early manufacturers of harvesting machinery. According to this plan small classrooms were arranged around and opened into a central auditorium which was usually connected with the main auditorium of the church by movable partitions. These classrooms gave a privacy which had not been possible in the old many-setteed "vestry" and served to make more prominent the instructional element in the Sunday school. But the uniform lesson was not easily adapted to pupils of different ages. The lesson helps with their questions and answers and Golden Text were an anachronism in the educational world. In a number of theological seminaries an attempt was made by such pioneers as St. John and Pease to apply educational principles to the Sunday school.

I

As I have already said, in our Divinity School Professor Henderson gave a course in religious education, but it was again President Harper who led in the more extensive and organized effort to improve religious instruction. He became Superintendent of the Hyde Park Baptist Sunday School in Chicago and under his influence the school was reorganized according to what were regarded as strictly educational methods. Professor E. D. Burton was made Superintendent of Instruction, Professor H. E. Slaught, Examiner, and I was made Director of Benevolence. We had also a Director of Public Worship. The pupils were arranged in groups according to their grades in school and we began preparing lessons for the various grades. The material for study was exclusively the Bible but was selected on the basis of the current belief in the intellectual development of the child. Each grade had its lesson. Pupils were passed from one grade to another by examination and the teachers were themselves instructed as to the use of the new material and the methods of instruction. With President Harper and Dr. Burton as editors a series of *Constructive Bible Studies* was set up and textbooks were prepared for all different grades. Their circulation in the course of time amounted to several hundred thousand. *The Life of Christ,* which Professor Burton and I prepared, after successive revisions, is still widely used. In this series questions and written work were to lead the pupil to genuine study of the scriptures. There were other series issued by denominational and publishing houses more or less based on the idea that pupils of different ages required different material for study not merely a different type of question.

In *The Biblical World* we had an organ for arousing interest in the reform of Sunday school instruction and under the secretaryship of Dr. Clyde W. Votaw the journal endeavored to show the significance of the new biblical studies to religious education. A series of editorials in which Professor Burton and I embodied the plans which we were testing in the Hyde Park Baptist Sunday school were published in 1903 under the title *Principles and Ideals for the Sunday School.* In this volume we were ready to grant that instructional material could come from non-biblical sources such as the history of the church and missions, but the basic material was to be drawn from the Bible with what seemed an intelligent recognition of different interests of the different ages of the pupils. It was frankly based on the importance of content of lessons. In this regard it represented the idea of religious education before it had been materially affected by psychology and educational experiments. We were later, in the *Constructive Series,* to feel the influence of educational advance, but never to the extent that later theories of religious education involved. In fact the series became two, one emphasizing content and the other the pupil's interest and experience.

II

So widespread became the conviction that educational methods should be applied to the Sunday school that the time seemed ripe for organizing a movement. The existing Sunday school organizations were indifferent, if not unfriendly, to the abandonment of the uniform lessons and naturally the attitude of the publishing houses was the same. The American Institute of Sacred Literature under the leadership of President Harper called a conference of outstanding biblical scholars and such Sunday school leaders as were sympathetic with educational advance and it was decided to call a convention in the interest of religious education. The plans for this step were entrusted to a committee, but most of the work was done by President Harper and a small group of us whom he asked to co-operate. Preparations for the first convention of what became the Religious Education Association were made in detail. It was held in Chicago on February 12, 1903. The general meeting filled the great Auditorium. There was considerable anxiety on the part of some of the officials of the Sunday School Association lest the movement should become actively hostile. Those of us who were immediately concerned with its organization had no such ideas, however. To avoid mistakes I prepared the paper on the curriculum which embodied the results of the experiments in the Hyde Park Baptist Sunday School, as well as the views of specialists in the new field. For the same reason I prepared the address read by Dr. Frank W. Gausaulus. We wanted the co-operation rather than the hostility of the Sunday school organizations for there was no intention of developing religious education as a rival to the church. Dean Frank K. Sanders of Yale Divinity School was elected President of the Association, and President Harper chairman of the Executive Committee. Ira Landrith was elected General Secretary, Professor Clyde W. Votaw Editorial Secretary, and Wallace N. Stearns Financial Secretary. For a number of years the Religious Education Association held conventions in which notable men took part. As I look over the *Proceedings* of these conventions I am impressed with the breadth of interest and the thoroughly scientific treatment which was given to the various topics. Some time after the death of President Harper the Association came under the leadership of Henry F. Cope as General Secretary, and he showed real ability in carrying on its affairs. I was for years a member of the Executive Committee and was in position to observe as well as co-operate in the extension of its influence. The Religious Education Association, as the center of widespread movement, mirrored the changes which were taking place in the field of education. The curriculum as originally proposed by the Association was strictly biblical. It was not long, however, before the religious education movement came under the influence of persons who were not primarily interested in the Bible but were more concerned with the psychological aspects of education. The outstanding figure was Professor George A. Coe of Union Theological Seminary. His interest was genuinely scientific and he organized an experimental school not connected with a church. To some extent religious education became an independent movement, the educational significance of a church was minimized, and a new profession emerged. The International Sunday School Association itself recognized the strength of the movement and became the International Council of Religious Education. Its members are fully alive to modern needs and methods. Today most of the denominations have scientifically trained Secretaries of Education.

III

It must be admitted that in its earlier stages religious education was secular education dressed in a Prince Albert coat. Its representatives felt that the educational principles which were being so voluminously discussed in teachers' conventions and teachers' colleges could be carried over into the field of religion. Nor was such an extension as rash as it may seem. Education had not become as mechanized as it later became. The influence of John Dewey made the conception of education as a preparation for social living revolutionary. Why then was anything like religious education needed when general education was doing so much for the development of character? The only distinct difference which a committee of educational experts could discover was that the duty of religious education was "to put the fear of God into the youngsters." It is not strange that the professional educator looked with suspicion, if not distrust, upon the first movement in religious education, for much that it undertook to do could have been undertaken, and in many cases was undertaken, by those who made no claim to being religious. Much of the instruction was superficial but self-satisfied. The appeal to young men and women to become Directors of Religious Education was stimulated by various sorts of publicity. In Boston a store window was filled with an exhibition of the gowns and hoods of various degrees which were open to those who took the course in religious education. Throughout all this period of inexperienced enthusiasm I maintained that a distinct mistake was being made both on psychological and practical grounds in recasting religion into the psychology of ethics, the omission of lessons about God and the failure to see that a church as an institution had religious education as one of its major functions.

The dominance of the psychologist in the field of religious education has affected the conception of religion itself. Whereas Christianity as an organized religion has emphasized the influence of God upon human life, the psychologist either ignores God or with the scientific gesture of indifference consigns God to the metaphysician. It is not surprising, therefore, that religion is thought of as "the good life" to the neglect of the universal attempt on the part of man to gain help from that which is superhuman. The organization of "the good life" is highly desirable and for its accomplishment the gathering of facts by questionnaires and observation is indispensable. But it by no means exhausts that human behavior to which we give the name religion than a comparison of conclusions drawn from experiments denies cosmic activities. I cannot help feeling that until religious education passes beyond psychology to religion as a technique of relationship with those cosmic activities which we conceive of as God, it will fail to perform a much-needed function. In the long run morals will need something more for a basis than a psychology. Righteousness must be rooted in something more than interest or social convention, important as each is. Walter Lippmann, in the opening chapters of his *Preface to Morals*, describes vividly how "the acids of modernity" have eaten into the moral authority which was based upon the biblical religion. However unsatisfactory is his attempt to furnish moral authority with a new religion I do not see how such a statement can be questioned. It is indispensable that the representatives of religious education should understand Christianity as a religion and not as a phase of psychology.

It seemed to me that the movement was in distinct danger, and in 1927 I published an article in the *Christian Century* to which the editors gave the title "Let Religious Education Beware." In this article I pointed out what seemed to me certain unfortunate tendencies which needed to be corrected. The chief of these seemed to be the tendency to minimize churches as institutions, to hide God behind a smoke screen of psychology, to neglect theology by those who had had no thorough theological training, to revert to an atomistic use of biblical texts to illustrate ethical principles, and to over-emphasize techniques and questionnaires. I ventured to close my criticism with these words:

. . . A generation that is indifferent to the church, that treats the Bible unintelligently, that does not pray as Jesus taught men to pray, no matter how much it may be interested in worship and ritual, that does not seek definite results in the way of sacrificial commitment to Jesus and his ideals, is not likely to possess any morality other than that which is dependent upon contemporary *mores* and uncontrolled "self-expression." No permanent civilization has ever been built upon that sort of morality. Our hope will lie, not simply in developing religious education as a technical science and vocation, but in the training of church members and transforming and energizing church institutions to bring youth into an uplifting and transforming relationship with God and a practical, intelligent loyalty to the example and teachings of Jesus. It is to these ends that religious education is confessively devoted, and, unless it loses itself in scientific introspection, it is these ends it will serve.

I see no reason to modify this warning, but within the last two years the danger has been somewhat met by the influence of the International Council of Religious Education which is directly connected with the churches. Reaction of many pastors against immature and often tactless Directors of Education has resulted in a new interest on the part of the churches themselves in the Sunday school and of pastors in the field of religious education. We have come to see more clearly that the church itself is the institution to carry on religious education. There is, however, still a tendency among the specialists in this field to neglect the possibilities which lie in the historical study of the Bible and to make little use of biblical material for the development of morals. Such neglect is in part due to the biblical teachers themselves whose interests have too often been centered upon problems of technique rather than upon methods of introducing the results of biblical study to the rank and file of church members. The fact that the Bible cannot be handled as a body of authoritative oracles has not been sufficiently faced, and it seems as if there were real danger that religious education in our churches should revert to a use of the scriptures which is neither intelligent nor authoritative. If the teaching of the Bible is to be limited to those who are out of sympathy with the scientific method, it will be the fault of those who, having a leadership in educational fields, have neglected to put the findings of biblical study at the disposal of those who are concerned with the development of the moral and religious life of the young.

IV

A church will find its chief field of influence in the moral and religious education of the young. Those touched by the Sunday schools are much more numerous than church members. Many of them never become identified with church life and about their only source of moral idealism, as distinct from enthusiasm for some economic or cultural cause, is derived from the instruction given them by churches in their early years. The situation is very much like that in the schools. Whatever rudiments of culture the great mass of people hold are given them during the school age. There is, of course, a growing interest in adult education, and church membership might be described as adult education in Christian ideals. But it is with children that education has primarily to do. Even indifferently religious parents want their children sent to Sunday school.

I have sometimes irritated representatives of technical religious education by insisting that it is good pedagogy to have children commit to memory that which they do not understand, but which in the course of time will be influential in their lives. However much one may criticize catechetical instruction, it does lodge in the young minds material which can give content and direction to their later lives. They may cease to believe the formulas, they may evaluate them intelligently, but their ideas of religion have what might be called a quantitative content. Important as is discussion as a phase of educational discipline, it is not likely that wisdom can come from the interchange of ignorance. However scientific the methods of religious education may become, it should not neglect giving content to moral and religious instruction. If one can judge the tendencies at the present time it would seem as if this necessity was better realized than formerly. The Sunday school is one, but ideally it should not be the only means of such education. Preaching and worship can make their contribution. Such recognition of the educational function of the church will help make Christian morality an effective element in those cultural and social trends which determine social process.

Nor can religious education as a character-forming process be detached from the family. Although the public school develops some sense of citizenship and some experience of co-operative life, the child leaves the family to go to school. Such admirable societies as the Parent Teacher Association cannot obviate this fact. Unfortunately, there is the same tendency to delegate the religious education to the Sunday school. Even religious people find it easier to teach their neighbor's children than their own. But in view of what psychiatrists have shown to be the influence upon the children of tensions between parents, it becomes the elementary duty of a church to extend its educational influence into the relations of husbands and wives. Such investigation in this field as has been made indicates that the disintegration of the family cannot be measured by statistics as to divorce. The institution itself is being questioned. Its influence as a social force is being lessened without the appearance of a moral equivalent. It is encouraging to see that the trend in religious education now includes these relations which the family represents. No very significant improvement can be expected, however, if attention is centered on sex rather than on the family as a social institution wherein one generation carries over its ideals to another.

CHAPTER XVI

MODERNIZING THEOLOGICAL EDUCATION

THE ATTEMPT to bring religion into touch with modern life did not displace my interest in teaching or the development of the Divinity School of the University of Chicago. It rather deepened my conviction that a church needed intelligent leadership quite as much as pious living on the part of its minister. However well the old scholastic training may have been adapted to the less complicated world in which it was organized, it certainly is anachronistic in our modern world. The churches are leaking at the top. Bible Institutes and similar institutions which distrusted modern culture are flooding the country with religious workers whose literalistic interpretation of the Bible limits the appeal of Christianity to those unaffected by contemporary intellectual forces. I did not go as far as I heard one distinguished educator say, that one of these schools was doing more harm than good, for Christianity even though it be unintelligent will inspire generous and clean living. But Protestant churches cannot deal with the masses of people like Roman Catholicism. The Protestant would make the masses theologically minded while the Catholic church leaves theological discussion to a technically trained priesthood and demands of the laity an implicit faith in the doctrines of the church and the performance of prescribed duties. There is undoubted efficiency in such policy.

But what is to be the relation of the Protestant churches with men and women who have lost belief in the supernatural claims of both the priest and the minister and yet need religion for

255

moral efficiency? An anachronistic religion may deal with anachronisms; makers of tomorrow need a religion that is creative. But how shall it be creative without ministers who have an intelligent, though oftentimes critical sympathy with social trends, and who have acquired at least some degree of professional training in meeting the conditions of a world in which they actually live. The attitude of the clergy will inevitably become that of the people. But conversely the clergy are influenced and in some cases controlled by church authorities or by congregations. In consequence they do not display initiative in social change and their relations with the community are generally social. Their attempts at reform are generally limited to attacks on evils from which church members are exempt. If they are conservative they are more apt to have the support of church membership but if they are progressive they can become centers of influence around which the more progressive minorities may gather. In consequence the training of those who are to become religious leaders is a matter of extreme concern. If church circles are to center their attention upon preparation for heaven and the avoidance of certain practices of contemporary social life, they will have little wisdom, even less enthusiasm for the development of a better social order.

I

The importance of training young men for wise leadership in a period of rapid transformation has always been uppermost in my conception of the task of the Divinity School. It was not difficult to set up personal friendships with students in the school. Many of them were older than I when I began my theological teaching and we represented about the same social group. We could understand each other. A real difficulty arises, however, as the theological professor himself grows older. He is less in touch with the changes within the world from which his students come and to which they must go. He is in danger of diverting his students from clearly understanding the function of their task as leaders of religious movements to technical problems in which he has become interested. As time passes he loses his sense of comradeship with younger persons who increasingly represent new social situations. I have seen theological professors, who, starting out thoroughly *en rapport* with men of their own age and sensitive to the needs of their own generation, have gradually lost touch with the ambitions and problems of another generation. They no longer belong to a world that is passing beyond them. They may stimulate individual piety, they may further theological scholarship, but they do not contribute to an intelligent religious leadership.

II

One problem in the Divinity School at the University of Chicago was always before us. On the one hand we were determined to keep abreast of scientific procedure in our field and on the other hand we were to function as a professional school. How could these two interests be combined? It would have been comparatively easy to develop along lines of conventional theological training, adding certain advanced courses for those who wished to become specialists. That in general describes the policy of progressive schools when I first came to the University of Chicago. Nor would it have been difficult to develop into a graduate school of religion in which research was dominant and no more attention would be given to the practical concerns of our students' careers than was given by the Graduate School of Arts and Literature, where the fact that practically all its students were to become teachers did not lead to the consideration of teaching as a profession. The fact that we enjoyed full academic freedom and were constantly publishing the results of our study led the friends of strictly denominational seminaries to describe our efforts in the latter term. I remember being at an alumni meeting of one of these seminaries in which the President stated that if men wanted to become specialists in Hebrew they ought to go to the Divinity School of the University of Chicago, but if they wished to become pastors, they ought to go to his seminary. Indeed, so far were we misrepresented in the competition for students that it was stated that we had given up preparing men for the ministry—and that too in the face of the fact that we were giving more courses in preparation for the pastorate than almost any theological seminary in the country.

As a matter of fact, we were endeavoring to introduce into the training for religious leadership something of scientific interest in the field of religion. It was clear that theological training which did not begin with dogmatic authority must needs develop confidence in methods of reaching reality. The tentative character of research had to be recognized and adjusted to religious teaching and church organization. It was a genuinely educational problem, all the more difficult since the authority of revelation and doctrinal formulation was—as it still is in most seminaries—commonly regarded as the proper point of departure in theological teaching. Liberals in religion needed to be taught how to organize effective churches.

We set our faces in the Divinity School to answer these questions. I conceived of our mission as summarized in three terms—reality, efficiency and contagious faith. From one point of view we have always been on the defensive, but our defense has consisted in positive rather than controversial methods. Probably no group of theological teachers in our day has been subject to more bitter attacks than we, but we have almost never been drawn into controversy. At the beginning of the period of theological agitation I sought to organize my attitude in accordance with a conviction which has been repeatedly justified by experience. I have been humanly sensitive to misrepresentation, and I dare say I have said things that I had better have left unsaid; but my religious optimism has precipitated itself in a general formula—honest men may differ while seeking the same ends but when reconciliation comes the other person should have nothing to forgive.

I am not so self-righteous as to think that in our effort to combine the scientific attitude with institutional efficiency we have altogether avoided that condescension which too often characterizes religious teachers who have no institutional responsibility, but in our experimenting with theological education we have honestly endeavored to make reliable results contribute to religious efficiency.

We felt our way cautiously. Our first step was to reorganize biblical studies. At the suggestion of President Harper, who was himself the head of the department of Semitic Languages and Literature, courses in the content of the Old Testament and the history of the Hebrew people were substituted for Hebrew as a requirement for the D.B. degree. For a number of years Greek continued to be required for that degree, but increasingly students who came to us had no more knowledge of Greek than they had of Hebrew. High schools and colleges no longer insisted on the study of the classical languages and it seemed a waste of time to compel mature men to study the elements of Greek when there was every probability they never would achieve any real efficiency in the use of the language. Consequently at the suggestion of the New Testament department a course in the teaching of Jesus was substituted for the Greek requirement. At the same time the two departments offered many elective courses which involved the use of the original languages of the Bible.

The test of efficiency by which these changes were made in the study of the Bible was extended to other fields. Courses were prescribed for a degree which seemed especially needed by those who were to organize religious life through the churches. An understanding of the religious value of the Bible, courses in the relation of church and society, the history of

Christian ethics, thought and institutions, church management, music, public speaking, the technique of religious education, the psychology of religion, some acquaintance with psychiatry and the organization of one's own theology we believed contributed directly to efficient religious leadership. Women were admitted on the same basis as men. As far as practicable the remunerative work by our students was made a part of the curriculum. At the same time we organized and directed research work on the part of advanced students who were studying for the doctorate.

III

My relation to these progressive changes in curriculum was set largely by circumstances. In 1899 as an inducement to remain at Chicago rather than accept the presidency of an Eastern college I was made Junior Dean of the Divinity School. My particular duty was oversight of the first-year students. But it was not long before I found myself undertaking a good many tasks outside that field. My responsibility was not very taxing, for President Harper was the dominant influence in the school and Dr. E. B. Hulbert, its great-hearted Dean, had no particular ambition to strike out along other lines than those which the President suggested.

During the early years of my association with the University I became a sort of chore boy, never refusing a task however uninteresting it might be. I visited churches and associations in the interest of raising funds to assist the all but universally impecunious theological students, served on committees, and at the same time worked feverishly at critical problems and preparation of lectures on subjects which were entirely new to me. I was constantly reminded of the young professor of anatomy who, being asked how he was getting on, replied that he was doing splendidly, he was always one bone ahead of his class.

At Dr. Harper's suggestion I engaged in an interesting educational experiment—the organization of a class to study biblical history in Palestine. I was responsible for all the details and found myself a combination of a traveling courier and lecturer. The class which finally organized numbered seven and only three could be fairly described as theological students. One of the others was Walter Williams, Dean of the School of Journalism and later President of the University of Missouri. I had visited Palestine in 1897, and in 1902 the country had not greatly changed. Archaeological exploration had been going on for a number of years but nothing on its present scale. The influx of Jews was already considerable but political difficulties were not serious. The Turkish rule was not friendly to change and with the exception of few roads about Jerusalem there were no carriage roads in the country. The Bedouin still drove their flocks into the Jordan valley. It was possible, therefore, to get historical feeling which would help in understanding biblical material.

Enjoyable as was the experience I have never since had any ambitions to lead parties, although opportunities have not been lacking. The University continued these classes, giving residence credit to those who wished to do the necessary work and take examinations, but in the course of a few years they became hardly more than tourist parties and upon my suggestion they ceased to be aspects of University life.

At the death of Dean Eri Baker Hulbert in 1908 I was made Dean of the Divinity School. In the University of Chicago a Dean is a professor who undertakes certain tasks while maintaining his classwork. This rather unusual policy was intended to prevent the detachment of deans from academic interests. Personally, for instance, I have always carried a professor's load of classroom instruction. The relation of the departments with the President's office was direct and questions of the budget were referred by them to him. In the case of the professional schools circumstances tended to make the Dean rather more directive than in the case of the Graduate Schools of Arts, Literature and Science, but I always regarded myself as the administrative officer of the faculty. Changes in curriculum and in organization were not taken without essentially the unanimous vote of the faculty. It became clear, however, that department organization in the Divinity School was artificial and I felt that the real basis of organization was fields of interest in which various departments could co-operate. Some progress was made in this direction.

In 1931 the committee on the study of ministerial education in America made under the joint auspices on the Conference of Theological Seminaries and the Institute of Social and Religious Research proposed a rearrangement of courses in three divisions; the first included those disciplines giving the historical approach to religion and Christianity; the second those concerned with the interpretation of Christianity, including theology, religious psychology and social aspects of Christianity; and the third, those covering the work of the church and the ministry. Under my successor, Dean Shirley J. Case, the Divinity School completed the organization of group instruction in fields rather than departments.

IV

We have been able to experiment without being subject to denominational or other control. Many of our changes were tentative and some of them did not meet the needs of students. Fortunately in our student body there have been those who have specialized in the field of education and their reactions both to existing and proposed methods have been decidedly helpful. In one case I was waited upon by a group of these advanced students who, with the utmost consideration, reported to me that in their opinion one of our departments was doing unsatisfactory work. The situation obviously had within it serious possibilities. I did not wish to hurt the feelings of the department concerned and yet the criticisms seemed too just to be neglected. In consequence I asked the faculty to appoint a committee on curriculum which would consult with a similar committee appointed by the Student Council. Nothing could have been more admirable than the resulting discussions and the department concerned never suspected the real situation. The co-operation between students and the faculty became helpful. It is perhaps worth noticing that these critical students are at present holding important positions on college and seminary faculties.

In the field of sociology Professor Charles Richmond Henderson was, by virtue of his experience and his acknowledged leadership in the field of charities and correction, particularly well fitted to arouse the students' interest in human affairs. He gave only one or two courses especially for theological students, but those which he offered on the family and various forms of social amelioration and charity were invaluable for men who were to become pastors. At his death his work was taken over and expanded by courses which I gave in the relation of church and society, and more technical courses offered by Professor Arthur E. Holt of the Chicago Theological Seminary who was appointed as a member of our faculty. After the establishment of the School of Social Service Administration in the University it was possible for our students to enter its courses. For a number of years a member of its staff gave a course each year specially intended for our students, and the two schools co-operated in open lectures in the field of psychiatry. Formal courses in the latter field were given by Dr. Boisen of the Chicago Theological Seminary. We made plans for the establishment for a scientific study of the psychology of religion and called a man to a professorship. Much to our regret he declined the call and the depression has made it impossible to do more than employ guest professors. In planning for this type of work we had the hearty co-operation of members of the

University departments of psychology, sociology and education.

It was characteristic of President Harper and Professor Henderson that they foresaw the development in the field of Sociology and there was organized in the University a College of Religious and Social Sciences co-ordinate with the other colleges. I was entrusted with its administration but it was too far in advance of its time to be successful, and with the establishment of the school of Social Service Administration it passed out of the picture. I fear that its inefficiency was due to a failure on my part to see its possibilities quite as much as to the practical difficulties which such a school then faced. Social service had not become a vocation. When that did occur there was little or no appreciation of the need of an intelligent understanding of the function of the churches on the part of social workers.

Professor Henderson was one of the very first to see the importance of religious education and gave one course in that subject, although he was not technically trained in education methods. His course was the beginning of the development of a large and influential department.

V

On the university campus where one met such men as Von Holt, Michelson, Laughlin, Dewey, Small and where the air was charged with the incredible activity of its president, it was impossible to escape the impulse to write. The members of the Divinity Faculty and Conference have published something like three hundred volumes. At the time I joined the Faculty the University Press was publishing a number of journals, among them two and, in the course of a few years, three which were edited by those immediately associated with the work of the Divinity School. I have already mentioned my first writing was for the *American Journal of Sociology,* a series of articles subsequently published as the *Social Teaching of Jesus.* I was the professor of

New Testament history. The seminaries generally gave a sketch of the inter-biblical period but I doubt if any scholar in America forecast the influence which historical study was to have upon views as to the New Testament and its theological bearing. German scholars were dealing with the factual elements of the period with characteristic precision. Schürer had already published the first edition of his great work, and Harnack was producing those extraordinary essays and volumes which it is now the fashion of theologians who have little historical feeling to treat rather superciliously. But his influence and that of Hatch were felt in the field of early church history rather than in the historical approach to the New Testament itself.

Without any one's giving it serious attention there was being developed an antithesis between the inherited view of the New Testament as a body of oracles and as a group of writings selected from the stream of early Christian literature. The traditional view determined the departmental organization of theological schools, but in the University of Chicago there was a New Testament Department in the Divinity School and a Department of Biblical and Patristic Greek in the Graduate School of Arts. Professor Burton was the head of both departments and the instructors were the same, some of them being carried on the budget of the Divinity School and others on that of the Graduate School. The two departments were more interested in the philological, critical and literary study of the New Testament than in the attempt to locate the literature in a historic movement. It was only gradually that the recognition of Christianity as historically conditioned by its contemporary life influenced the study of the New Testament. It was Professor Burton's ambition to develop an English lexicon of the New Testament, and during one winter a number of us worked on the scheme. But my social and historical interest soon outweighed that in lexicographical details.

I published a volume on *The History of the New Testament*

Times in Palestine. It was largely in the method of Schürer, although written by the use of sources which were available. A few years ago I rewrote the book from the point of view of social psychology. The period from Alexander to Hadrian called for a study of revolutionary psychology which furnished the thought patterns and point of contact of Jesus.

VI

Associations within our faculty have always been helpful. We did not attempt to get absolute agreement in our teaching and in some cases the differences were distinctly marked. Among those devoted to the scientific study of religion such differences are inevitable and it would have been contrary to academic freedom to attempt any coerced uniformity. At the same time we constantly exchanged opinions and I owe much to the suggestions of my colleagues. No attempt has ever been made to enforce our views upon the student body. We have asked only to be understood. Agreement was wholly within the students' choice. During my administration we had something like ten thousand students. They were drawn from all denominations of Christians. I remember only a few cases of students who changed their denominational relations and of these three became Episcopalians. Many students would have preferred to be told what to believe rather than to be taught how to believe. Religious faith is quite as emotional as intellectual. Perhaps even more so. Loyalty to a religious organization seldom changes. If our freedom of thought and emphasis sometimes confused students, it at least made plain that Christianity was not a mass of authoritative dogma but a moral and religious social movement. I remember one student complained, "One professor teaches one thing and another teaches something different. I don't know enough to choose between the views and I am going to join a church that will tell me what I ought to believe." He did this and has won success in his new relations.

Mature students deserve to be treated as mature. For them personal relations with different professors make the best approach to dealing with intimate problems. It was one of my privileges as Dean to have students come to me for brotherly and later, I dare say, fatherly advice in regard to all sorts of perplexities. Some of my warmest friendships have been with these men and women.

If religious leadership were purely individualistic and Christianity were a philosophy instead of a religious movement, the problems of a scientific theological education would be comparatively simple. But in point of fact, whether they were to become teachers or preachers, students had to take into account the religious bodies with whom they were to work. If we can trust their own statements the atmosphere of the Divinity School, the historical and social approach to religion enabled them to see the permanent elements in their ecclesiastical inheritance. Our efforts have been constructive rather than negative. Changes in religious beliefs were to be the outcome not of the abandonment of doctrines but of the development of a new sense of their real meaning for the religious and moral life. John Dewey somewhere says that the problems of philosophy are not solved but are outgrown. That is equally true of the problems of theology.

Some of the most satisfactory experiences of my life have been the building up of friendships with young ministers who never were our students but who have confided to me their theological restlessness and have found in the type of thought which we were developing in the Divinity School a help in the adjustment of their denominational relations. When they came to see that doctrines were functional rather than final they were able to co-operate with those from whom they otherwise might easily have become estranged.

VII

The needs of our Divinity School were always evident. It was not possible to draw more heavily upon the general funds of the University and we needed better accommodations for our married students, for our religious and academic work, and above all increased endowment for the expansion of our research. The University in a way met the first need by putting at our disposal several apartment buildings so that in the course of time we had something like thirty apartments, from four to seven rooms, most of them furnished, in which our married students could live. It was one of my hopes that funds could be found for the erection of a building better adapted to such purposes, but as yet the want has not been filled. But, thanks to the generosity of Mrs. Anna Swift and her family, the school was provided with a splendid building which in a most satisfactory way meets our needs. The generosity of Mrs. Joseph Bond also made it possible to erect a beautiful chapel as a memorial to her husband, a man whom I had respected and admired. The endowment needs were met by a gift of $100,000 by Mrs. Swift and of a million dollars by John D. Rockefeller, Jr. With this addition to our funds it was possible to increase our faculty in numbers, and thus furnish opportunity for study by the graduates of other seminaries and especially by those who were planning to become teachers in seminaries and religious departments of colleges. Our former students are now teaching in more than a hundred theological seminaries and in a much larger number of colleges. They are serving as pastors in hundreds of churches and extending Christian influence to intellectual and social life. Some of them have made noteworthy contributions to theological literature. It is probably correct to say that generally they represent a realistic view of religion and I like to think that our emphasis upon a scientific approach to contemporary individual and social needs has helped forward a morally vital rather than a merely doctrinal conception of Christianity.

While our students would generally be regarded as sympathizing with the more liberal and progressive school of theological thought, they have seldom engaged in controversy. The most anti-religious persons with whom I have been acquainted, almost without exception, are men who have been educated in a rigorously authoritative seminary and have never been taught a method of intellectual readjustment.

VIII

We have been able to experiment also in Christian co-operation in theological education. In the first years of the University there was founded a Disciples' Divinity House. While not treated as another Divinity School it became the center of influence in the Disciples' body. Its students are registered in the Divinity School, but the House has its own endowment and an admirable building. The influence of such men as Professor Edward S. Ames of the Department of Philosophy and of Dr. Herbert L. Willett who was for years dean of the school, has permeated their denomination, and in the face of much opposition has found expression in the Campbell Institute which represents the liberal wing of the Disciples.

The Cumberland Presbyterians established another House, but it never met with success and finally ceased to exist. The Universalists moved their theological seminary from Galesburg and built a fine building on the campus. It had only a few students and only one professor. Finally it was combined with Meadville Theological Seminary.

For a number of summers the Unitarian seminary at Meadville, Pa., held its summer sessions in connection with the Divinity School and furnished one professor for the faculty of the Summer Quarter. In 1926 the seminary was moved to Chicago and erected or bought buildings in the immediate neighborhood of the University. Its students are usually registered also in the Divinity School.

A close affiliation has grown up between the Chicago Theological Seminary, a Congregational institution of distinguished history, and the Divinity School. The Congregational Seminary was established in good buildings on the west side of Chicago. As a detached seminary, however, it ceased to attract students who preferred schools in connection with a university like Yale or Union or our own Divinity School. It was one of the plans of President Harper to affiliate this school and bring it to the region of the University, but negotiations fell through because of unfortunate circumstances. With the coming of Dr. Ozora S. Davis, as President of the seminary, however, the project was revived. He and I worked out a general plan of affiliation which was satisfactory to the authorities of the University and the seminary, and in 1912 the seminary moved to the vicinity of the University and there was an interchange of courses between the two institutions. At first the Seminary did not have adequate buildings, but its students had the free use of those of the University. Its friends, however, made possible a dormitory, assembly hall and library which now have been supplemented by three residences for women students and married students. By the will of Victor Lawson the seminary was left a very large sum of money and its work was developed. It has been able to co-operate with the Congregational City Mission Society, and under the guidance of Dr. Arthur E. Holt and Dr. Samuel C. Kinchelow it has made notable contributions to a scientific understanding of church life in Chicago and vicinity. Dr. Holt also has been deeply interested in various phases of economic struggle, especially those concerned with the milk supply of the city. His experience made him the inevitable choice as chairman of the Committee of Social Action which the National Council of the Congregational and Christian Churches has established. With its endowment, magnificent buildings and intimate contact with the life of the community, the Chicago Theological Seminary has become one of the significant denominational schools of America. Our relations have been marked by uniform consideration and co-operation. When points of uncertainty arose they were never allowed to develop into disagreements and there has been geniune fellowship on the part of both the faculty and students.

IX

Attempts to have students of the University planning to go as medical missionaries study in the Divinity School were not successful. The pressure of medical courses left no time for our courses. As a class they seemed uninterested in religious education although they were to work in religious affiliations. I suspect, too, that many religious bodies whose students were thus preparing for medical mission work were afraid of exposing their students to our liberal influence.

In endeavoring to prepare other workers for the mission field we were brought face to face with a policy of missionary Boards against which I repeatedly protested. Thanks to the wealth of courses throughout the University and to our own department of Missions, we were in position to prepare students for specific fields. But after completing an education which did not differ from that of those preparing to go into the pastorate or teaching in America, they were assigned mission fields in countries about which they knew practically nothing. We soon found that it was impossible to prepare men as missionaries because of this opportunist policy on the part of the Boards. In the case of missionaries on furlough, however, the situation is fortunately very different. Men and women who had been in the foreign field have come to feel the need of special study and the Boards are ready to permit them to take up graduate study with us as well as with other institutions that offer opportunity for research and special training. We must have had seven hundred such missionaries studying with us. One of the pleasures of travel in Asia was to meet former students in practically every city to which I went.

We endeavored to get the co-operation of those specially interested in the matter in a research project concerned with the actual relationship of the Christian movement to the cultures of the East. Several missionaries were given special training in the department of Sociology and Anthropology for that purpose. We went so far as to prepare a very elaborate questionnaire on the general status of Eurasians. The results of our efforts were not satisfactory, although in one or two cases our former students have made distinct contributions to the scientific study of non-Christian religions, and the civilizations to which they belong. Our general point of view has been admirably set forth by our professor of Missions, Archibald G. Baker, in his work, *Christian Missions and New World Cultures*.

X

The more I came to understand the relation of theological seminaries to the world with which I had become acquainted in my other activities, the more I felt that there was distinct need of an inventory of their efficiency. In 1924 I proposed to the Conference of Theological Seminaries that there should be appointed a committee for the purpose of studying the efficiency of the seminaries. As a result a committee was appointed of which I was a member and Wm. Adams Brown was the chairman. For a year or so very little was done and President Eislin of Garrett Biblical Institute, President Davis of the Chicago Theological Seminary and I determined to carry on an independent investigation so far as our own institutions were concerned and obtained the necessary funds. I called on Mr. Galen Fisher, secretary of the Institute of Social and Religious Research, to get his judgment on our plans which were in the nature of "job analysis," and found that the Institute was considering a proposition to make such an investigation along lines suggested by Professor Brown. A conference was called of a number of men interested in the matter. Discussion showed some difference of opinion as to just what was needed, but the Institute undertook to finance an investigation which covered the various proposals. Mark A. May was put in charge and Professor Brown was made theological adviser. I was a member of an Advisory Committee which not only co-operated in the work itself but acted as an editorial board. This report, when it appeared, was in three volumes entitled *The Education of American Ministers,* with a fourth volume written by Professor Brown which summarized the work of the Report. I do not know how much attention has been given the Report but I doubt if among all the publications of the Institute there is any more thorough or elaborate. Thanks to the interest of Professor Brown, the Conference of Theological Schools determined to develop interest on the part of the seminaries and Professor Sherrill of the Louisville Theological Seminary, has been designated to give part of his time for the secretaryship. The difficulties due to the denominational control on the part of most seminaries are considerable, but there are evidences that they realize that they are dealing with a modern world. Social service and religious education are now being given increased attention and outgrown disciplines are being abandoned. Denominational inertia and the over-supply of uneducated and so inexpensive ministers are the chief obstacles to a general reorganization of theological education.

I have been repeatedly asked whether the quality of theological students is improving or deteriorating. I cannot see any particular change. Theological students are about the same grade as students in Graduate Schools. The real difference between them and other professional students is chiefly between those who are and those who are not swayed by non-acquisitive motives. And averages are always misleading. I have had few stupid students—they would not be allowed to remain in the Divinity School. On the other hand I have had several men of genius. Not a few of those who entered teaching won widespread recognition. To judge from such statistics as are available, those who became pastors have been rather more efficient than others. But here again conclusions must be tentative. In overseeing the investigation as to ministerial success made by the Institute of Social and Religious Research I found the investigator forced to use multiple rather than single criteria. That is what would be expected if Christianity be a religious group behavior rather than a theological algebra. And the influence of a religion can never be statistically stated.

CHAPTER XVII

FUNDAMENTALISM AND MODERNISM

As ONE looks back over the years which lie between the world of my youth and that of today, the period seems to be not only transitional but creative. During it appeared epoch-making advance in the subjection of the natural forces to the production of wealth, new means of communication which all but abolished space, the concentration of capital, the rise of a new class-consciousness, mass production of almost every needed article, the over-extension of agriculture into marginal land, the beginnings of national control of corporations and a new sense of the inefficiency of the eighteenth century individualism. Due to the vast immigration the psychology of America was changing, and the country was rapidly ceasing to be isolated from European life. The problem of our relations with Asia took on a new character because of the modernization of Japan, the eastward expansion of Russia and the beginning of political ferment in China and India. It was inevitable that such momentous changes should have influenced Christian groups and that religious men should seek to give them moral direction.

I have already sketched the efforts which were made to accomplish this end. The lack of precedents made them naturally tentative and their success varied in about the same proportion as religious persons and institutions grew conscious of the new conditions and endeavored to treat them as data rather than as obstructions to faith. Gradually those who realized the new trends were known as Modernists and those who felt that the religious efficiency involved the maintenance of theological and ecclesiastical *status quo* became known as Fundamentalists. The

275

real difference between the two groups lay deeper than theology. It was the contrast of two religious attitudes toward cultural and social elements in the changing world.

The scholastic habit of speaking of the church as if it were a uniformly organized group of Christians obscures the fact that the history of the Christian movement is one of repeated differentiation. So long as the idea of the Catholic church prevailed, this differentiation was largely limited to the rise of monastic orders and these were usually brought under the control of Rome. With the rise of nationalist churches the differentiation varied largely in proportion as the state was accustomed to democratic procedures. In Lutheran countries there was practically no emergence of non-conformist groups with the exception of Moravians. In England, on the contrary, non-conformity triumphed over opposition and by the eighteenth century was well grounded in English society. It was, however, in America that the differention was most in evidence. The absence of state churches and the spirit of liberty natural in a new country with expanding frontiers, led to the establishmnt of religious bodies responsive to the democratic trends. Theological differences led to organization of great numbers of sects, some of which grew into considerable denominations. With the exception of the Unitarian and Universalist denominations, these new bodies were as a rule, theologically evangelical.

I

It was a new phase of this differentiation when minorities in various denominations undertook to reinterpret their religious heritage in the light of new knowledge and social trends. Had they lived in the first half of the nineteenth century they would probably have organized a new denomination. As it was they became a leaven of religious adjustment within the churches themselves. It was natural that those who had not come under the influence of scientific method and social ideals should oppose the movement. The opposition had already begun before the outbreak of the World War, but the conflict-psychology which the war stimulated focused the enmity to change and led to a determined effort in several denominations to force the so-called Modernist group out from the churches. That theological differences did not lead to ecclesiastical schism was due to the fact that the Modernist group attempted to avoid controversy by insisting upon its right to remain in a denomination, its loyalty to the permanent values of Christianity and its support of the work of denominations represented by mission boards and other institutions.

Where a church had a constitutional basis like the Westminster Confession, controversy was more formally legal than in the case of denominations organized on the basis of Congregational polity without any authoritative Confession. But its psychology was the same. To the orthodox, Christianity was based upon the Bible as authority. The absence of an authoritative Confession did not affect the general position of a denomination but it left the door open for the minority to insist upon the right to its own interpretation of the Bible as a guide for faith and life. In the Baptist denomination the struggle was particularly intense because of the efforts of the so-called Fundamentalist group to induce the Northern Baptist Convention to adopt some Confession as a basis for the exclusion of the Modernist group. But in so doing, they chose a position in which they could be opposed on the basis of the historic refusal of the Baptist churches to accept an authoritative Confession or creed. To adopt one meant the abandonment of denominational liberties. On this ground the Convention finally acted, insisting that the Baptist denomination accepted only the New Testament as a basis for belief and practice. Throughout all these controversies a practical issue was whether or not dissenters should continue to support existing boards. In the case of the Presbyterians a reactionary group established its own theological seminary and endeavored to set up its own mission operations. This led to the trial of a number of clergymen on the charge of disloyalty to existing denominational agencies and theological questions were thus side-tracked to the discussion of denominational solidarity.

As in other periods of tension in Christian history, decision was being made as to the general direction of evangelical Protestantism. Both parties recognized this fact and each undertook to shape the future of the various denominations in accordance with what seemed to it to be the ultimate conception of Christianity. The Fundamentalist movement was orthodoxy struggling to preserve not merely its doctrines but the inerrant authority of the Bible. To succeed it had to oppose science and other elements of a developing culture. The Modernist movement regarded doctrines as relative to the needs begotten by new social and cultural conditions. Both alike regarded themselves as loyal to the Christian religion.

II

It may have been because of my sympathies, but it seemed to me that the tactics of the Fundamentalist group were those of the period in which the orthodox formulas were drawn up. It is, of course, true that they made no recourse to force, but their language was often intemperate and their actions were repeatedly open to ethical criticism. But it is to be borne in mind, that the issue touched the very depths of human emotions. The future of Christianity seemed at stake. From the point of view of orthodoxy Modernism was attacking the basis of Christianity itself.

This opinion was especially strong among pre-millenarians. To them the Bible was not only a collection of proof texts but it was a revelation as to the future. The early Christians expected that their own life-expectancy was the measure of the world's existence and that Jesus would return from Heaven visibly with a trumpet blowing to call the dead up from the under-world, change all believers into likeness to his spiritual body and establish a judgment day for all mankind. These events, of course, did not take place but the expectation was in the Bible and regardless of any chronological difficulty it was transferred to our own day. Exegetically I think the pre-millenarians are more correct than the post-millenarians, but they gave orthodoxy the emotional intensity to be expected on the part of those whose central religious interest is in the Book of Revelation. The good effect of such loyalty to Jesus is to be seen in well-ordered lives, a devotion to those who are in distress and piety which is as sincere as it is self-denying. But pre-millenarians have introduced into church life the intolerance of those whose faith is not susceptible to rational examination and churches in which they are numerous are apt to be divided.

Before the war I had foreseen the serious consequences to organized religious life which lay in the development of this belief. The more it grew the more would the interest in the constructive extension of Christianity in social life be threatened. The extraordinary program for the future which became elaborated into a succession of miraculous events, all of which were supported by quotations from the Bible, convinced me that somebody ought to face the situation frankly. The attempts of liberal minded conservatives to combat pre-millenarianism by post-millenarianism, that is to say, to show that the Bible implied that the millennium would precede rather than follow the coming of Christ, were unsatisfactory, for they still preserved the Messianic expectation of the primitive church. For those who hold that the center of Christianity is the Nicene Creed such a view was a relief. At first I found it so myself, since it enabled one to think of the coming of the Kingdom of God as a social process in which it might be said that there were a series of judgment days and a spiritual coming of Christ. But my study of Jewish messianic hope made such a use of New Testament conceptions possible only by exegetical violence, if not casuistry. It seemed imperative that the issue should be definitely stated as one which involved the abandonment of the early Jewish expectations found in the New Testament literature. Such a view was not difficult for those who had the historical and critical approach to the Bible, but it was bound to be opposed not only from the point of view of official orthodoxy but particularly from the point of view of those who found in the expectation of the second coming of Christ a blessed hope. To avoid involving the Federal Council and the Northern Baptist Convention in what I expected would be certain attack, I waited until my term of office as President of both bodies had expired and in 1917 published a little tract entitled *Will Christ Come Again?* In this I showed that the pre-millenarian view was a restatement of the Jewish expectations preserved in the New Testament and that it was inconsistent with actual facts. The American Institute of Sacred Literature has issued many thousands of this tract. The response of the leaders of pre-millenarian movement was prompt and sometimes bitter. In fact, a considerable pamphlet literature grew up about it, and after the war the issue was so sharply drawn that more elaborate discussions followed, notably the two volumes by my colleague, Professor Shirley J. Case, *The Millennial Hope* and the *Commentary on Revelation*.

III

The true approach to Christian religion has seemed to me to be through an understanding of the values it conserved and participation in organizing its operations for larger efficiency in dealing with individuals and groups. To approach Christianity from the point of view of some philosophy seems less realistic than an understanding of the concrete Christian movement itself. My training as a historian has made me dubious as to any explanation or justification of Christianity indifferent to its nature as a religion conserving permanent values in patterns susceptible to historical evaluation. Despite the fact that I have been a rather special object of attack, my participation in religious activities made me more sympathetic with conservatives than was the case of some of my friends who approached problems of religion from the point of view of some current philosophy. The study of the various religions and of Christianity in particular has convinced me that the task which confronts the church is not so much the discovery of truth as the organization of life in loyalty to the realistic view of men's relation to the universe and to one another, as persons. However valuable and inspiring a philosophy of religion may be, religion itself is concrete.

From such point of view theological change follows an extension of the Christian religion itself. Its history has repeatedly been marked by such extension both in doctrines and institutions. As I have already pointed out the first movement toward the historical and literary study of the Bible was not theologically critical. Its representatives became increasingly interested in technical matters of Biblical study but believed heartily that they were contributing to a better use of the Bible in the religious life. The critical scholars of the last decade of the nineteenth century and the first years of the twentieth century were dominated by the belief that they were giving the churches a new appreciation of the Bible.

One has only to read such books as Dodd's *Origin and Nature of the Bible,* the various volumes of George Adam Smith, Salmon's *Introduction to the New Testament,* and Kent's volume on the *Origin and Permanent Values of the Old Testament,* to speak only of a few, to see how sincerely the leaders of the critical school believed that they were setting forth the Bible as a "concrete revelation of God's character and will through the life and experiences of a race from the hearts of inspired men," to quote Kent's statement relative to the Old Testament. What they did not realize was that such a study took away from the

Bible its supernatural authority as a divine revelation and made it a contribution to religious life with only such authority as might be found within experience. It furthermore failed to recognize the significance of the Christian religion itself as distinct from the Biblical literature. I shared in this indifference because I had not realized the real significance of history as something more than a presentation of facts. My *New Testament Times in Palestine* in its first edition was hardly more than a presentation of what might be called a historical background of the gospel. In writing my *Messianic Hope in the New Testament* I first appreciated the fact that the ideas and conceptions of Jesus and the apostles were those of contemporary Judaism. But even then I did not clearly see the real bearing of this fact. When I was transferred from the field of New Testament history to that of theology I had very little acquaintance with theology. Yet Ritchlianism had indirectly influenced me and for a number of years I undertook to teach theology as the "content of the gospel." So far as I knew, the method I adopted was novel. My lectures fell into three parts. The first was a presentation of the teachings of the New Testament in the spirit of biblical theology. The second part dealt with an evaluation of such teaching and the third was a constructive statement. The method was pioneering, ignoring Christianity itself as a religious movement. *The Gospel and the Modern Man* published in 1910 was an elaboration of the evaluating process. The modern man I regarded as one who was under the influence of the forces that were making the future. After describing these forces as best I could, I undertook to show how the gospel as set forth in the New Testament could be accepted by one who was sympathetic with scientific and social trends. The total effect was a restatement of evangelicalism as if there had not been any contribution to Christianity from the days of the New Testament. In 1907, however, I gave a course of lectures at Harvard summer school of theology on the "Social Aspects of

Christian Doctrine." I undertook to show how Christian doctrines had social as well as individual application. Something of the same thing had been attempted by President William De-Witt Hyde of Bowdoin College in his volume *Social Theology,* and President Henry Churchill King in his *Theology and the Social Consciousness,* but their methods and mine were different. The same is true of Rauschenbusch's *Theology of the Social Gospel,* which appeared several years later. But further study led me in a different direction. I came to see that theological doctrines had a social origin, that they were the product of group action in the interests of group solidarity and that they were really analogies which were the outcome of what I called creative social minds. In 1915 I published in the *Biblical World* a long outline study of the history of doctrine from this point of view. The constructive forces in western civilization, imperialism, feudalism, nationalism, democracy, were clearly moulds in which not only the organization but the doctrines of the Christian religion were shaped. Such a view substituted historical relativity and efficiency for inspired authority. What was more important it showed how impossible it was to pass immediately from the gospel as it is found in the New Testament to the religious needs of today. If Christian doctrines were to be regarded as the outcome of historical process, then the process itself conserved values which groups of Christians had found in Jesus and expressed in patterns which could be permanent only through recourse to authority. The practical question had to do with the discovery of these values carried along in the stream of historical Christianity. The New Testament as literature could not be a test of truth for its own formulas were relative to the world in which Jesus and the apostles lived.

Thus the issue between Modernism and Fundamentalism resolved itself into this: Granting that the Christian religion carried values which should be embodied in the life of today, were those values always to be expressed in formulas and conceptions which came from the life of the past? Or would it be possible to re-express them in analogies more effective in our modern world?

I endeavored to set forth this issue in 1924 in a volume called *The Faith of Modernism.* It was an attempt to put forth positively the belief that Christianity consisted in a life of service controlled by the attitudes and convictions which from the days of Jesus have been the heart of the continuous Christian community. I did not believe that the Modernist would come to any authoritative theology, for in the nature of the case the scientific method would be tentative. The volume was intended to be expository and conciliatory. I suspect, however, that its emphasis upon permanent evangelical values did not appeal to those of liberal tendency who were more interested in denying the formulas of orthodoxy than in methods of theological reconstruction. Of course the Fundamentalist could see in such a method only a denial of that which he regarded as the very quintessence of Christian truth. Yet Modernism in my use of the term was a method of discovering and applying the basic values carried in Christian religion to the needs of the modern day. It was constructive rather than critical. It could sympathize with orthodoxy as a historical phase of the same process, and objected to it only because it insisted upon the permanence of the formulas in which a Christian group of the past had rationalized its loyalties.

IV

The pressure of historical method and the growing perception that Christian values to be recognized needed to be expressed in other than political analogies finally unified in the conclusion that theology could be understood only from the point of view of social psychology. As a form of group action it utilized the patterns of successive stages of social process. In my two volumes *The Atonement and the Social Process* and *The*

Growth of the Idea of God, I attempted to show how successive theological ideas have been the extension of social techniques into the field of religion. From such a point of view theology is not a philosophy but the result of a group's utilization of unquestioned ideas and practices of contemporary social life as patterns by which to describe adjustment with cosmic activities upon which men feel they are dependent. Historically speaking a doctrine has been born of the dominant interest and experience of some religious group. Theology by its very purpose is functional rather than metaphysical, although in the nature of the case it leads up to the frontier of metaphysics.

Such a view is not likely to be held by those to whom the history of doctrine is factual rather than a record of ways in which men have been religious in the light of what seemed to them to be reality. For the historically minded theologian doctrines of orthodoxy have their worth, but only for those who find them helpful. The values of evangelical Christianity cease to be dependent upon formulas and become effective only as they are seen to be in accordance with that which we feel is real. Even the term God ceases to be metaphysical and in the light of religious history becomes the conception of those personality producing activities of the universe with which men are organically connected and with which they can set up personal relations.

For those whose thinking has been set by scientific method and who see the historical relativity of doctrines, the whole conception of religion will change. Whether or not they remain interested in a church will depend in most cases upon how far they feel that it is an agency for developing ethical and religious attitudes which are independent of doctrinal precision.

v

An ethical question was involved in our attempt to give religious and moral rather than theological direction to the life of the churches. We have been repeatedly told that while we have a perfect right to believe what we wish, no one has a right to stay in an evangelical church who rejects the inerrancy of the Bible and orthodox doctrines. The proper program for such persons, we are told, is to form a new organization or join the Unitarians. This demand is plausible, but it lacks justice unless one holds that orthodoxy is identical with Christianity however much such a view would be opposed to scientific and social findings. But it is just that major premise of the identity of orthodoxy with Christianity that is untenable. Coercive authority in religion is as much opposed to the principles of love as to the ideals of democracy. The members of a church are certainly entitled to participate in shaping its policies and adjusting it to conditions in the midst of which it must live. The only just basis of withdrawal is a rejection of those basic values and conditions which lie beneath and are expressed in organized Christianity. A man who disbelieves in reason and purpose and personal response in the universe, who thinks that force is more truly ultimate than love, who regards Jesus as a neurasthenic or a weakling, who believes that injustice is never to give way to righteousness, and that there is no escape from mechanistic cycles, is certainly denying that for which the churches have always stood. To undertake to convert a church to such views is to ask the Christian religion to commit suicide. No corporate right can be pled which would justify such policy. But his attitude is the very opposite of those who are seeking seriously to impregnate social change and individual lives with the ideals and principles which have been expressed in Christian doctrines but which do not rest on any supernatural authority of the scriptures or of a church. Those of us who have been compelled by study and experience to distinguish between the values perpetuated in the Christian religion and the formulas and practices in which they have been expressed, believe that we are neither obstinate nor hypocritical in our endeavor to relieve the Chris-

tian from the burden of outgrown patterns of thought and enforced loyalty to that which hinders religious faith. We have
no quarrel with those who find moral inspiration and guidance
in sincere acceptance of orthodoxy. They, as truly as we, are
working for the same ends. If, like Peter they have the duty of
evangelizing one type of persons, we like Paul have the duty of
evangelizing another. As in the case of the apostles, Christian
principles should lead us to give each other the right hand of
fellowship and work for the enrichment of human life.

Doctrinal agreement is not necessary for co-operation in
good works. Friends can co-operate when systems may conflict.
When men of different intellectual habits and cultural back-
grounds possess the same ambition to serve their day and generation, co-operation is possible at the point where their ideals
meet. The pity is that men with the same purposes so often find
co-operation hindered by emotional attitudes born of doctrinal
differences. I know the difficulty that lies in attempts to co-
operate with those whose views you distrust and who in turn
distrust yours. I once attempted reconciliation with a bitter
critic only to have it refused, until I had "a different spirit." On
the other hand some of the warmest friendships I have known
have been with men of radically different views regarding
religion. It is a narrow view of life that makes co-operation
depend upon agreements which do not affect an immediate
objective.

VI

Theologians like physicians should have a Code of professional ethics. There are some men who do not seem sure that
they are telling the truth until some one gets angry with them.
What they claim as conscience is a combination of prejudice and
pugnaciousness. To other men the will of God means their own
plan of action. Such human traits are inflamed by controversy.

Indeed, there seems to be an "unwritten law" in religion as truly as in domestic relations. In the name of the Lord one can say things which are little better than libel. I recall only too plainly how a minister of the gospel declared he would like to burn an irritating opponent at the stake.

Liberally minded persons are not vindictive, but they are sometimes contemptuous of those whose views they have themselves rejected. But such an attitude, while probably less worthy of condemnation than downright anger, is not conducive to that unity of the spirit which is the bond of peace. The admonition to love one's enemies must certainly apply to theological opponents.

Yet human nature being as it is, conflict is one method of progress. A dictatorship in morals is as much an enemy of the rights of individuals as a dictatorship in politics. It is always in danger of overlooking facts which are elements in a situation. If Christianity were a system of truth the case might be different, for nothing can be truer than an absolute. Behavior and attitudes, however, are the very essence of a religion and the methods by which they are intellectually justified are relative to one's intelligence. Convictions and formulas which justify the faith of one group might seem actual disbeliefs to other groups whose religious loyalty is as thoroughly genuine. Most of the struggles of the church with heretics have been over ways of establishing some belief both parties declared was true. So long as the struggle for ideals is expressed in the pattern of military campaigns and the attainment of desirable ends is pictured as a victory, the recognition of the efficiency of co-operation through mutual concessions will be lacking.

My experience in dealing with men of different religious convictions is the basis of the assurance that the way to get unity of action among those of identical purpose but of different theologies is not that of conversion but of co-operation for practical ends. The way to get together is to work together. If Christians cannot agree as to the mode of baptism or the nature of the eucharist they can at least co-operate in emphasizing the basic moral ideals of Christianity and unitedly combat those evils which threaten the well-being of a community. To use Sabatier's expression, this is to substitute the religion of the spirit for the religion of authority. And this one has to admit is difficult, requiring self-control and willingness to make sacrifices in any justifiable compromise.

Generally speaking non-combativeness is good strategy in religion. A young minister once urged that I head up a movement looking toward the establishment of open membership in Baptist churches. This, of course, involved the whole question of the mode of baptism which he and I alike had come to feel was a matter of secondary importance. I declined to take any such step on the ground that controversy would not only consolidate opposition but make central that which ought to be secondary. It would be wiser, I held, to let a trend already discernible work out its own results while as members of a denomination we all united to further those moral and religious ends which we felt were of first importance. As it turned out my reading of the situation was correct. Matters of first importance were faced without the confusion which would have resulted from an attempt to force an issue which was bound sooner or later to work itself out.

Leadership consists largely in using secondary enthusiasms to further primary ends. If religion on the part of the individual were a matter of detached and solitary attitudes, some form of theological anarchy might be justifiable, but Christianity as a religion involves group behavior and the united support of ideals. Emotions are likely to precede their intellectual vindication. If changes within a religious body are to be directed toward the moral and religious ends for which the body really stands, its backward as well as its progressive members must be recognized. The discussion of differing methods and formulas, if conducted in the spirit of mutual respect, is an educational process which leaves no memory of bitterness and carries a cause further than can victorious coercion.

CHAPTER XVIII

AND TOMORROW?

FOR A man in health, retirement is like entering a new life. Farewell dinners, over-generous words of appreciation of former students, resolutions of boards, a complimentary volume of essays by friends, almost make one feel like Charles V watching rehearsals for his own funeral. The lack of a routine which has been the vertebral column of one's activities, is a temptation to lapse into reminiscence and detective stories. One hardly knows whether to regret or to be gratified that the world gets on so well without him! Yet retirement is not a prolonged academic vacation. True, we find it a little more difficult to make immediate decisions and perhaps initiative is quieted. When I was a young man I cheered myself against old age by Browning's "Rabbi Ben Ezra" and Tennyson's "Ulysses" but both were written when the authors were relatively young. Life does not permit old age to rival youth. One may not quite be ready to sit by the fireside but neither is one keen to face the Cyclops and the sea.

The large group of university colleagues who like myself have reached the age of retirement have not turned idlers. There are still researches to be made, books to be written and good causes to be championed. Our experience may suggest caution when the inexperience of others breeds optimism, but we know that it is the future rather than the past that counts. If we have done our work well our successors will not need to do it over again but can face new conditions and plan new advances. We can at least urge that a philosophy of futility is futile, that broadcasting frustration is a gospel of cowardice and that detachment from

291

social movements and religious institutions leads to inefficiency. If one is to become a tradition it need not to be a tradition that hinders progress.

I

As when one sails toward the sea the confusion of the dock disappears and the mountains and headlands rise against the sky, so in retrospect the major accomplishments of religious change come into proper outline. The controversies between men who ought to have presented a common front to all sorts of evil, the defection of champions and the lassitude of leaders which rise in memory as a dust storm only partially obscure the events of real importance. Any change in public opinion or the organization of new attitudes is not accomplished mechanically. Each is the work of innumerable individuals. And in many cases religious change which should be a divine comedy becomes human tragedy. A religious belief cannot be changed or thrust aside as if it were a matter of mere clothing. Whether rational or superstitious it becomes so identified with a man's fears and hopes as to become a part of himself. Religious doubt is something like the shock of an earthquake. That which has been a very foundation of security is itself insecure. It is not strange that men should oppose violently those who question authority. It is a mistake to see merely conflict between the older and the younger generation. It often happens that youth is more relentlessly acquisitive and therefore more conservative than maturity. Social and intellectual changes which have been made during the last fifty years have done more than produce religious indifference. They have established a social climate within which religious faith must exist. Acquaintance with the past makes one hesitate to affirm that our day is peculiarly anti-religious. The lamentations of the past were as frequent as those of the present. Then as now religious uncertainty was born of the failure to adjust religious urge to the disappearance of what had seemed to be real and to the emergence of realities hard for men to accept.

Whoever looks upon an organized religion as one aspect of a social process will project observable trends and counter-trends into the future. It might almost be said that he discovers a Mendelian law in history, which makes more probable a forecast of future development than is possible for one who treats religion in the abstract, independent of human behavior.

The changes of the last half century certainly must be interpreted as including the process of social differentiation within the area of religion. Undoubtedly there has been a general modification of Christianity in view of those economic and cultural changes to which the entire social order is subjected. Even in the case of unqualified Catholicism there has been, at least in the United States, an extension of the religious conception in parochial schools, the Knights of Columbus, Daughters of Isabella, Peace societies and social studies. There could not be a more serious mistake than to think of the Roman Catholic church as concerned exclusively with life after death, important as is its power of the keys. Within Protestantism the differentiation is more marked. It is not accurate to say with Machen that liberalism is a different religion from Christianity, but it is possible to say that there is developing a new species of Christianity. The older forms of Christianity will continue with their appeal to an infallible and authoritative Bible, their insistence upon the virgin birth, the substitutionary atonement, miracles, the physical resurrection of Jesus and his visible return from Heaven to judge the world. The great masses of men and women show little desire to have their religion freed from a supernaturalism that demands an implicit faith and ecclesiastical loyalty. One may well question how far such views will hold the allegiance of a second and third generation educated in public schools where religious teaching is forbidden. However one may question the policy from the point of view of democracy, there is no denying consistency in the establishment of parochial schools by Catholics and Lutherans. They serve to develop mind-sets on the part of children which will make them suspicious of social and cultural tendencies at variance with inherited beliefs and institutions. Ecclesiastical conservatism is a prophylactic against radical social theory. I can see no evidence that it is lessening among the rank and file of Americans. Any forecast of the future should not overlook its influence. For theologically conservative Christians, while not sufficiently realizing the extent to which Christian principles can be applied to group action, certainly contribute to society moral ideals and genuine reliance upon divine help. To them Jesus is something more than a historical figure. He is the revelation of God in human life. However foreign early evangelicalism may seem to those who have always been under the influence of today's intellectual and social trends, it had undoubted power to evoke emotional support for moral idealism and to develop attitudes that aid social co-operation for human welfare. From its circle most socially minded pioneers have come.

II

Liberal Christians will not be interested in theological regularity or in authoritative creeds and confessions, but theologians will continue their attempts to find a theoretical basis for what they practically accept. Such rationalization is inevitable, for the professional mind naturally turns from action to theoretical justifications of action. But while the dogmatizing of evangelicalism may go on apace, its spirit and devotion to spiritual values will be carried forward by those who are interested in religion as a factor of social process. Churches without religious convictions are not apt to survive their eloquent pastors. Christians who are loyal to the principles enunciated by Jesus and dramatized in his life and who make intelligent faith in God a basis for hope and courage, will carry forward the results of the past fifty years.

Too often a discussion of the immediate duties of the churches is indifferent to the fact that moral leadership must be exercised in a contemporary world and that the praise of methods efficient in the past may be as academic and romantic as the praise of medieval trade guilds in a world of machines and mass production. Anachronisms cannot make a future. Tomorrow's creative Christianity will not be a reversion to the methods and ideals of the evangelicalism of my boyhood. Nor will it merely repeat the methods and accomplishments of the generation that pioneered in social and religious reconstruction. Religious education will not revert to the methods of a generation ago; biblical scholars will not abandon the principles of historical criticism; churches will not be indifferent to the ethics of political and economic groups; the tendencies away from sectarianism toward a larger Christian unity will not disappear; but such conditions will be the starting point for new faith and new advance. Neither the past nor the present should be a mould in which the future is to be cast. Those of us who have had a share in the transformation of religious life welcome every sincere attempt to make religion vital in the new conditions which are so rapidly appearing. We give our successors the same right to criticize us which we exercised in criticizing our predecessors. But they need not begin where we began. When we compare the Christian influence of today with that of a half century ago it is clear that the teaching of Jesus is much more a ferment in human relations than when he was treated as the vicarious sacrifice satisfying the justice of an offended deity. In the application of Christian principles, the new generation of religious leaders has at its disposal the rapidly increasing knowledge of the universe, of social processes and of the human person. Individualism in the sense of the nineteenth century liberalism is being replaced by an individualism that recognizes group action.

The ethics of these new relations, it is to be hoped, will not be a resuscitated utilitarianism, a pious pessimism, a recourse to coercion or a social theory that would make a religion merely a detached search for "the good life."

III

In forecasting the future by projecting the trends of the last half century, allowance must be made for the fact that a second generation cannot begin with the conditions in which those trends were developed. Particularly is this true in our contemporary life. The natural course of all reconstructive processes has been disarranged by the Great War and those who are now entering middle age have grown up in an age of disillusionment and struggle. Their confidence in democracy has been rudely shaken. The inability of individuals to withstand group pressure has induced among some theologians an almost psychopathic attitude of pessimism and the elevation of crisis above process. It is no accident that such a feeling should originate on the continent of Europe, or that it should reappear among those who have reached maturity in the midst of the rapid changes in the United States. I cannot believe that such a mood is either healthy or conducive to religious faith. It is more akin to the eschatology of a subject Jewish people and savors too much of defeatism and distrust of intelligently implemented love. One might almost describe it as premillenarian liberalism.

Such a theology lays emphasis upon those elements of Calvinism which minimize the worth of human nature and emphasize the transcendent absolutism of God. As such it is opposed not only to the spirit of democracy which Calvinism engendered but also to the extension of the values of Christianity to the social process. It is to overlook the growing opposition to war, the attempt to further the personal welfare of under-privileged classes through social legislation, organized philanthropy, revolt against the economic interpretation of history and the mechanistic interpretation of the universe, the application of religious faith to health, experiments in shaping a morality which presumes human equality. Such a new social mind, of course, cannot be wholly credited to organized Christianity, but it has the qualities of the moral idealism of the prophets and of Jesus. It will be the task of a younger generation to implement such ideals wisely.

Such a task will be especially difficult because it has become so much the fashion to magnify a sense of frustration as a characteristic of the generation that has been born since the Great War. Those thousands of young men who a generation ago became aware of social questions and came to treat Jesus as something more than a theological doctrine are now middle-aged persons whose responsibilities are steadily increasing. They have already experienced the difficulty of adjusting their ideals to the exigencies of life. Many of them have succumbed to influences which they themselves would condemn. It was they who felt the chief brunt of the World War and its resulting cynicism and what is popularly called disillusion. Their early enthusiasm to make the world better by the extension of democracy has been somewhat cooled. Individualism has become rather a term of reproach. They are becoming possessed of a fear that the church in forwarding a social gospel may be moving toward communism, and at the same time find themselves in the midst of political changes which make them fear the destruction of business initiative. They are in fact an intermediate generation which must determine very largely the direction in which the social process will move.

It is not strange, therefore, that the third generation, that is to say those young persons who have been born since the war, should experience a sense of frustration. They have inherited a depression and must adjust themselves to conditions which only gradually offer opportunity. Even more than their parents they need encouragement. If they discover that the churches are indifferent to their needs and are incompetent to arouse their hopes, they are likely to drift either toward moral indifferentism or revolutionary programs.

Many of the potential enemies of Christian ideals are developing into social movements opposed alike to democracy and belief in God. They have the advantage of all revolutionary movements in so presenting ideal conditions as to arouse discontent and justify class hatred. Such passions are tremendously forceful. As compared with their promises the gospel of Jesus seems abstract. But none the less it has the support of cosmic process. The one condition of its effectiveness is sacrificial social mindedness on the part of the privileged. The churches will need to justify their existence as social groups by producing such an attitude of mind. It does not require any great power of observation to see how fatal to a church is its refusal to participate in all efforts to further personal welfare. But equally fatal would be the transformation of a church into a non-religious society. There certainly is danger that a church of the more liberal sort should be swept away from its theistic moorings and become one of many reform movements. My experience convinces me that for a church to become primarily an agent of economic and political change is to compromise its future. To organize the moral gains of the past rather than to extend the frontiers of religion means self-satisfaction and institutional decay. Unless churches can become centers of a genuinely religious idealism they will be outmoded. Those who are earnestly seeking to abolish social evils, extend justice and enrich individual life will leave organizations in which religious interest is hardly more than vestigial, and will turn to institutions whose programs are not obscured by rhetorical piety. Academic freedom and scientific thought must do something more for religion than raise problems. There is no efficiency in a god who is under investigation.

The future will decide for itself how much it needs churches or a religion such as that which men of my generation have attempted to organize. For myself the social necessity for religious organizations that will not divorce religion from social process seems indisputable. So long as men are dominated by their emotions there must be institutions to direct such emotions. The defection of socially minded persons from the churches would leave organized religion in the hands of those who are more concerned with the past than with the future and who make their belief in God an excuse for indifference to social needs. That would indeed be a misfortune. Religion would be set over against the new age and the churches would be left to oppose atheism and secularism with outgrown formulas and practices.

I envy a generation that will be called upon to defend the individual from absorption into social process and to direct that process toward personal rather than economic efficiency. For I cannot doubt that in the future as in the past there will emerge that vicarious tenth which, according to its best intelligence, seeks at its own expense to democratize privilege and justify reliance upon love as an expression of that cosmic activity we know as God. To it I would say, as in the words of Alfred Noyes Tycho Brahe said to Kepler:

> *"Take thou the splendor, carry it out of sight*
> *Into the great new age I must not know*
> *Into the great new realm I must not tread."*

INDEX

Academic freedom in religion, 55, 58 sq., 65
American Institute of Sacred Literature, 61, 74 sq.
Andover Theological Seminary, 28
Atkinson, Henry A., 213

Bailey, W. S., 39, 46, 49
Baptists, 107 sq.
Baptist City Mission Society of Chicago, 154
Baptist Executive Council of Chicago, 116-118
Baptist Theological Union Seminary, 57, 61, 67
Barrows Lectures, 238
Bible, significance of to orthodoxy, 278, 281 sq.
Biblical World, 72
Bitting, William C., 116
Brett, George P., 97
Bryan, William J., 198, 227, 229
Brown, William Adams, 272 sq.
Brotherhood of the Kingdom, 50
Barton, Ernest De Witt, 26, 50, 58

Carnegie, Andrew, founds Church Peace Union, 195
Chamberlin, Georgia L., 74, 76
Chautauqua Institution, 76
Chicago Theological Seminary, 270
Christendom, 91
Christianity and war, 206, 207, 210 sq., 216
Christianity and Social Process, 129, 239
Church and State, theories of relations between, 172 sq.
Churches, function of, 286; outlook for, 296.
Church Peace Union, 195, 196, 213
Church Unity, beginnings of, 152; Catholic conception of, 167
Colby College, 16 sq., 39
College of Religious and Social Sciences, 264

Committee on Social Action of the National Council of the Congregational and Christian Churches, 132
Community Churches, 161
Conference of Theological Seminaries, 262, 272
Constructive Bible Studies, 246
Contributions of Science to Religion, 224
Co-operative Council of City Missions, 155 sq.
Creative Christianity, 129
Curry, S. S., 27, 40

Darrow, Clarence, 228
Denominations, origins of, 107, 151
Dictionary of Religion and Ethics, 98
Disciples' Divinity House of the University of Chicago, 269
Divinity School of the University of Chicago, 56 sq., 256 sq.
Doctrines, origin of, 285

Education in latter part of the 19th Century, 15 sq.
Education in Asia, 240
Elden, Mary P., 42
Evangelicalism, late Victorian period, 9-14, 44
Evolution, 18, 226 sq.

Federal Council of the Churches of Christ in America, 161, 165
Federated Churches, 160
Foreign missions, 238, 241; training for, 271
Foster, George B., 67 sq.
Fundamentalism, 277, 283

Goodspeed, George S., 41, 98
Gulick, Sidney L., 198, 199, 213
Gunsaulus, Frank W., 167

Hall of Religion, Century of Progress Exposition, 139 sq.

301